The Politics of Education Reform in China's Hong Kong

Education reform has become a highly political issue in the Hong Kong Special Administrative Region (HKSAR) since the transfer of sovereignty to the People's Republic of China (PRC).

Lo and Hung focus on the political struggles among stakeholders, including the government of Hong Kong, the Catholic Church, parents, students, teachers, the central authorities of Beijing, and even the bureaucratic politics between Beijing, the Hong Kong government and the Examination Authority. They examine the key elements of education reform in the HKSAR, including language and curriculum reform, national security education, civic and patriotic education, the rise of the pro-Beijing education elites and interest groups, and the revamp of examination questions and examination authority. The entire education reform in the HKSAR has pushed the Hong Kong education system toward a process of mainlandization, making Hong Kong's education system more similar to the mainland system with emphasis on political "correctness" in the understanding of Chinese national security, history and culture.

Highlighting the political struggles among the various stakeholders, this book is essential for scholars of Hong Kong and China, especially those with an interest in the relationship between education and politics.

Sonny Shiu-Hing Lo is Professor of Politics at HKU SPACE.

Steven Chung-Fun Hung is Assistant Professor in the Department of Social Sciences at the Education University of Hong Kong.

Routledge Contemporary China Series

China's Energy Security and Relations With Petrostates
Oil as an Idea
Anna Kuteleva

Ethnic Identity of the Kam People in Contemporary China
Government versus Local Perspectives
Wei Wang and Lisong Jiang

China's Globalization from Below
Chinese Entrepreneurial Migrants and the Belt and Road Initiative
Theodor Tudoroiu

Civil Society in China
How Society Speaks to the State
Runya Qiaoan

China's Foreign Policy since 1949
Kevin G Cai

China's Carbon-Energy Policy and Asia's Energy Transition
Carbon Leakage, Relocation and Halos
Edited by Akihisa Mori

Ecocriticism and Chinese Literature
Imagined Landscapes and Real Lived Spaces
Riccardo Moratto, Nicoletta Pesaro and Di-kai Chao

Work Safety Regulation in China
The CCP's Fatality Quota System
Jie Gao

The Politics of Education Reform in China's Hong Kong
Sonny Shiu-Hing Lo and Chung Fun Steven Hung

For more information about this series, please visit: https://www.routledge.com/Routledge-Contemporary-China-Series/book-series/SE0768

The Politics of Education Reform in China's Hong Kong

Sonny Shiu-Hing Lo and
Chung Fun Steven Hung

LONDON AND NEW YORK

First published 2022
by Routledge
4 Park Square, Milton Park, Abingdon, Oxon OX14 4RN

and by Routledge
605 Third Avenue, New York, NY 10158

*Routledge is an imprint of the Taylor & Francis Group,
an informa business*

© 2022 Sonny Shiu-Hing Lo and Chung Fun Steven Hung

The right of Sonny Shiu-Hing Lo and Chung Fun Steven Hung to be identified as authors of this work has been asserted in accordance with sections 77 and 78 of the Copyright, Designs and Patents Act 1988.

All rights reserved. No part of this book may be reprinted or reproduced or utilised in any form or by any electronic, mechanical, or other means, now known or hereafter invented, including photocopying and recording, or in any information storage or retrieval system, without permission in writing from the publishers.

Trademark notice: Product or corporate names may be trademarks or registered trademarks and are used only for identification and explanation without intent to infringe.

British Library Cataloguing-in-Publication Data
A catalogue record for this book is available from the British Library

Library of Congress Cataloguing-in-Publication Data
A catalog record has been requested for this book

ISBN: 978-0-367-70624-1 (hbk)
ISBN: 978-0-367-70623-4 (pbk)
ISBN: 978-1-003-14726-8 (ebk)

DOI: 10.4324/9781003147268

Typeset in ITC Galliard Std
by KnowledgeWorks Global Ltd.

Contents

List of Figures — vi
List of Tables — vii
List of Abbreviations — ix
Acknowledgment — xi

1 Toward an Analytical Framework of Studying the Political Context and Content of Education Reform — 1

2 Education Reform in Hong Kong from British Rule to the Post-1997 Period — 42

3 The Mainlandization of Education in Hong Kong: Impacts of the national security law on education reform — 65

4 A Hong Kong-Style of Cultural Revolution in the Education Sector — 108

5 Adaptation to the Mainlandization, Decolonization, Legalization and Migration — 151

Conclusion — 188
Bibliography — 193
Index — 204

Figures

1.1	An Analytical Framework Understanding the Context and Content of Education Reforms in Hong Kong	36
2.1	Changing Population of Hong Kong, 1841–2021	44
5.1	Student Enrolment in Day Schools by Level, 2002 to 2020	166
5.2	Demographic Characteristics of One-Way Permit Holders: Implications for Education, 1998–2019	168
5.3	Percentage of Students Studying Outside Hong Kong after S6 Graduations, 2012–2020	173

Tables

2.1	The Evolution of Education Policy in Hong Kong, 1945–1997	47
2.2	The Content of Education Reform in the HKSAR Soon After July 1, 1997	52
2.3	Comparing the Examination Subjects in HKCEE and HKDSE	54
2.4	Recent Education Review, 2014-2021	59
2.5	The Chief Executive's Policy Address, Education Policy and Education Reforms	60
3.1	The Scope of National Security Education	75
3.2	Comparisons of Liberal Studies with Citizenship and Social Development	79
3.3	The Number of Media and Organizations in Hong Kong, 2018 and 2021	89
3.4	Internet Media and Their Facebook Popularity	90
3.5	The Transformation of Pro-Beijing Schools in Hong Kong after 1997	94
3.6	Major Teachers' Unions in Hong Kong	95
3.7	Membership of Education Unions, 1955–2019	96
3.8	Educational Interest Groups that Are Not Registered as Teachers' Unions	98
3.9	Elites from the Thirty Members of Education Section in the Election Committee	99
3.10	Composition of the Education Professional Alliance, 2021	101
4.1	Events Leading to the Dissolution of the Professional Teachers Union	124
4.2	Chronology of the Controversy over the History Examination Question, May-June 2020	131
5.1	Education Reforms in the PRC	152
5.2	Student Activists and the Costs of Their Political Participation	159
5.3	Operating Classes, Accommodation and Student Enrolment in Primary and Secondary Schools by Religious Background of School, 2019 and 2020 (Numbers in Primary Schools/Secondary Schools)	167

5.4	Student Enrolment (Headcount) in University Grants Council-Funded Programs at Hong Kong Universities from 1996–1997 to 2019–2020	170
5.5	The Number of Schools and Student Enrolment in Day Schools by Type in 2019 and 2020	178
5.6	The Pay Scale of School Teachers in Hong Kong	179
5.7	Teaching Vacancies Advertisement from June to Early September 2021	181

List of Abbreviations

ACCA	Association of Chartered Certified Accountants
ASIPECS	Assessment System for Ideological and Political Education for College Students
ASL	Advanced Supplementary Level
BNO	British National Overseas
CCP	Chinese Communist Party
CCTV	China Central Television
CDC	Curriculum Development Council
CGA	Certified General Accountants
CHKU	Council of the University of Hong Kong
CHRF	Civil Human Rights Front
CityU	City University of Hong Kong
CPA	Chartered Professional Accountants
CPPCC	Chinese People's Political Consultative Conference
CSD	Citizenship and Social Development
CUHK	Chinese University of Hong Kong
CYL	Communist Youth League
DAB	Democratic Alliance for Betterment and Progress of Hong Kong
DSE	Diploma of Secondary Education
DSS	Direct Subsidy Scheme
EDB	Education Bureau
EdUHK	Education University of Hong Kong
EEGU	Education Employees General Union
EPA	Education Professional Alliance
ExCo	Executive Council
FEW	Federation of Education Workers
GBA	Greater Bay Area
GESU	Government Educational Staff Union
HKASPDMC	Hong Kong Alliance in Support of Patriotic Democratic Movements of China
HKASTA	Hong Kong Aided School Teachers' Association
HKBU	Hong Kong Baptist University
HKCEE	Hong Kong Certificate of Education Examination

List of Abbreviations

HKDSE	Hong Kong Diploma of Secondary Education
HKEAA	Hong Kong Examinations and Assessment Authority
HKEWU	Hong Kong Education Workers Union
HKFS	Hong Kong Federation of Students
HKNP	Hong Kong National Party
HKSAR	Hong Kong Special Administrative Region
HKSSPA	Hong Kong Secondary School Principals Association
HKTA	Hong Kong Teachers' Association
HKU	University of Hong Kong
HKUST	Hong Kong University of Science and Technology
HKUSU	Hong Kong University Student Union
HKUSUC	Hong Kong University Students' Union Council
ITE	Information Technology in Education
JPCHKCD	Justice and Peace Commission of the Hong Kong Catholic Diocese
KMT	Kuomintang
KNFA	Kaifong and Neighborhood Friends Association
LegCo	Legislative Council
MCE	Moral and Civic Education
MNE	Moral and National Education
MoE	Ministry of Education
MoF	Ministry of Finance
MoI	Medium of Instruction
NPC	National People's Congress
NSE	National Security Education
NSS	New Senior Secondary
OCMFA	Office of the Commissioner of the Ministry of Foreign Affairs
OHKF	Our Hong Kong Foundation
PISA	Program for International Student Assessment
PLA	People's Liberation Army
PolyU	Polytechnic University
PRC	People's Republic of China
PTA	Progressive Teachers' Alliance
PTU	Professional Teachers' Union
RTHK	Radio Television Hong Kong
SCNPC	Standing Committee of the National People's Congress
SMI	School Management Initiative
SSSPP	Secondary School Students Preparatory Platform
STEM	Science, Technology, Engineering, Mathematics
TAR	Tibet Autonomous Region
TSA	Territory-wide System Assessment
TTRA	Targets and Target-related Assessment
UIC	United International College
WTO	World Trade Organization
XUAR	Xinjiang Uyghur Autonomous Region

Acknowledgment

The authors wish to express their gratitude to Simon Bates, the Editor of Routledge, for his staunch support of our book project from the process of writing up a proposal to that of finalizing the entire book manuscript.

We also thank six of our former students who were willing to chat with us informally on their feelings and insights on Hong Kong's education reform after the promulgation of the national security law in late June 2020. Two of them had already left Hong Kong for the United Kingdom and we wish them the best of luck in their new endeavors.

This book was completed at a time when national security education and national education began to be implemented in Hong Kong in September 2021. We utilize lots of materials, including government documents, website sources and news reports, to describe the unprecedented education reform in the city under China's sovereignty and tremendous political influence.

By adopting a political science perspective, we hope that this book can fill in a crucial gap in the existing literature on Hong Kong's education. If politics, as Harold Laswell defined, refers to who gets what, when and how, this book strives to analyze in detail the politics of education reform in the Hong Kong Special Administrative Region.

Sonny Shiu-Hing Lo
Steven Chung-fun Hung
September 18, 2021

1 Toward an Analytical Framework of Studying the Political Context and Content of Education Reform

The objective of this book is to use the case of Hong Kong, whose sovereignty was transferred from Britain to the People's Republic of China (PRC) on July 1, 1997, to demonstrate that the transformation of education reform proceeded gradually in a liberal fashion until late June 2020, when the enactment of the national security law propelled education reform in the Hong Kong Special Administrative Region (HKSAR) in a far more mainlandized, nationalistic, politically patriotic manner than ever before. The mainlandization of education reform in the HKSAR from late June 2020 onward has become educationally and politically significant because the PRC government and authorities responsible for Hong Kong affairs have firmly believed in the necessity of changing the education system of the HKSAR to an ideological direction.

Ideologically, the mainland's socialist education system has been characterized by political indoctrination. A similar pattern of education reform has been conducted in the HKSAR since late June 2020, although the results remain to be observed and assessed. At the time of writing this book, the mainlandized education reform in the HKSAR is entering its second year; nevertheless, the period from late June 2020 to November 2021 has laid the foundation of the mainlandization of the education system in Hong Kong from 2021 to 2047, when the Sino-British Joint Declaration over Hong Kong and the Hong Kong mini-constitution, the Basic Law, will expire.[1] Under the PRC regime led by General Secretary of the Chinese Communist Party (CCP) Xi Jinping since November 2012, the PRC policy toward the HKSAR has shifted to a more hardline and politically conservative position.[2] The reasons for such change were complex, including not only the PRC's domestic shift to a more politically hardline and conservative position but also the rise of Hong Kong's localism that resisted and opposed Beijing's policies and the HKSAR government. Localism – a strong sense of local identity among some Hong Kong people – has been seen as the enemy of the HKSAR government and the PRC party-state, for many localists launched social and political movements to oppose the policies of the Hong Kong authorities, ranging from the 2012 anti-national education campaign to the September–December 2014 Occupy Central Movement, and from the early 2016 Mongkok riot to the provocative oath-taking behavior of two localist legislators-elect, and from the 2019 anti-extradition bill movement

DOI: 10.4324/9781003147268-1

to the persistent lobbying efforts of some localists for foreign support of Hong Kong's anti-extradition campaign in the latter half of 2019.[3] All these localist movements have been viewed by the PRC as politically subversive, leading to the necessity of imposing the national security law onto the HKSAR in late June 2020. In short, the mainlandization of Hong Kong's education reform, in the eyes of PRC leaders, is a must to "correct" and "reverse" the local education system, which has been seen as nurturing and producing politically "subversive" activists who plunged the HKSAR into social disorder and political chaos.

It is not the objective of this book to probe the dynamics of student participation in protests and social movements. Indeed, not all students participated in social and political movements – a phenomenon that has not been clarified by some politicians supportive of the PRC-initiated education reform in the HKSAR. Pro-Beijing politicians in the HKSAR have tended to adopt a lopsided view of Hong Kong's education system, putting the blame on the "politicization" of Hong Kong on the students at the primary, secondary and university levels. Their intention has been political; most of them are opportunistic and attempt at climbing up the political ladder of the HKSAR, where the political system is increasingly patron-clientelist.[4] In a patron-clientelist system, political clients obedient to their bosses and authorities are destined to be the loyal actors of the PRC state so that they can and will become the most influential ruling elites of the HKSAR. However, as this book will discuss later, the education system of Hong Kong is more complex than many pro-Beijing politicians have portrayed. In other words, student participation in politics was triggered by a multiplicity of factors rather than because of a particular curriculum, such as the Liberal Studies subject, which became the target of criticisms. Indeed, the Liberal Studies subject, as will be examined, was formulated and implemented without being free from any problem.

On the other hand, pro-Beijing politicians and PRC officials argued consistently that Chinese history as a subject in the senior level of secondary schools of Hong Kong was devalued by making it an elective rather than compulsory. Such a criticism was, objectively speaking, valid from the perspective of enhancing the Chinese national identity of Hong Kong students. The weak sense of Chinese national identity of many Hong Kong students was attributable to the underdevelopment in the study of Chinese history and culture. Yet, the factors shaping student participation in the politics of Hong Kong from 2012 to 2019 were far more complex than the pro-Beijing elites portrayed. These factors embraced, for example, the unpopular policies of the HKSAR government, notably the extradition bill in mid-2019, and the clumsy way in which such policy, like the national education curriculum in 2012, was explained and promoted. Putting the blame on Hong Kong's education system and its Liberal Studies curriculum was to simplify the entire picture of education politics in the HKSAR.

The key elements of mainlandizing Hong Kong's education reform, as this book will discuss, include the dilution of the Liberal Studies curriculum, which was heavily politically criticized for "politicizing" Hong Kong students; the replacement of this curriculum with Citizenship and Social Development (CSD);

the reform of the Chinese history curriculum; the enhancement in the content of national security education; a gradual emphasis on the history and contribution of the CCP to the PRC's socio-economic development and international status; and finally the consolidation of the Chinese culture in Hong Kong's curriculum reform. All these reforms aim at enhancing the dual objectives of making Hong Kong students imbued with a stronger sense of Chinese national identity and a stronger sense of political patriotism.

This book examines how the context of education reform has changed in the HKSAR by focusing on the China factor and how the content of education reform has been redesigned and formulated. By focusing on the context and content of education reform, this book can fill in an existing gap in the literature on Hong Kong's education because an overwhelming majority of the literature has centered on the educative aspects without linking the content and context of education reforms to the rapidly changing political environment and dynamics. This book can contribute to our deeper understanding of Hong Kong's education reform by bringing back the role of politics, including the political considerations of the PRC authorities responsible for Hong Kong matters, the political role of the Hong Kong education bureaucracy in altering the curricula after the imposition of the national security law, and the political adaptation of schools, teachers, students and parents to the new politics of Hong Kong after late June 2020.

This chapter is going to conduct a literature review on the context and content of education reform in both the PRC and Hong Kong. In the process of reviewing the literature, the authors will reflect on how the previous findings have implications for Hong Kong's education reforms. Then this chapter will build up an analytical framework for us to comprehend and understand the context and content of education reforms in the HKSAR.

The Evolution of Mainland China's Political Education

In the PRC's education reform, some university subjects have become more internationalized in their content than ever before. A good example is the broad field of accounting education, which has been developing quickly since 1949.[5] Yet, the changes in the content of accounting education reflected the transformation of its political and social context. Guohua Zhang, Gordon Boyce and Kamran Ahmed have delineated the process of change in the content of accounting education in China. They have noted that China's accession to the World Trade Organization (WTO) in 2001 was a turning point in the rapid expansion of university accounting education. More university-qualified graduates have sought to serve local and international needs in the accounting profession. In particular, university accounting education has taken on an internationalized dimension, reflecting domestic economic changes and wider developments outside the PRC.[6] The mainland's accounting education was heavily influenced by the CCP and the direction of the central government, whose Ministry of Finance (MoF) and Ministry of Education (MoE) have been playing a crucial role in internationalizing and modernizing the content of accounting education.[7] The MoF's administration of accounting education embraces two aspects: the organization of professional in-service training and professional certificate education with invited lecturers from universities; and diploma and degree education in vocational, technical and higher education institutions in cooperation with the MoE. Yet, accounting education objectives are not only subject to the requirements of the MoF and MoE but also accommodate changes in the CCP's education policies. The MoE supervises all aspects of university supervision and leadership, ranging from the approval of curriculum and textbooks to the endorsement of university teaching and research personnel.

Since 2001, market mechanism has increasingly been entrenched in the economy, leading to the revisions of accounting standards in 2006 and their convergence with International Financial Reporting Standards – a change reflecting China's openness to international influence even though such transformation was under the watchful eyes of PRC authorities. Today, many PRC accounting academics have overseas qualifications, ideally placing them to accommodate changes within the university accounting education. Many mainland universities have forged cooperation with international professional bodies, with new majors in international accounting programs and examinations, including the integration of Chartered Professional Accountants (CPA) programs and Association of Chartered Certified Accountants (ACCA) and Certified General Accountants (CGA) examinations. In the early 2000s, China established national accounting institutes, speeding up the internationalization of Chinese accounting and university education through sponsorship and collaboration with overseas and domestic accounting educational institutions. In 2005, the MoF initiated a Leading Accounting Talents Project to build up high-quality and comprehensive advanced accounting skills across the nation.[8] In a nutshell, the internationalization of Chinese accounting education was a mirror of the PRC's process of opening its economy and joining the WTO.

The process of internationalizing the content of university education, however, has been accompanied by another extreme, namely the utilization of political re-education, especially in the case of Xinjiang province. In the summer of 2017, reports on large-scale internments of Muslims (Uyghurs, Kazakhs and Kyrgyz) in China's north-west Xinjiang Uyghur Autonomous Region (XUAR) emerged.[9] By the end of the year, reports on the detention of some ethnic-minority townships up to 10% of the entire population emerged, including the internment of 120,000 people in the Uyghur-dominated Kashgar prefecture alone. Despite increasing media coverage from 2017 to 2020, the Chinese government denied the existence of Xinjiang's re-education camps. Based on the available documentary evidence, Adrian Zenz argued that the region's current re-education system exceeded the size of China's entire former "education through labor" system, which was officially abolished in 2013. Zenz contended that under the XUAR party-secretary, Chen Quanguo, the scale of internments reached "unprecedented levels" with the Muslim majority regions being "assigned detention quotas" and resulting in the internment of a large Muslim population "without due process."[10] China's re-education efforts at the Muslims, to Zenz, are tantamount to the "biopolitics" of the "war on terror."[11] Xinjiang is China's largest administrative territory, and it is strategically located along a 5,600-kilometer border with eight nations. As such, China's sensitivity to the separatist activities in Xinjiang is understandable, especially after the September 11, 2001 terrorist attack on the World Trade Center in New York. After the suicide car's bomb attack in Beijing's Tiananmen Square in October 2013, the terrorist attack at a train station in Kunming in March 2014, and the market bombing in Ürümchi in April 2014, China's sensitivity to all these separatist activities was heightened. Zenz concluded that the XUAR then "embarked on a massive human and technological securitization drive that turned the region into one of the most heavily fortified and policed regions in the world."[12] Re-education in XUAR has been conducted in the context of "de-extremification work."[13] Zenz reminded us that the concept of re-education had a long history in Communist China, which established "reform through labor" (*laodong gaizao*), commonly referred to as *laogai*, during the 1950s. While the *laogai* system is part of the formal prison system, the "reeducation through labor" system (*laodong jiaoyang* or *laojiao*) was established in 1957 as an administrative penalty and internment system.[14] *Laojiao* was revised in the 1980s and has been widely used for dissidents, petitioners and criminal elements.

In the early 2000s, another term for re-education emerged to convert Falun Gong followers away from their spiritual beliefs, namely "transformation through education" (*jiaoyu zhuanhua*). Moreover, some "problematic students" are subjected to "transformation through education." In the case of Xinjiang, the term "transformation through education" is restricted to (a) political re-education of the population, especially Muslim minorities, (b) political re-education of cadres and (c) persons detained for "coerced detoxification."[15] Xinjiang's political re-education is conducted through a network of centers (*zhongxin*), bases (*jidi*) and schools (*xuexiao*).[16] Locals often refer to reeducation as attending classes, especially since 2014. According to Zenz, the increasingly widespread application of "transformation through education" to the Uyghur or Muslim population arose in tandem with the "de-extremification" (*qu jiduanhua*) campaign.[17] The phrase "de-extremification" was first used by Xinjiang's former party-secretary Zhang Chunxian in January 2012 at a meeting in Khotän prefecture, where a local legislation was enacted in April 2015 to enforce the policy. In 2015, Chapchal County in Ili Prefecture, which had a 66 percent minority population (28 percent Uyghur), held a 15-day transformation through education training class using a fully closed-style management with training activities in military drill, patriotic singing, criminal law, marriage law, patriotic videos, writing personal reflections, and drama performance. Participants emotionally announced that they must "repent and become new persons."[18] This kind of personal repentance, according to Zenz, was reminiscent of self-criticisms in the Maoist era. Re-education bases were later set up at the county, township and village levels, in which participants had to pass onto the base at the next higher level.[19] Before Chen Quanguo became Xinjiang's new party-secretary in 2016, he had already acquired a reputation in Beijing for successfully pacified the Tibet Autonomous Region (TAR) through a mixture of "intense securitization and penetrating social control mechanisms."[20] In Xinjiang, Chen implemented the same policies, according to Zenz, including massive deployment of police and cadres to monitor villages. The "de-extremification ordinance" embraced the implementation of individual and centralized education, legal education, thought education, psychological counseling, behavioral correction and skills education.[21]

According to Zenz, China's re-education drive in Xinjiang has become "arguably the country's most intense campaign of coercive social re-engineering since the Cultural Revolution."[22] It was a testimony to the PRC's securitization in its western and strategic minority regions, especially as Xinjiang remains the core area of the PRC's Belt and Road initiative. While securitization reduced the officially reported violent incidents from 2017 to the present, the mainland authorities, as Zenz has argued, insist on the utilization of political re-education as a tool of social control. As such, political reeducation also aims at conducting united front work on the Muslim ethnic minority in Xinjiang, trying to win the hearts and minds of the Uyghurs in particular.

Zenz's findings cannot be found in Hong Kong, where political education takes a much softer approach, as this book will argue. Unlike the Uyghurs who had to undergo political reeducation in camps, the Hong Kong Chinese youths are mostly Hans and ethnic minorities embrace South Indians, thereby making it difficult for the HKSAR authorities to implement the style of massive political reeducation as with the Xinjiang case. As this book will show, the Hong Kong experiences show that, after the imposition of the national security law in June 2020, a new national security education has been formulated and implemented at all the schools, ranging from primary to the university levels. Although there is evidence to prove that Hong Kong's education system is undergoing a process of mainlandization – making its curriculum and pedagogy more similar to the mainland – the Hong Kong approach to injecting national education is much softer than the more hardline, massive and camp-style approach adopted in Xinjiang.

As with Zenz, Raza Zainab has argued in 2019 that the PRC's "detention of around one million" Uyghur Muslims in the far-western Chinese province of Xinjiang constituted "considerable human rights abuses [which] were being committed by the Chinese government."[23] Zainab argued that by 2019, 1.5 million were "incarcerated," representing approximately one of every six Uyghur Muslims in Xinjiang.[24] Additionally, there was evidence that the PRC state expanded its "re-education" campaign to children, with nearly every three to six-year-old child was exposed to "a state-controlled educational environment."[25] Some were forced into orphanages and boarding schools under surveillance. The PRC government asserted that the extremist elements "distorted" the facts and that Xinjiang has been traditionally a Chinese territory since the third century. Zainab has claimed that Uygur were frequently visited by Han Chinese relatives who intended to "assimilate them into a homogenized Chinese culture and ensure their loyalty to the government above all else, especially in matters of religion."[26] Zainab wrote that people who did not conform to their minders were sent to camps and that the Hans relatives "teach them Chinese and praise the virtues of Beijing's policies."[27] In other words, political education, ideological indoctrination and attempts at cultural assimilation were conducted.

In fact, ideo-political education is commonplace in the PRC. As a compulsory course at universities throughout the mainland, ideo-political education aims at safeguarding university students' political loyalty to the CCP.[28] In 1951, the MoE mandated that all universities placed ideo-political education at the core of teaching pedagogy and that ideo-political education should be organized by the academic director of the university. Its core courses were "Marxist Political and Economic Theory," "Marxist Philosophy" and "History of the CCP" – usually regarded as "The Three Old Political Courses (*laosanmen*)." The courses emphasized Marxist and Mao Zedong Thought and promoted political leaders' charisma with the objective of legitimizing the PRC's political system and ideology. During the Cultural Revolution from 1966 to 1976, the "Three Old Political Courses" were suspended until 1980, when all universities were required to teach the "Marxist Theory" course again, including "Philosophy," "Political Economy" and "History of the CCP." In 1982, the PRC MoE issued "The Announcement on the Gradual Offering of "Communist Ideo-virtue Courses" at the higher education level," stating that the course's aim was to nurture vision and culture of the CCP in the psyche of university students. Students were expected to be self-disciplined and devoted to the CCP while simultaneously expanding their professional knowledge. In the process of implementing the Four Modernizations during the 1980s, the CCP promulgated "The Announcement on Reforming the Teaching of 'Ideo-virtue' and 'Political Theory' in Schools."[29] Three new political courses were established: "Principles of Marxist Theory," "Construction of Chinese Communism" and "History of Chinese Revolution." By the 1990s, most Chinese universities offered two courses to replace the previous three: "Ideo-political Education" and "Marxist Theory" – commonly known as the "Two Subjects" (*liangke*). In 1998, ideo-political education was expanded to include eight courses: "Principles of Marxist Philosophy," "Principles of Marxist Political Economy," "Introduction to Mao Thought," "Major Ideas of Deng Xiaoping Theory and the Three Representatives," "Nurturing ideo-virtue," "Foundation of Law," "Trends and Policies" and "Contemporary World Economy and Politics" (only for those in the arts stream). The addition of "Foundation of Law" indicated the need to raise juridical awareness due to the process of China's legal modernization and economic development. In 2005, the PRC MoE and Propaganda Department promulgated the "Reform of Ideo-political Curriculum in Higher Education," which said that ideo-political education should take on a greater role in indoctrinating university students on national development and in guiding students to understand not only the developmental objectives of Chinese socialism but also China's international competitiveness. The policy document was guided by Marxist-Leninist Theory, Mao Zedong Thought, Deng Xiaoping Theory and the Three Representatives. Under the new curriculum, six courses were merged to constitute four new compulsory courses: "Basic Principles of Marxism," "Introduction to the Major Theories of Mao, Deng and the Three Representatives," "Principles of Contemporary Chinese History" and "Nurturing Ideo-Virtue and the Foundation of Law." Moreover, a course on "Trends and Policies" and an elective course on "Contemporary World Economy and Politics" were offered. Teachers were expected to replace the old mode of one-sided teaching with new student-centered learning, utilizing case studies and engaging in group discussions and debates. To facilitate the development of teaching and learning pedagogy, some universities organized collective teaching preparation to unify the teaching plan. The MoE produced a teaching film on the best lecture and provided model PowerPoint files and case studies for teachers.

In 2011, Manhong Lai and Leslie Lo found that mainland students expressed strong resistance to compulsory ideo-political courses.[30] From the outset, teachers had to change students' negative perceptions of ideo-political education; they could not attract student interest if they strictly followed the state's designed textbooks.[31] One challenge to their teaching was student bias toward the subject. To attract student interest, teachers found that they had to adjust the course content and their teaching approaches. The aim of ideo-political education was to enhance university students' political ideologies. It was hoped that students would internalize social responsibilities. Some teachers chose to cover topics they found more interesting and to discuss social issues in their lectures – a kind of autonomy some teachers maintained. However, the quality assurance mechanism was imbued with restrictions on their teaching pedagogy, meaning that the question of whether teachers could retain their autonomy depended on the understanding and support of key senior academics.[32]

Lai and Lo's findings have important implications for the HKSAR. The authors' discussions with four teachers, as will be elaborated in this book later, have found that they formerly relied on class discussions in the previous Liberal Studies course and that they are now abandoning such lively discussions in the currently new subject of CSD (which replaced Liberal Studies).[33] It is doubtful whether some teachers who teach CSD will really use current topics to stimulate students' interest, especially as the new curriculum guideline does not encourage teachers to use ongoing events as examples to discuss with students. In short, after the introduction of the national security law in late June 2020 and the implementation of national security education in the HKSAR, the autonomy of teachers has apparently been reduced and their teaching pedagogies tend to be far more politically cautious than ever before.

Party control over higher education in the PRC has been a relatively neglected topic in the literature on the relationships between education and politics in China, except for a few articles, one of which was written by Qinghua Wang.[34] Wang has focused on the post-1989 regime's efforts at strengthening and professionalizing political education at universities by intensifying its "disciplinary construction (*xueke jianshe*)."[35] Yet, such efforts were "partially successful in meeting the regime's objectives."[36] Apparently, the training of political education teachers was professionalized; the related courses became more attractive and effective; and more students tended to accept the party-sponsored views and policies taught in political education courses and to support the CCP leadership. The professionalization of political education, according to Wang, was among the most important measures adopted by the post-1989 regime in the PRC, which sought to consolidate its own legitimacy. These measures embraced, for example, the strengthening of CCP leadership by reverting from the "Presidential Responsibility System," which had been proposed in 1985 on an experimental basis, back to the "Presidential Responsibility System under the Leadership of the University Party Committee."[37] The role of the party committee was to promote patriotic education and accelerate CCP recruitment of party members. Another important measure was the disciplinary construction of political education, namely treating political education work as a science and training the related personnel (such as teachers, theorists, political advisors, workers for public bodies and party cadres) in a scientific manner through political education programs at universities.[38]

Political education, Wang stressed, has become the "lifeline" of the CCP since 1921.[39] It not only persists in the military, economy and various social sectors but also ensures students' political reliability.[40] Political education was a hallmark of Maoist political campaigns and remains an instrument of the CCP to legitimize its rule in the mainland. Wang has alerted us that, in the era of globalization, the PRC regime "has frankly acknowledged that because of the global hegemonic position of the West, Western culture will continue to appeal strongly to students and to Chinese society as a whole, keeping China in a defensive stance."[41] As such, from the regime's perspective, "the Western enemy forces' peaceful evolution (*heping yanbian*) plot toward the CCP will continue to be a grave threat."[42] To prevent Western ideological infiltration into the mainland, political education in universities is of paramount importance. As with Lai and Lo, Wang has observed the significance of disciplinary construction of political education, but he added that political education has become "an academic discipline" with disciplinary status at national, provincial and ministerial levels where teachers and researchers are expected to contribute to its disciplinary development, including curriculum design, training scheme and teaching pedagogy.[43] A large number of undergraduate, master's and doctoral students of this political education discipline have to be trained. However, in the 1980s, the two former CCP party-secretaries, Hu Yaobang and Zhao Ziyang decided that because economic construction was the PRC's national focus, political education was relegated to the level of secondary importance. After the Tiananmen incident in June 1989, and especially after the late Chinese leader Deng Xiaoping's instruction in 1993, political education has reemerged in a more prominent way in higher education.[44] In 1994, the CCP put forward a policy framework to improve moral education in schools, reasserting that political education was a "science." In October 1995, the MoE stipulated that the teaching pedagogy of political education courses should be reformed and that Deng Xiaoping's theories on socialist construction with Chinese characteristics should be regarded as the central content.

In 1996, political education was upgraded to a doctorate-conferring discipline; famous universities like Renmin, Tsinghua and Wuhan Universities became the first institutions admitting doctoral students. Political education, according to Wang, was renamed as the "Marxist Theory and Political Education" and was designated a "second-order discipline" in the "List of Doctorate and Master's Degree-Conferring Disciplines and Majors" promulgated in June 1997.[45] After the 15th Party Congress in 1997, during which the Deng Xiaoping Theory was added to the CCP constitution as one of the guiding theories, political education was reformed to include a course on Deng Xiaoping's theory. By 1997, over 70 universities had bachelor's programs of study in political education, 35 had master's programs, and 3 had doctoral programs.[46] In December 2005, the "Marxist Theory and Political Education" was renamed as "Marxist Theory" and officially upgraded to a "first-order discipline," which consisted of six "second-order disciplines": "Essential Theories of Marxism," "Research on Sinicized (*zhongguohua*) Marxism," "Research on Essential Issues in Modern and Contemporary Chinese History," "Political Education," "History of the Development of Marxism" and "Research on Marxism in Other Countries."[47] In July 2007, the "Marxist Theory" was upgraded to a level with post-doctoral research centers and 25 post-doctoral related programs were established. If socialist education systems are characterized by some degree of political education and indoctrination, the case of the PRC was a typical example.

Political Implications for Hong Kong: From Depoliticization to Politicization

Qinghua Wang's findings are important in our study of Hong Kong's education reform. The Hong Kong case, as will be discussed, does not witness the direct implantation of the mainland Chinese model in which party control is entrenched at university administration, the curriculum is restructured in such a way as to inject a strong element of political education, and the study of Marxism is by no means a compulsory subject at the university level. However, the Hong Kong style of education reform, especially the period immediately after the introduction of the national security law in June 2020 and the implementation of the national security education, is much "softer." It is softer in the sense of emphasizing the Chinese culture, the history of China's war of resistance against Japan during the Second World War, and the emphasis on a whole range of national security issues that impinge on the PRC regime.

Wang has also found that, in the PRC educational setting, Marxism-related programs at the master and doctoral levels have produced a batch of graduates and political education workers, who are the staunch supporters of the PRC regime.[48] The academics who supervise master and doctoral students "possess higher social status and therefore face stricter demands for publication."[49] Moreover, the regime "hopes that PE teachers will conduct more research on issues that arise in their teaching, research that may provide theoretical support for more convincingly answering students' questions."[50] If research can strengthen the teaching of political education, it contributes to the consolidation of political education as a discipline. Academics and graduate students trained under the discipline of political education have gradually become the ideologues supportive of the regime.

In the case of Hong Kong, secondary school teachers who have written up textbooks and references on national security education are gradually becoming the elite of the pro-establishment and pro-national security apparatus. Some principals, vice-principals and secondary school teachers grasp the opportunity of advancing national security education and deepening the students' understanding of Chinese culture and history to contribute to the development of the related curriculum. As a result, they have become the "vanguard" of education reform in the HKSAR.

Furthermore, as will be examined in this book, the Education Bureau (EDB) of the HKSAR government revamped the Liberal Studies subject shortly after the introduction of the national security law in June 2020 and replaced it with the CSD subject. The new CSD subject, as will be discussed in detail, has strong components of Chinese culture, history and national security. As such, the newly reformed subject of the CSD and the emphasis on national security education in Hong Kong have both the shadows and elements of political education. In other words, the combination of National Security Education with the CSD can be seen as a Hong Kong style of political education.

Regarding the attitudes of students toward political education in the PRC, Wang conducted a survey in 2002 during which the respondents were 935 students from five Hunan universities. He found that 35.2 percent of the students said they liked political education courses, 36.7 percent said they did not care (*wu suowei*), and 27.4 percent answered that they were not interested.[51] Furthermore, in a 2005 survey of Wuhan-area university students who were asked if there was a need to have political education courses, 8.6 percent of the 968 respondents wrote "very much so" (*feichang you biyao*) and 37.8 percent chose "there is a need" (*you biyao*), making a total of 46.4 percent.[52] Wang has made the following observations on mainland students: "They embrace Western democratic ideals but will not take political risks to oppose the Party. They do not think highly of communist beliefs but nevertheless actively exploit opportunities and patronage associated with the regime (e.g. by joining the Party)."[53] According to Wang, most mainland students expressed the view that "although China is an authoritarian state, it does not mean that democracy does not exist in China."[54] Given the fact that China remains different from the United States in terms of history, culture and national conditions, there is no point in discussing which political system is the best – a view that, to Wang, is in conformity with the government's perspective. In brief, mainland students' political socialization has been proceeding in such a way that their political culture tends to buttress the regime in power.

In the context of Hong Kong, due to the high degree of political sensitivity in 2020 and 2021, the authors could not conduct any large-scale survey to tap the views of secondary school students toward the replacement of Liberal Studies with the CSD and the introduction of the national security education, for many students preferred to adopt a low profile. However, we spoke to a few former students, whose views will be reported later in this book.

The political objectives of reforming Hong Kong's education system are to achieve several functions: (1) strengthening the legitimacy of the HKSAR government, whose legitimacy was questioned seriously by political activists in the July 1, 2003 mass protest, the 2012 anti-national education campaign, the 2014 Occupy Central Movement, and most importantly the anti-extradition movement in the latter half of 2019; (2) transforming the local identity of many Hong Kong students to a more nationalistic Chinese identity in the coming years; (3) consolidating the legitimacy of the CCP, which has been portrayed and stressed by Beijing authorities as the creator of "one country, two systems" and whose authority was challenged in the anti-extradition movement in 2019 and (4) protecting the national security of the central government in the HKSAR.

The Hong Kong case deserves our attention because of its traditionally strong student resistance to the hegemonic pressure and forces from the governing authorities. Gregory Fairbrother found that both university students in Hong Kong and mainland China reacted to national education as part of the state attempts at establishing and maintaining legitimacy.[55] In colonial Hong Kong, national themes were neglected in civic education, but they became prominent in the policy discourse after its sovereignty reverted to China in 1997. In contrast, national themes were not only significant in Chinese political education during the 1990s but also accompanied by the broadening of political education discourse to embrace other themes such as the rule by law, due process and individual rights.[56] The ultimate objective was to bolster the legitimacy of the CCP. In Hong Kong, the colonial state's claims to legitimacy were based on public consultation in the process of policy-making and the provision of public services; moreover, social stability had to be maintained by depoliticizing the people of Hong Kong and by shunning the promotion of Chinese nationality in society and schools.[57] Fairbrother has brought the concept of hegemony to his analyses, elucidating that the university students in China and Hong Kong became the targets of state hegemony. As with Wang, Lai and Lo, Fairbrother had identified the trends of expanding political education in the PRC. In Hong Kong, however, the colonial state in the 1980s diluted the curricular content pertinent to China and it focused on the Chinese language and the cultural themes in Chinese history courses before the revolutionary era in 1911. However, following the 1984 Sino-British agreement over Hong Kong, the 1985 Guidelines on Civic Education in Schools began to give more prominence to national themes in the entire curriculum, trying to arouse students' awareness of the PRC developments, their "love for the nation and pride in being Chinese," and their willingness to contribute to the PRC's economic development.[58] Then values such as civic awareness, responsibility and to a lesser extent civil and social rights were stressed in the civic education guidelines. Civic education was reshaped in such a way as to promote social and political stability rather than emphasizing "a potentially destabilizing nationality."[59] This depoliticizing approach was questioned by critics, who argued that national themes in education were underemphasized. In May 1996, the Legislative Council called for the government to formulate a comprehensive civic education policy. The first HKSAR Chief Executive, Tung Chee-hwa, said in 1997 that his government would promote the teaching of Chinese history and culture to strengthen the identity of Hong Kong people with China. Gradually, national themes in education appeared in Hong Kong's education reform, including the civic education curriculum, which was revisited in 2002. Other measures taken by the government from 2002 to 2004 embraced Chinese cultural projects, national flag-raising ceremonies in schools on the PRC's National Day, the teaching of the national anthem in school music classes, the designation of Putonghua in 2000 as a public examination subject, and the inception of student and teacher exchanges with mainland China. Fairbrother observed that while the CCP and state organs in the mainland issued various directives on political education after 1979, the public fear of indoctrination among Hong Kong people prevented the post-1997 government from promoting national themes in education.[60] In the early 2000s, civic education was not mandated, while flag-raising ceremonies were compulsory in a small number of government schools.

The politicization of education in the PRC was a contrast to the continuous depoliticization of education in the HKSAR. However, Fairbrother noted that during the 1990s, some mainland students' resistance to the process of hegemony was exhibited primarily through their skeptical attitude toward the accuracy and purpose of political education.[61] Yet, with a broadening of the discourse over citizenship education and an increase in the emphasis on legality and individual rights, the PRC state sought to maintain its hegemony through "an accommodation to subordinate ideologies."[62]

Following the transfer of sovereignty in Hong Kong, nationality has increasingly gained priority as an indispensable element in the new HKSAR state's hegemony.[63] However, this governmental shift did not lead to a change in students' attitudes toward the mainland Chinese nation-state. Fairbrother argued in 2008 that "resistance to national education among the students theoretically would have manifested itself, and in fact did, as a reaction of a stronger sense of skepticism toward education for nationality, having an effect opposite to what the state intended."[64] His observation turned out to be accurate in 2012 when the government's introduction of the national education curriculum met the fierce resistance and opposition from many parents, students and intellectuals. Fairbrother's conclusion that there was resistance from students to political education was valid until late June 2020, when the national security law was imposed by the PRC onto the HKSAR. Since then, as this book will discuss, the push for political education in Hong Kong has been so strong that even students, parents and intellectuals cannot resist it. Resisting it means an act of disobeying the national security law – a cost too high for students, parents, intellectuals and those democrats imbued with a strong sense of local Hong Kong identity. If political education represents a kind of ideological hegemony from the state,[65] then the national security education and national education imposed by mainland China on the HKSAR since late June 2020 symbolize the hegemonic pressures exerted by the strong PRC state on the local Hong Kong city-state.

In another work, Fairbrother compared and contrasted the attitudes of Hong Kong students with their mainland counterparts, arguing that the former were characterized by their curiosity toward mainland China and the latter punctuated by their skepticism about mainland schooling and governmental indoctrination.[66] In other words, Hong Kong students generally believed that their knowledge of mainland China would be deepened after they enrolled in universities, while mainland students generally perceived that what they learned outside schools was different from their political socialization in their school years. With the benefit of hindsight, especially considering the developments in the HKSAR after the imposition of the national security law in late June 2020, the PRC authorities are determined to re-politicize the Hong Kong students, who were depoliticized by the colonial government and, to some extent, the HKSAR government shortly after the handover in July 1997 in such a way that they lacked, in the minds of Beijing, sufficiently strong Chinese nationalism. The inculcation of a stronger national Chinese identity in the mind of Hong Kong students is now deep-rooted in the psyche of PRC officials responsible for the HKSAR.

Students as the CCP's Key Targets of Mobilization and Politicization: Implications for Hong Kong

After decades of strenuous efforts, the CCP has established a multi-tiered system, including co-option, surveillance and monitoring, and ideological and political education, to ensure its domination of Chinese college students.[67] Traditionally, mainland college students were playing a crucial role in leading and mobilizing political movements in 1895, when they promoted reforms in the Qing Dynasty, in 1919 as they initiated the New Culture Movement, in 1935 as they advocated a unified front against Japan, in 1966 as they rebelled against the bureaucratic establishment, in 1976 when they protested against the Gang of Four, and in 1989 when they exerted pressure on political reform and anti-corruption. To buttress its legitimacy, the CCP mobilized and recruited college students as allies in the competition against the Kuomintang (KMT) in the 1940s, as contributors to its policies of industrialization and collectivization in the 1950s, as players in its political campaigns during the 1960s and 1970s, and as supporters for its market-oriented reforms in the 1980s.[68] Nevertheless, "the power of college students is Janus-faced, which could turn violent and threatening if not effectively guided and shaped."[69] Most importantly, the CCP learned a bitter lesson from the May and June 1989 incident when the power of college students was unleashed and when it had to be suppressed by the military force. To win the hearts and minds of mainland students, the CCP had to resort to indoctrination by strengthening ideological and political education in China's higher education. Deng Xiaoping remarked on June 9, 1989, that the "biggest mistake in the past ten years" was the lack of effective "ideological and political education."[70] As a result, the CCP made strenuous efforts at co-opting and recruiting college students. By the end of 2014, college students occupied about 2.56 percent of the 87.8 million CCP members – about 37 percent of the newly recruited CCP members in that year.[71] Furthermore, the Communist Youth League (CYL) provided an additional recruitment channel and surveillance tool for the party to co-opt the youths. Through the establishment of *xueke jianshe* (disciplinary construction) for ideological and political education, the CCP made an investment in grooming high-quality personnel to nurture more young people loyal to the party-state than ever before.[72] Gradually, the political culture of college students in the PRC changed from being critical questioners of the party to its loyal supporters.

After Xi Jinping became China's top leader in 2012, he has paid special attention to the role of political ideology and education to ensure the longevity of the CCP in governing the PRC. In 2012, the MoE and the CCP's Publicity Department jointly distributed the trial version of the Assessment System for Ideological and Political Education for College Students (ASIPECS).[73] Apart from the 20 indicators of assessing higher education institutions, ASIPECS added 12 indicators for assessing provincial and municipal governments, which were responsible for higher education's performance. In 2014, the CCP issued a guideline on how to strengthen and improve ideological and political education in higher education institutes, where a new program was later launched in 2015 to call for innovations in establishing political theory courses. All levels of the party committees would be responsible for all issues pertinent to ideological and political education in higher education institutes. During a national meeting on political and ideological work at universities and colleges in late 2016, President Xi personally emphasized the importance of political education and called for strengthened ideological work in all higher education institutes. As instructed by President Xi, the primary goal of political and ideological work in mainland universities and colleges is to consolidate the CCP's leadership in higher education. The CCP's political education focuses on the CCP's history, development and its policies, indoctrinating students at higher education institutes, and exerting pressure on the local government leaders to put ideological work on the top of their agenda. In other words, local leaders are more likely to get career promotion and advancement if their political education work is seen as satisfactory. Above all, mainland surveys showed that the CCP's revived ideological and political education in higher education contributed to curbing the power of college students.[74] A large percentage of college students found the ideological and political education courses "interesting and attractive" with high attendance rates and higher trust in central and local political authorities and institutions.[75] Most significantly, the support for China's existing political system is strong among college students, who "are also quite responsive to the CCP's political mobilizations via strategically staged political events (e.g. the 2015 military parade)."[76] Despite the Internet's growing influence, the majority of college students acquire their information on the CCP and key socio-economic policies through official channels, such as ideological and political education courses, which are effectively and skillfully controlled by the CCP.[77] All these channels offer the CCP "a critical upper hand in China's political communication."[78] Thanks to the CCP's cooptation of college students through recruitment, surveillance and through the activities of party branches and student work system on campus, "the power of college students has been fairly tamed and effectively controlled."[79]

The mobilization of college students and CYL members to participate in major events, like the centennial celebration of the CCP on July 1, 2021, could stimulate their patriotism and nationalism and boost their support of the PRC's political system. In fact, President Xi Jinping's speech on July 1, 2021, appealed to the youth to support the Chinese renaissance, meaning that the young people should not only support China's economic rise but also the CCP, which to Xi is the major contributor to the Chinese renaissance.[80] A closer reading of President Xi's speech showed how he, as the Party's General Secretary and the Chairman of the Central Military Commission, induced the patriotic and nationalistic sentiment of the young people. He emphasized that the CCP led China to "fully establish a *xiaokang* (an affluent) society" and that it is keen to construct the PRC into a "socialist, modernized and powerful country in the second 100 years."[81] This is the "great honor" of not only the Chinese people but also the CCP.

President Xi harped on the theme of stressing Chinese nationalism, saying that, with 5,000 years of civilization, China suffered from national humiliation after the 1840 Opium War. As such, the realization of the "Chinese Renaissance" is the "greatest ideal of the Chinese people and the Chinese nation."[82] President Xi invoked the historical nationalistic sentiment of the Chinese people by referring to how the Chinese people fought for their national survival, ranging from the Taiping rebellion to the Hundred Days Reform and from the Boxer rebellion to the 1911 revolution. Amid these difficult paths of modernization, the CCP emerged, thanks to the Sinification of Marxism-Leninism. He praised all the previous Chinese leaders who adapted Marxism to the Chinese circumstances and who developed the CCP further, including Mao Zedong, Deng Xiaoping, Jiang Zemin, Hu Jintao, Zhou Enlai, Liu Shaoqi, Zhu De and Chen Yun. Ideologically, President Xi laid the emphases on the need to persist in the belief in Marxism-Leninism, the Mao Zedong Thought, the Deng Xiaoping Theory, the three scientific representatives, the insight of scientific development, and the new era of "fully implement the Chinese-style socialism."[83] He believed that Chinese Marxism would have to be developed further in the twenty-first century.

On the role of the CCP, President Xi remarked that the Party realizes the Chinese renaissance, solidifies the Chinese people, liberates their thoughts, and achieves the great success of the open-door policy and socialist modernization. He said: "Without the CCP, there would not be the new China and there would not be the Chinese renaissance."[84] The CCP coordinates "all the interests of the nationalities" in the entire country.[85] It must persistently "elevate the standards of the Party's scientific governance, democratic government, the implementation of law and the full development of the Party's coordination and provision of core leadership."[86]

President Xi added that while the party represents "the root interests of the people," it does not represent any interest group or privileged stratum. As such, "any attempt to separate the CCP from the Chinese people and to make their relationships confrontational is bound to fail and is destined to be rejected by 95 million CCP members."[87] He also stressed the importance of having a strong military to ensure national safety and security. The Party must lead and instruct the military, while China must insist on the need for a strong military with Chinese characteristics.

Finally, President Xi stressed that to unify the Chinese people inside and outside China, the CCP must put its united front work on top of its agenda, consolidating all the forces and achieving the objective of the Chinese renaissance. To strive for success, the Party must inculcate a strong political consciousness of governing itself effectively and assertively by eradicating "all the viruses that erodes the health and skin of the CCP."[88] Under these circumstances, the Party "will by no means change its quality, color and taste," while simultaneously becoming the "strong core leadership" in the path of developing Chinese-style socialism.[89] Xi's powerful speech appealed to the young people to stick to patriotism and nationalism and to support the CCP loyally.

Apart from the utilization of powerful speeches and the mobilization of students to participate in CCP events, the PRC has indoctrinated children by relying on role models as a means of political socialization and moral education. Ray Garland Reeds had long observed that mainland Chinese students were encouraged to learn from the socialist role model, Lei Feng.[90] In answer to the question "What are the children really learning from Comrade Lei Feng?," Reeds found that Chinese children in post-1949 China "were actually learning a set of core virtues that have their roots in the Confucian tradition and that individual Chinese constructed their own versions of the role model in accordance with their own beliefs."[91] Although the socialist role models such as Lei Feng would disappear as China becomes increasingly capitalistic, the use of role models as a pedagogical tool will not fade away.[92] Reed noted that cultural heroes, role models and moral exemplars were the means through which the continuity of Chinese culture had been expressed over the centuries. The incorruptible scholars, officials and loyal servants were recognized literary types whose standards for behavior imparted the values and ideals of the Chinese culture.

These prototypes, according to Reed, were employed as models by emperors, magistrates, teachers and parents to inspire moral rectitude for others to emulate. These models have encouraged filial piety, generosity, diligence, chastity and integrity, providing a means through which ruling elites and regimes can perpetuate their authority. As a historical model, Lei Feng was "a man of modest consequence" without power and strength.[93] Nevertheless, he was diligent and loyal to the Party and Mao Zedong, serving the people and the socialist motherland. In 1963, when Mao called upon the nation to learn from comrade

Lei Feng, the CCP, CYL, the propaganda department of the People's Liberation Army (PLA) and the Party leadership all joined forces to portray him as a model of national emulation. As such, the Confucian virtue of learning from role models was intermingled powerfully with the socialist mobilization of individuals and groups to worship Lei Feng. It could be argued that mainland Chinese children were learning "a set of proletarianized Confucian values."[94] In the Maoist era, some teachers who portrayed Lei Feng as a model used slide shows and pictures in their teaching pedagogy, while others used art projects to encourage students to draw Lei's portrait. However, students whose class background was regarded as "undesirable," such as parents having a middle-class or landlord background before CCP came to power in 1949, could be denied entry into the CYL.[95] Indeed, not all students in the Maoist era liked Lei Feng; a minority saw their own family members as role models rather than those models politically sanctioned by the government.[96] Overall, the utilization of role models and the inculcation of values such as loyalty, filial piety, modesty and frugality constituted the means through which the CCP conducted political education and ideological indoctrination among the mainland citizens.

In regions populated with ethnic minorities, such as the Tibetans, the PRC government cultivated talents, induced political loyalty, and sped up development there by establishing Tibetan *neidi* (interior region) classes and schools in many parts of China from the mid-1980s onward.[97] The origin of this education policy, according to Zhu Zhiyong and Deng Meng, could arguably be traced back to the Tang dynasty and the Republican period. The methods used by the CCP fluctuated between "culturalization" and "politicization."[98] There are two basic school educational systems for young Tibetans in the TAR: the state-run school system within TAR and the Tibetan *Neidi* Boarding Schools (classes) for TAR students located in different parts of China. Altogether 55 ethnic minority groups are officially recognized. According to Zhu and Deng, "ethnic identity was increased with ethnic recognition in the political and ideological thinking."[99] To maintain the political rights of ethnic minorities, autonomous institutions and preferential policies were implemented in minority regions. The PRC government realizes the need to integrate all ethnic groups into the Chinese nation. Under this circumstance, the Tibetan *Neidi* Classes were established, and the state's ideology and culture have been emphasized in the design of the curriculum for Tibetan students. However, the lack of Tibetan culture through the school curriculum has ironically enhanced the ethnic identity of the Tibetan students.[100] Therefore, amid the propagation of state ideology and culture, ethnic minority students in the PRC can develop their cultural identity through their own practices, discussions and interactions.

The gradual increase in the student population in the PRC, and the radical transformation from an elite to a mass education system, have since the early 2000s put great pressure on China's higher education institutions to redesign its citizenship education programs for the sake of encouraging their civic learning and participation in the wider society.[101] A survey of 12 mainland universities conducted from May to June 2007 found that the majority of students valued their civic responsibility and viewed it as a crucial motivation of social participation.[102] When asked how they benefited from their associational life, more than 91.4 percent of students viewed networking or socializing as their major benefit out of civic engagement. Next to networking was social learning, but the development of leadership ability was perceived as relatively less important. The findings pointed to the phenomenon that students mostly benefited from civic engagement through socialization, which was motivated by their civic responsibility. Moreover, there were 52.9 percent, 82.4 percent and 87.5 percent of Chinese college students who believed that they had a clear idea of the concept of civil society, of being patriotic and loyal to China, and of having an obligation to actively participate in activities that benefited their society, respectively.[103] For the reason why fewer students showed their positive attitude toward civil society, Li Jun hypothesized that they were under the influence of "strong ideological-political education dominating course offerings and campus culture in Chinese universities."[104] As such, Chinese college students "may be exposed to less citizenship education in terms of broader concepts of citizenship and civil society but to more ideological–political education on campuses."[105] Unlike Hong Kong students, who generally had a weak sense of national identity, mainland Chinese students generally had relatively "very strong and firm feelings towards their nationality."[106]

Li Jun's findings are politically significant for our study of the politics of education reform in the HKSAR. If Hong Kong students are generally imbued with a weaker sense of national identity, it is natural that PRC authorities, and the HKSAR government, are keen to inject a much stronger sense of national identity into the psyche of Hong Kong students than ever before. This governing mentality explains why the HKSAR government after the promulgation of the national security law by the Standing Committee of the National People's Congress (SCNPC) in late June 2020, has become very active and assertive in not only the introduction of the national security education but also the consolidation of Chinese history and culture at the primary and secondary school levels – a phenomenon that this book will examine in detail.

In China, according to Li, "ongoing political campaigns for patriotic education centered on nationalism in formal and informal schooling mandated by the CPC-led Chinese government might be the most obvious."[107] Patriotism stems partly from relatively independent grassroots movements, which include groups, individual citizens and netizens, as evidenced from time to time in the fluctuating relationships between China and Japan on the one hand and the PRC and the United States on the other hand. Yet, these movements were of sporadic nature and subject to the CCP's surveillance. Most importantly, Li Jun has observed that "patriotism is usually narrowed and blurred by nationalism, and [that it] has become a double-edged sword for the stability and legitimacy" of the CCP.[108] Popular nationalist groups could rise and threaten the CCP legitimacy. Li has concluded that Chinese college students tended to see their civic commitment as the most important motivation for civic participation and that most of them benefitted from their political socialization with special appreciation of networking and personal socialization opportunities.

The double-edged nature of popular nationalistic groups in the PRC has implications for the HKSAR. During the anti-national education campaign in the summer of 2012, popular groups that emerged in Hong Kong were not nationalistic and patriotic, but they were of critical and liberal nature, such as the student group Scholarism led by young activist Joshua Wong Chi-fung. During the Occupy Central Movement from September to December 2014, popular groups that sprung up in the HKSAR were pro-democracy, post-materialistic (supportive of human rights and civil liberties) and liberal-minded, but they had a weak sense of Chinese patriotism and nationalism. Similarly, the radical groups and individuals that confronted the police in the 2016 Mongkok riot, such as the Hong Kong Indigenous, were localist or nativist in nature, but their sense of Chinese nationalism was weak. Most importantly, localist groups from 2012 to 2016 were anti-CCP – a phenomenon that explained why PRC authorities later were determined to impose the national security law onto the HKSAR, especially after the violent confrontations between radical localists and police during the anti-extradition movement from June to December 2019. If the CCP legitimacy was challenged and undermined by localist groups in Hong Kong from 2012 to 2019, then the imposition of the national security law and its related national security education would be necessary in the eyes of CCP authorities dealing with Hong Kong affairs.

Judging from the participation of hundreds of thousands of students from primary, secondary and university levels in the anti-extradition movement in the latter half of 2019, many Hong Kong students participated in politics due to their strong sense of local Hong Kong identity. Many of them perceived the extradition bill as an erosion of civil liberties in the HKSAR. Their civic participation, to use Li Jun's term, stemmed from a strong sense of civic commitment. Nevertheless, since the extradition bill was utilized by the HKSAR government and the PRC authorities to pursue the corrupt mainland people who laundered their dirty money in Hong Kong,[109] the anti-extradition movement was naturally seen by Beijing as anti-CCP, anti-China, anti-HKSAR government and "unpatriotic." As such, the crackdown on the activists in the anti-extradition movement is understandable.

The Politics of Educational Reforms in Mainland China: Implications for Hong Kong

In the PRC, there were three notable phases of educational reform since the adoption of its open-door policy in 1978.[110] The first phase from 1978 to the 1980s was efficiency-oriented because the PRC state rebuilt the education system from the ruins caused by the Cultural Revolution. In 1986, the NPC enacted the Compulsory Education Law, which stipulated that every child should complete nine years of formal schooling, including six years for primary and three years for junior secondary schools. The PRC government also promoted economic reform and slowly established the socialist market mechanism. The CCP saw education as a means of developing the economy. At the same time, Deng

Xiaoping's policy of allowing a minority of the people to become rich first put elite education as a priority of the CCP agenda. In education policies and documents, the concepts of efficiency, effectiveness and competition emerged in the early 2000s. The second phase from the 1990s to the early 2000s was equality oriented.[111] The PRC government focused on not only better public access to basic education and the right to education for every child but also the responsibility for compulsory education. Key schools were abolished and integrated into the system of compulsory education. The priority was to minimize the disparity in education between urban and rural areas, between eastern and western regions, and among the affluent and less well-off groups. The third phase from the early 2000s to the present is innovation-oriented stage characterized by a shift of the strategy from "made in China" to "innovation in China" – a response to the era of globalization and the need for a knowledge-based economy.[112] The current period is also marked by a focus on creativity, research, sustainable development and life-long learning capabilities. Education reform must be carried out to sustain China's socio-economic development. It has to cultivate the global awareness of Chinese students, who can have their international competitive capabilities. The current period of education reform is punctuated by internationalization with cooperative and exchange relations with various countries and international organizations. Although the sour Sino-American relations during the US presidency of Donald Trump affected educational collaboration between the two countries, the overall education reform in China has moved toward the path of globalization and internationalization.

Huang, Wang and Li have noted that amid the process of internationalization of education, two ideological discourses persist in the PRC: neo-liberalism and the new left.[113] Neo-liberals embrace the interests of the newly rising wealthy classes, support the deepening of market reforms and "identify globalism with universal freedom and democracy."[114] The new left, however, articulates the interests of workers and farmers, arguing that the PRC state should protect the poor and the needy and resist the forces of globalization. To the neo-liberals, globalization can coexist with local Chinese values. To the new left, globalization is equivalent to Westernization – a process that must be resisted. The challenge for the PRC's education reform is how to strike a balance between globalization and indigenization. In 2009, Shanghai students participated in the Program for International Student Assessment (PISA) for the first time – a sign of educational globalization.[115] The Shanghai Municipal Education Commission was the department leading this project in collaboration with the Shanghai Academy of Educational Science, the Shanghai Examination Institute, the Shanghai Educational Evaluation Institute and District Education Bureaus.[116] The intention was to monitor the outcome and effectiveness of Shanghai's education reform, assess the city's position in international benchmarking tests and promote further reforms.

Huang, Wang and Li have observed that the PRC has a long tradition of centralization in its education reform.[117] Education has been traditionally regarded as an instrument to promote socio-economic development and to disseminate the official ideology. As such, the Party-state has monopolized the provision, financing and governance of education.[118] This situation remained in the 1960s and 1970s until the introduction of market reforms in the early 1980s when decentralization was considered as necessary in education reform. This process of decentralization revealed a paradox of the forces between decentralization and centralization. The first stage of decentralizing education reform focused on educational administration and the coordination between central, provincial and local governments during the mid-1980s. Local governments were responsible for the provision of primary and secondary education; nonetheless, the central government shifted the financial responsibilities to local authorities rather than delegating decision-making power.[119] Therefore, local governments found alternative funding sources to support schools, including tuition fees, donations, and school-run enterprises.

The second stage of educational decentralization, according to Huang, Wang and Li, was to coordinate the relations between education and society.[120] Delegation and devolution were experimented, including the empowerment of parents, the presence of more choices, and the implementation of school-based management. In 1993 the central government came up with a new program for education reform, shifting the primary focus from economic development to human resource development. In 1997 the State Council published the Regulations for Running School by Social Forces, trying to diversify education providers by encouraging corporations, enterprises, social organizations, groups and individuals to contribute to the establishment and management of non-state schools. Gradually, some private and non-state schools emerged. The third stage of decentralization of education reform began in the early 2000s, involving legislation and the privatization of education. In 2002, the SCNPC enacted the Law of Privately-Run Education Promotion (or *minban*, non-state education), conferring upon private schools the same status as with public schools. The legislation defined the rights and duties of private institutions, teachers and students. Huang, Wang and Li have cautioned us that the PRC's education reform is characterized by the coexistence of centralization, decentralization and recentralization.[121] They wrote: "The processes of decentralized centralizations do happen in areas of education such as fiscal reform, school management and curriculum reform. With fiscal reform, the central government diversifies the education providers and allows various institutions or individuals to participate in establishing or managing schools."[122] On the other hand, the central government sponsors various programs and provides loans and subsidies for schools and teachers' professional development. Moreover, it moves village-based, town and city government finance in education to the county and provincial government levels. Most importantly, the central government promotes a national education inspection system, monitoring the efficiency and effectiveness of expenditures and evaluating the outcomes of education. Hence, the role of the central government in education reform shifted from "an omnipotent to a limited government, from regulation to deregulation, from command/control administration to guided governance."[123] Overall, the process of decentralization has remained top-down with the feature of "decentralized centralization."

The decentralized nature of education reform within China's centralized education system can be seen in curriculum reforms. In 1988, the MoE initiated reforms to change the unified national curricula to diversified textbooks; some publishers and provincial education authorities were allowed to compile their textbooks for provincial and local use. Shanghai, Guangdong, Zhejiang and Sichuan were asked to develop local curricula. Three years later, the Outline of Basic Education Curriculum Reform was issued, implementing curriculum reforms at the national, provincial and city levels. The new policy encouraged principals and teachers develop school-based curricula, while local education authorities could choose from the centrally approved textbooks. Some degree of school autonomy and teacher professional autonomy were encouraged, but some observers believed that this reform was not decentralization, but it was a process of recentralization that could consolidate governmental control and auditing.[124] The national curriculum could be seen as a mechanism of central control over local education reform, for the central authorities set the parameters and limits clearly. Such control includes, for example, the competitive national college entrance examination for senior high school graduates or the annual *gaokao*. Another example of central control is the teaching quality evaluation conducted by MoE from 2003 to 2008. In short, central control has been intermingled with selective decentralization in China's education reforms. Most importantly, education reform in the PRC is by no means neutral, but it is "fundamentally political" and "highlights the importance of dealing with the relationship between education and the state."[125]

The findings of Huang, Wang and Li have important implications for Hong Kong's education reforms. Firstly, the ideological divide between neo-liberalism and the "new left" can be seen in the HKSAR's education reforms, especially after the imposition of the national security law in late June 2020. While the education authorities in the HKSAR prior to the introduction of the national security law adopted a largely neo-liberal ideology, their successors since late June 2020 have been characterized by leftism, namely an ideological drift toward the mainland Chinese approach of reforming the education system, including the injection of national security education, the strengthening of the content of Chinese culture and history, and the dilution of the Liberal Studies curriculum introduced by the post-1997 liberal-minded education authorities. In other words, since late June 2020, there has been a process of rolling back the neo-liberal reforms introduced by the early post-1997 education authorities. The neo-liberal education reforms, in the eyes of the PRC officials responsible for Hong Kong matters were politically hostile and detrimental to the legitimacy of both the HKSAR administration and central government in Beijing. The Liberal Studies subject was seen as producing politically disobedient, defiant and "rebellious" students who constantly challenged the legitimacy of the dual states, namely the central state in the PRC and the local state in the HKSAR.

The second important finding of Huang, Wang and Li is the dynamic relationship between centralization and decentralization. The final years of the British colonial administration in Hong Kong introduced education reforms by implementing some degree of decentralization – a practice inherited by the post-1997 education authorities until June 2020. A process of recentralization from the central authorities in Beijing has become obvious since late June 2020, forcing the local education officials in the HKSAR to implement drastic education reforms. The objectives are to inculcate a strong sense of Chinese patriotism and national identity and to indoctrinate more Hong Kong young people on their need to understand the PRC history and to respect, if not necessarily support, the CCP. This book will later examine how political education and indoctrination have been conducted since late June 2020.

Education Reforms in Hong Kong

Michael Lanford's recent study of the perceptions of higher education reform in Hong Kong has shown that policy-makers, faculty members and administrators felt the necessity of such reform.[126] He interviewed administrators and professors who were aware of the need for constant re-evaluation of reform issues and who expected that lessons could be drawn from the learning experiences. Writing before the introduction of the national security law in the HKSAR in June 2020, Lanford observed that a liberal arts education was "fundamental to the development and longevity of a knowledge economy" in Hong Kong.[127] He identified an emerging international market of liberal arts education, a phenomenon different from the United States. However, Lanford's observation was valid for only a short period of time, for the Liberal Studies curriculum in Hong Kong's secondary schools was quickly perceived as producing students not only critical of the HKSAR government and Beijing authorities but also harmful to the legitimacy of the local and central states, especially from 2012 to 2019 when social movements in Hong Kong were thriving. As a result, liberal arts education in Hong Kong's secondary schools after the introduction of the national security law in June 2020 has been limited, although liberal arts subjects persist in local universities.

Neo-liberalism was an ideology shaping education reforms in the HKSAR from July 1, 1997, to late June 2020, when the promulgation of the national security law changed the neo-liberal ideology to the ideology of Chinese patriotism and nationalism. Wai-Chi Chee has identified the trends of marketization and neo-liberalism in Hong Kong's education reforms.[128] The post-colonial state regulated teachers who negotiated their professionalism and were imbued with the "oppositional cultures against the new governance."[129] While neo-liberal reforms in education can enhance class power and the rising inequality between high-ranking and low-ranking schools, the case of Hong Kong did show the features of neo-liberalism. Elite schools have been traditionally regarded by students and parents highly, whereas low-ranking schools have found it difficult to climb up the status ladder. Chee observes that the post-1997 education authorities used narratives to describe some schools as failing to provide quality education and lacking sufficient public scrutiny in how they spent public money. As such, the post-1997 education authorities developed the penchant of deploying not only quality assurance mechanism as governing tools but also the declining student population as the "state disciplinary apparatus."[130] However, teachers countered the "hegemony" of the post-colonial state through negotiations and organizational resistance.

Chee's findings are important in two crucial aspects. First, PRC authorities regarded neo-liberalism as a politically undesirable and hostile ideology detrimental to the legitimacy of the HKSAR government and the central state in Beijing. Neo-liberalism fostered some degree of pluralism in the Hong Kong education system, where students and teachers as individuals and groups were empowered to resist the post-colonial government's policies, such as the 2012 national education policy, the 2015 political reform blueprint, and the 2019 extradition bill. As such, PRC authorities were determined to impose the national security law in June 2020 as a turning point to reverse neo-liberalism and transform it into political education that instills a greater sense of Chinese patriotism and nationalism into the psyche of teachers and students. Second, Chee's finding on the resistance of teachers to the "hegemony" of the post-colonial state is politically significant. Given the hegemonic nature of the socialist regime of the PRC, and due to the strong leadership of the CCP in mainland China, PRC authorities naturally saw the anti-hegemony tendency of many Hong Kong teachers as a "rebellious" political culture that has to be changed.

Teachers play a crucial role in any education reform. In the case of Hong Kong, Pattie Yuk Yee Luk-Fong and Marie Brennan found that teachers experienced a lot of new forms of "glocal" practices, namely the mixture of global and local practices in the implementation of education reforms.[131] While global education reforms embrace pupil centeredness, curriculum reforms and school-based assessment, Confucian traditions included teacher-centered pedagogy, emphasis on academic achievement and high-stakes examinations. Education reforms globally exhibit features of managerialism, standardized curricula and accountability mechanisms. In response to the globalization of education reforms, Hong Kong teachers not only translated these reforms into practices but also interpreted their experiences in the context of Hong Kong. Specifically, the unique circumstances of Hong Kong witnessed the interplay between Western values and Chinese cultural traditions.

These findings on the interplay between Western practices and Chinese cultural tradition can be applied to our deeper understanding of the contextual environment of Hong Kong's education reforms after July 1, 1997. From 1997 to June 2020, the post-colonial education authorities adopted the global trend of education reforms, emphasizing managerialism, standardized curricula and accountability measures. However, the turning point came in late June 2020, when the national security law was imposed onto the HKSAR. Since then, education reforms in Hong Kong have taken a Chinese spin, displaying more mainland Chinese features than ever before. These Chinese features include, for example, the strengthening of national security education, the emphasis on Chinese history and culture, the obedience of students to political authorities, and the inculcation of national Chinese identity into the psyche of both teachers and students. The 2019 anti-extradition protests and movements have been viewed by Beijing as illegal and politically undesirable. Hence, if the interplay between the Western and Eastern cultures characterized education reform in the HKSAR from 1997 to June 2020, then the predominance of Chinese political values has become increasingly preponderant over Western values since July 2020, when the national security law began to be implemented.

Historically speaking, Hong Kong's education reforms borrowed much from other systems. Katherine Forestier, Bob Adamson, Christine Han and Paul Morris have found that Hong Kong benchmarked internationally by participating in such international tests as the Organization for Economic Co-operation and Development's Programme for International Student Assessment (PISA) and the International Association for the Evaluation of Educational Achievement's Trends in International Mathematics and Science Study and Progress in International Reading Literacy Study.[132] Although Hong Kong's international testing was ranked high in the 1980s, it embarked on further education reforms during the 1990s, culminating in the launch of a new academic structure and new school leaving qualification, namely the Hong Kong Diploma of Secondary Education (HKDSE). From the beginning of these reforms, Hong Kong's education authorities indicated that they would borrow the policies from elsewhere. The Hong Kong approach to implementing education reforms involved not only a practice of referencing and borrowing from the international systems, tests and assessments but also an increasing speed of policy transfer in the context of globalization.[133] Hong Kong's education policy-makers adapted the Western practices to the setting of the HKSAR, for there was "a determination to resolve dichotomies between East and West and the so-called traditional and progressive approaches to education, and to work through collaborative networks that bridge policy, practice and academia."[134] A strong degree of collaboration between policy-makers, practitioners and academics was found in the Hong Kong experiences of referencing and borrowing the Western practices.

Mainlandization of Hong Kong's Education Reforms

The finding on the mixture of Western and local Hong Kong practices has implications for the imposition of the PRC-initiated education reforms in the HKSAR since late June 2020. If borrowing and referencing practices from the West were commonplace in Hong Kong's education reforms from July 1, 1997, to late June 2020, the mainlandization of education reforms in the HKSAR has become both a new and prominent feature since July 2020. The practices of referencing and borrowing have since June 2020 come from the mainland rather than the West. The mainlandization of Hong Kong's education reforms is characterized by (1) the dilution of the neo-liberal elements in the Liberal Studies subject and its replacement by the CSD curriculum; (2) the strengthening of Chinese history and culture in the school curricula; (3) the emphasis on the Chinese national security in different subjects and at varying levels of schools (primary, secondary and tertiary); (4) the organization of various activities, ranging from exhibition to school events, that can and will consolidate Chinese patriotism and nationalism and (5) the retraining of both teachers and students on the need to not only respect the PRC's national security interest and sovereignty but also to understand the Chinese history and culture in a much deeper way than ever before.

The study of education reforms in Hong Kong must consider the role of students, whose local identity has been quite strong since the 1970s. Iris Chuiping Kam has found that the "new, modern and self-determining identity of the Hongkongese" was a prominent feature of the Hong Kong youths since the 1970s.[135] Such local identity was fostered by the colonial administration as a way of containing the political turbulence – a legacy from the riots in 1966 and 1967. After the riots, an inquiry commission was set up by the British colonial government to study its causes, coming up with the conclusion that there was a huge communication gap between the colonizers and the ruled. As such, apart from the introduction of social reforms, the inculcation of a strong sense of local identity began with the adoption of education reforms. Iris Kam has argued that to build up a stronger sense of civic belonging, the Hong Kong education system was depoliticized with a more "abstract" academic curriculum without reference to the national sentiments of local Hong Kong Chinese.[136] Instead, a strong emphasis on academic achievements in public examinations and the access to well-paid employment to private and public sectors after graduation could be seen. As a matter of fact, Hong Kong had a long history of examinations administered within the territory. The Cambridge Local Examinations were introduced in 1886 and they were replaced by Oxford Examinations in 1889. In 1937, the Education Department set up a local school certificate examination, which was later administered by a separate Hong Kong Examination and Assessment Authority (HKEAA) in 1977. The persistence of examinations provided the colonial government with the instrument to control the curricula of secondary schools, including the content and design of all curricula and impacting on the life and values of students. Nevertheless, under the British administration, Hong Kong's education lacked the China elements, except for the subject of Chinese history, until 1998 when the Curriculum Development Council revised the Chinese history syllabus and introduced modern China as a topic in personal and social education. Still, the element of Chineseness remained relatively weak until 2012, when the HKSAR government tried but failed to introduce the subject of national education. Iris Kam has observed that the injection of the China element in personal and social education reform represented an intention of strengthening the Chinese identity.[137] However, the reform was inadequate because the identity of students after 1997 remained ambiguous. Kam wrote shortly after the abortive national education policy in 2012: "Based on the assumption that the increase in the knowledge of China will lead to the increase of patriotic feelings among students, it fails to address a more fundamental and subtle issue of how an intensely unifying national identity promoted in the personal and social education reform is indeed differentiated from the day-to-day cultural experiences of students."[138] She observed that the "ambiguous identity" of students would continue after the introduction of the Liberal Studies subject in 2009 because the new subject placed much emphases on the development of generic skills and critical thinking of students.

Kam's observations had important implications for education reforms in the HKSAR during the abortive attempt at introducing national education in 2012. Because many students, parents and intellectuals perceived the government's national education policy as "brainwashing" the school children of Hong Kong, the new Chief Executive C. Y. Leung backed down by announcing just one day before the September 2012 Legislative Council elections that schools would be allowed to choose whether the national education curriculum would be implemented. This meant that, due to public opposition, the government made concessions and almost abandoned the new policy in September 2012. However, from the perspective of PRC authorities responsible for Hong Kong matters, the HKSAR government was politically weak, and the public opposition was stirred up by pro-democracy and anti-PRC politicians. PRC officials hoped that the Chinese national identity of Hong Kong school children should be enhanced by adopting the national education curriculum and policy. Hence, the consolidation of the Chinese national identity is often in the minds of the PRC authorities dealing with Hong Kong matters.

The eruption of the early 2016 riots in Mongkok, where some radical localists confronted the police violently, and the highly provocative oath-taking behavior of two localist legislators-elect, Baggio Leung and Yau Wai-ching, in October 2016 infuriated the PRC authorities dealing with the HKSAR. The 2016 Mongkok riot was characterized by violent attacks initiated by some radical localists on the police, leading to the arrest of some radicals.[139] The provocative oath-taking behavior of Leung and Yau, who used the term "Chee-na" to refer to China, led to not only the anger of PRC officials but also the interpretation of the SCNPC over Article 106 of the Basic Law governing the oath-taking of legislators. The SCNPC ruled that legislators-elect must take their oath solemnly, properly and seriously. Most significantly, PRC authorities believed that some Hong Kong youths harbored anti-China sentiment and that their localism became extreme and separatist. As such, after the 2019 anti-extradition movement, which was perceived by PRC officials as anti-China and anti-CCP, the national security law had to be imposed onto the HKSAR in June 2020. On top of the agenda of the national security law was the implementation of the national security education and the re-education of the Hong Kong youths through a renewed emphasis on Chinese culture and history, including the rise of the PRC and the CCP and the party-state's contributions to China's domestic development and international status. In short, the young people of Hong Kong must be re-educated so that their national identity will gradually increase, that their localism has to be toned down and controlled and that Hong Kong's education system has to be decolonized and re-politicized to instill a much great sense of Chinese patriotism and nationalism than ever before.

In terms of curriculum reform, the PRC government has since June 2020 been keen to revamp the curricula to integrate more elements of Chinese national security, history and culture. Gregory Fairbrother and Kerry Kennedy have studied Hong Kong's civic education curriculum reform, which was characterized by a new independent subject of Moral and National Education (MNE) in October 2010.[140] The plan was to introduce MNE to the primary and secondary school curriculum from 2013 to 2014, according to the government's policy address in 2010. This change, if it were successful, would bring Hong Kong into line not only with civic education curriculum provision in China but also with that of the UK, where similar concerns led to citizenship education being mandated as a statutory subject in the English school curriculum in 2002.[141] As mentioned above, unfortunately, the policy on MNE was opposed by student activists, parents, intellectuals and the pro-democracy politicians in the HKSAR. Fairbrother and Kennedy found that students in other societies who participated in the subject of civic education tended to score higher on measures of civic knowledge and patriotism but not on their knowledge of democracy.[142] Indeed, democracy is not a value-free concept and is subject to interpretation by students in different countries and places. However, in the case of Hong Kong, the fact that the post-1997 government failed to introduce MNE was seen by the central authorities in Beijing as a sign of weakness vis-à-vis the increasingly assertive, hostile and localist civil society in the HKSAR.

On curriculum reform, Eric Chong has found that the globalization of integrated and interdisciplinary curriculum shaped the way in which the post-1997 HKSAR government introduced the Liberal Studies subject in 2009; nevertheless, he did not see any straightforward linkage between Liberal Studies and student participation in politics and social actions.[143] Above all, curriculum planners were not aware of the fact that students had a shallow disciplinary knowledge base and that they lacked transferrable skills. As such, teachers played a crucial role in helping students to examine real-life issues. There was no evidence to prove that students who took Liberal Studies subject tended to be participatory in the society and politics of Hong Kong – a view that was held by the critics of the Liberal Studies subject. Critics argued that student activists, such as Joshua Wong of Scholarism, might have been stimulated and politicized by the Liberal Studies subject. However, in the era of the globalization of the Internet, many Hong Kong youth could understand the socio-political development of Hong Kong and mainland China without relying on formal curriculum training, textbooks and references. Indeed, supporters of the Liberal Studies subject perceived the critics, who were composed of mainly pro-Beijing and pro-government elites, as exaggerating the learning outcomes and the unintended consequence on the politicization of youths. Another study has found that the learning outcome expressed in the curriculum and assessment guide of the planned Liberal Studies subject in 2007 was that students should be able to demonstrate an appreciation of their own values, other cultures, universal values and of being responsible and conscientious citizens[144] Critics of the Liberal Studies, however, firmly believed that Liberal Studies subject politicized many students, that it produced anti-governmental students and that it had to be revamped because it lacked the elements of Chinese history and culture. Eventually, with the enactment and the implementation of the national security law, Liberal Studies had to be replaced by CSD – a change in the name of the curriculum and a renewed emphasis on the content of Chinese history and culture.

In the PRC, school party secretaries are responsible for leading and supervising citizenship education.[145] In socialist China, schools feature two intertwined leadership lines, namely political and administrative. Every school normally has a party secretary responsible for political work on the campus, including citizenship education, and a school principal dealing with the overall school administration. There are three main patterns of party secretary's leadership in citizenship education: (1) leading without a clear division of power and labor with principals; (2) leading through mediating between higher authorities and the school and (3) leading by cooperating and competing with principals.[146] The party secretary's leadership is politically significant, for the policies and values of the CCP must be transmitted and implemented in the campus.

In the HKSAR, schools ranging from primary to secondary and from tertiary to university levels do not really have the formal establishment of party secretaries. As such, the responsibility of implementing the CCP's policy directives – the enforcement of the national security law, the introduction of national security education, and the renewed curriculum emphases on Chinese history and culture – rests with the school administrators, including school principals, deputy principals and the teachers concerned. This book will later examine how national security education was implemented in the HKSAR in the year 2021.

Chitat Chan, Danping Wang and Kathy Wong have studied how youths were represented in the students' works in the Liberal Studies subject.[147] They found that most student works presented "a deficit orientation."[148] Young people were characterized in terms of what they lacked or in how they failed to meet the standards. In other words, student works focusing on "what young people lack" overshadowed those focusing on "what young people possess" or "what has been done within limitations?" Although the Liberal Studies curriculum shaped the official public discourse in education reform, it did not really reflect students' learning experiences at an operational level. If so, what was taught to the students in the Liberal Studies subject differed from how students perceived themselves – a phenomenon neglected by the critics who argued for a revamp of the Liberal Studies subject on the assumption that Liberal Studies influenced the political culture of students.

On the other hand, Dennis Fung, Wai-Mei Lui, Tim Liang and Angie Su have studied how teachers perceived the Liberal Studies subject.[149] They found that Liberal Studies teachers themselves recognized the important role they play in implementing the subject and influencing reform outcomes. Teachers encountered a heavy workload, while the lack of supply teachers and teaching assistants due to the withdrawal of government subsidies led to tensions in the subject's implementation. Tensions emerged between the aspirations for and the actual implementation of the subject. The heavy workload of teachers was attributable partly to the need for teachers to constantly update their teaching materials. The excessive workload meant that teachers did not have sufficient time and energy to cope with students' individual learning needs. Students felt confused about the examination's assessment criteria, and they sensed the necessity of seeking outside help and tuition. Their engagement in the "shadow education system" was in conflict with the subject's ideology, namely the need for the society to "cultivate independent thinkers equipped with creativity, critical thinking skills and self-directed learning abilities."[150] As with Fung, Lui, Liang and Su, Robert Spires has also explored the tensions in the process of reforming Liberal Studies.[151] These tensions included public examinations, the proliferation of shadow education and the expansion of self-financed tertiary education options for Hong Kong students. The Liberal Studies debate mirrored the broader economic, political and social tensions in the HKSAR. If so, many critics who advocated a revamp of the Liberal Studies subject might ignore the originally underlying tensions within the curriculum; they pushed for its reform mainly because of political reason, namely seeing the Liberal Studies subject as producing active citizenry resistant and hostile to the policies of the HKSAR government and the central authorities.

Dennis Fung and Wai-mei Lui have studied the Liberal Studies curriculum and compared it with the MNE curriculum introduced in 2011.[152] The Liberal Studies curriculum was characterized by the "Hong Kong Today" and "Modern China" modules, which were designed to strengthen students' knowledge of local and national affairs. Later, when national elements were considered as inadequate, Moral and Civic Education (MCE) was revised by incorporating such teaching materials as the "China Model" handbook and it was then repackaged as MNE. Both Liberal Studies and MNE were multidisciplinary subjects. However, while Liberal Studies was initiated with two rounds of consultation lasting for two years, MNE was given a short consultation that lasted for merely four months. Liberal Studies continued to thrive as a compulsory subject, but MNE remained an optional and school-based subject without an assigned syllabus. The different treatment between Liberal Studies and MNE meant that the China component in the secondary school curricula remained relatively weak. Fung and Lui's finding was important because pro-Beijing and pro-government critics of the Liberal Studies subject exactly saw it as failing to inculcate a strong sense of national identity among the Hong Kong youths. In other words, the criticism made by pro-Beijing elites on the inadequate training of students in China was valid. The question remained how to reform the related curriculum in such a way to enhance the Chineseness of the Liberal Studies curriculum.

Dennis Chun-Lok Fung and Wai-Mei Lui have also questioned whether the Liberal Studies subject was a political instrument in the reform of the secondary school curriculum.[153] Since the retrocession of Hong Kong in 1997, the postcolonial government tried to mold Hongkongers into "loyal" Chinese citizens and to educate them to love their motherland. Hence, the Liberal Studies curriculum at the secondary school level was considered a vital means through which national identity and patriotic sentiments could be cultivated among the young students. The subject, once a core curriculum in the New Senior Secondary (NSS) academic structure, was seen as a tool for consolidating both multi-disciplinary learning and citizenship education. When Liberal Studies was adopted in 2009, it was regarded as a "pro-China" subject, particularly the "Modern China" module, which put an emphasis on the PRC's rapid economic development. Contrary to this perception, however, rather than reinforcing students' Chinese national identity, the curriculum produced "a new sense of local identity."[154] Furthermore, even though the "Modern China" module was composed of the China elements, many Hong Kong students demonstrated strong critical thinking and independent judgment abilities.

Here, the observation from Fung and Lui was politically significant. The critical thinking and independent judgment of many students could be seen as a "success" of the Liberal Studies curriculum. However, once students participated in politics and social movement, the Liberal Studies curriculum was viewed as "subversive" and producing "disobedient" and politically "defiant" students, such as Joshua Wong and his Scholarism group that succeeded in delaying the introduction of the national education policy in September 2012. Hence, the perception of the Liberal Studies curriculum changed over time, even though it might succeed in stimulating the critical thinking and independent judgment of some, but not all, secondary school students.

Another important observation made by Fung and Lui was that Liberal Studies "could be considered to have failed to achieve its arguably implicit objective of promoting blind patriotism."[155] During the societal debate over how the political system of Hong Kong could and should be democratized in 2014 and 2015, the post-1950s generation tended to be more moderate and supportive of a government proposal for the Chief Executive to be directly elected in 2017 through a screening process of the candidates by an Election Committee. The idea of "pocketing it first" was advocated by the pro-government camp in 2014 and 2015. Yet, it was rejected by members of the younger generation, such as Joshua Wong and his like-minded young liberals, because they firmly believed that the Election Committee that would screen the candidates to two to three, who would then be directly elected by citizens, constituted a "pseudo-democratic" political arrangement. As such, the young liberals were opposed to such an electoral model of selecting the Chief Executive in 2017. Fung and Lui have also observed that "the contribution that Liberal Studies has made in opening up a platform for these young minds to acquire the multi-disciplinary knowledge and critical thinking skills essential for them to understand the issues involved in the election debate, as well as in major socio-political events such as the [2014] Umbrella Movement, cannot be denied."[156] Yet, they also cautioned us that "when Liberal Studies falls onto the wrong hands, such as the more vociferous members of the extremist groups who place excessive emphasis on such values as civic responsibility, social justice and democracy, it can quickly transform into a convenient vehicle for igniting democratic fever amongst the young and be used as a morally fault-free justification for violence and exclusivism for particular political purposes."[157] They also criticized the trend of Liberal

Studies in refraining from dealing with sensitive issues related to China, thereby creating a positive image of the PRC. It was unclear whether students taking the Liberal Studies subject shared their critical observation, but one thing was certain: Liberal Studies was increasingly seen by the HKSAR government and PRC leaders for provoking and stimulating local students to oppose the local state and the motherland. Yet, Fung and Lui found that "many teacher and student participants" in their interviews disagreed with this view.

In another study, Dennis Fung and Tim Liang have examined the legitimacy of curriculum development in post-colonial Hong Kong by focusing on the case of Liberal Studies.[158] Faced with the growing Communist influence worldwide in the latter half of the twentieth century, Hong Kong's British colonial government depoliticized education and distanced students from the PRC through the prohibition of political rituals, national songs, and ceremonies at the school level. As a result, a kind of identity crisis emerged among the Hong Kong students during the 1960s: they were confused about whether they were Chinese or Hongkongers. With the growth of the Hong Kong identity from the 1970s to the 1990s, Hong Kong students began to develop their strong local identity. After July 1, 1997, the HKSAR government sought to shape students into loyal citizens of the motherland through the introduction of the Liberal Studies curriculum. However, teachers played a crucial role as "policy executors" with "their capacity to influence the legitimacy of curriculum implementation."[159] While Liberal Studies had the potential of increasing the political awareness of students, politics might shape how Liberal Studies would move forward – a finding that was later confirmed by the developments. Fung and Liang identified the HKSAR government's resort to "subterfuge to force through the curriculum's implementation" and its "politically motivated proposals for changes to the curriculum (e.g. dissuading students from social participation)."[160] Yet, such governmental interference "undermined the legitimacy of the curriculum policy, which has in turn further eroded the public's trust in the government and further diminished its credibility."[161] The outcome was a vicious circle in which the government lacked credibility, whereas the curriculum lacked policy legitimacy. Fung and Liang suggested that the HKSAR government should improve its public consultation by making it more transparent than before. Although their suggestion had good intention, the HKSAR government's weak capability meant that not only its national education policy was opposed and postponed in 2012, but its attempt at revising the Liberal Studies curriculum had to be pressured by the PRC shortly after the introduction of the national security law in late June 2020. Fung and Lui advocated a review process that ideally should follow a bottom-up and decentralized mode, but the reality was that the curriculum reform, not even review, was conducted in a top-down and centralized fashion immediately after the imposition of the national security law in the HKSAR in late June 2020.

Fung and Lui used the example of the abortive attempt at introducing MNE to primary and secondary schools in 2012 to show that "when educational policies are tainted by politics, they are very likely to trigger public outrage and place reform efforts at risk."[162] The policy was an explicit move to promote "a pro-China identity among Hong Kong citizens, an identity rendered conspicuously absent by the city's colonial past."[163] Yet, given the one-sided presentation of the PRC socialist polity in the "China Model" handbook, MNE was quickly seen by many students, teachers and parents as explicit attempts at "brainwashing" school children. Teachers, parents and students formed 24 interest groups to boycott and oppose the MNE, forcing the HKSAR government to shelve the curriculum. However, in the eyes of PRC authorities, such opposition revealed the anti-PRC and anti-CCP identity of many Hong Kong students. The anti-national education movement in 2012, albeit successful in delaying the implementation of MNE, was regarded by Beijing as "unpatriotic" and "anti-nationalistic." If MNE represented a kind of citizenship education designed to reintroduce and enhance the Chinese national identity into the psyche of Hong Kong students, its policy failure in 2012 left an indelible imprint on PRC authorities, who later were determined to impose the national security law and its related national security education onto the HKSAR in late June 2020.

Fung and Liang also found that teachers perceived the Liberal Studies curriculum as being driven by political motivations and entailing tenuous legitimacy. If the legitimacy of the post-1997 administration and its education reform were challenged by students, teachers and parents, PRC authorities ingrained in political education and indoctrination naturally saw these political actors as "subversive." This perception of PRC authorities explained why Beijing has been keen to see the HKSAR government implement education reforms immediately after the introduction of the national security law in late June 2020.

Education Reform in the HKSAR as Power Struggles

If education reform in the HKSAR represents a gradual attempt, at least before June 2020, by the government to inject the ingredients of Chineseness, nationalism and patriotism, then its content since early July 2020 has been marked by a triumph of the PRC's political authority over localist resistance and opposition. In a sense, the mainlandization of education reform in the HKSAR since late June 2020 has been characterized by a persistent power struggle whose result is tipped in favor of the sovereign power, the PRC.

Thomas Kwan-choi Tse has captured the political dynamics of education reform in the HKSAR sharply in terms of the efforts at remaking the Chinese identity and the hegemonic struggles over who had the power to force through all the reforms.[164] He identified accurately that the change in national education policy could be viewed as a barometer of the political climate in the HKSAR. Being a polity dependent on the PRC's powers conferred upon the local administration, Hong Kong displayed "peculiar features from a conventional model of citizenship education – most notably an absence of national education in the past and a salience of national education in the post-colonial era."[165] Against the background of the transfer of sovereignty, the deepening process of the economic integration of Hong Kong and China, the cultivation of both Chinese nationalism and patriotism have increasingly become the new official ideology adopted by the HKSAR government to demonstrate its political loyalty to the central government in Beijing. If the HKSAR government and its ruling elites are the clients of Beijing, they are naturally keen to be the loyal agents formulating the national education policy and implementing it fully to the satisfaction of PRC authorities. This top-down policy mode has been enhanced by the policy directive of the PRC authorities from the CCP and the State Council's Hong Kong and Macau Affairs Office. Once Beijing has decided to impose the national security law and national security education onto the HKSAR since late June 2020, the local government authorities must follow suit and are under pressure to demonstrate their effective implementation.

Utilizing Antonio Gramsci's concept of hegemony, Tse sharply identified the ideological dimension of the post-colonial state in the HKSAR, which has to impose its hegemonic power over the civil society to implement the policy directives of the central government, especially after the imposition of the national security law in late June 2020. If student leaders and intellectuals, such as law professor Benny Tai and sociologist Chan Kin-man who launched the Occupy Central Movement in 2014, could be seen as the "organic intellectuals" resisting the state power, then a severe power struggle over ideological and political hegemony took place in the HKSAR.[166] This power struggle was temporarily tipped in favor of the student and parent interest groups in September 2012, when the national education policy was postponed and left to the primary and secondary schools to decide its implementation. The power struggles between the "organic intellectual" and localist groups on the one hand and the HKSAR government and PRC authorities, on the other hand, persisted in 2015, when the political reform plan introduced by the Hong Kong administration was rejected by the young liberals and democrats, and in late 2016, when legislators-elect Baggio Leung and Yau Wai-ching challenged the hegemonic power of the PRC by using the term "Chee-na" to refer to China in their oath-taking ceremony. The power struggles between the liberals on the one hand and the conservative elites in Hong Kong and the mainland on the other continued in the latter half of 2019 when the HKSAR government eventually decided to withdraw the extradition bill in the face of severe protests. However, grasping the opportunity of the emergence of Covid-19 in early 2020, when Hong Kong had to enforce restrictions on crowd gathering, the PRC authorities pushed forward the national security law and the SCNPC enacted it to stabilize the Hong Kong development, to penalize the liberal democrats, to arrest and imprison some of the "troublemakers," and to warn the young local people that they cannot be "organic intellectuals" seeking to overthrow the HKSAR government and "subvert" the PRC's party-state. If an assertive civil society in the HKSAR before late June 2020 was partly the outcome of its education system, then a clampdown on its civil society and the related education reform is necessary after the imposition of the national security law. The implementation of the national security law and education in Hong Kong after late June 2020 represents a victory of the CCP hegemony over the HKSAR.

Toward an Analytical Framework of Understanding the Context and Content of Education Reform in Hong Kong

Figure 1.1 depicts our analytical framework of understanding the political context and content of education reforms in Hong Kong under the PRC's sovereignty. The China factor is arguably the most prominent shaper influencing the political context and content of education reforms in the HKSAR. Beijing's political clients include not only the HKSAR government but also the pro-Beijing politicians, elites, groups and organizations. The pro-Beijing elites and groups are important vehicles through which the central government in Beijing exerts pressure on the HKSAR government to implement education reform, which includes the enhancement of Chinese culture in curriculum reform and the acceleration of national security education in schools. All these pressures have the dual objectives of enhancing the degree of Chinese nationalism and patriotism in the psyche of the Hong Kong people, especially the young people at the primary, secondary and university levels. Education reform is composed of three main elements: (1) school-based reforms focusing on administrative change, the operation of school boards, the participation of parents in running the schools; (2) teachers' professionalism, which is expected to facilitate the implementation of school reforms introduced by the government and (3) curriculum reform in conformity with the national security law, national security education, and the enhancement of Chinese culture and history knowledge. Utilizing this framework, we will be able to understand the political dynamics of education reform in the HKSAR.

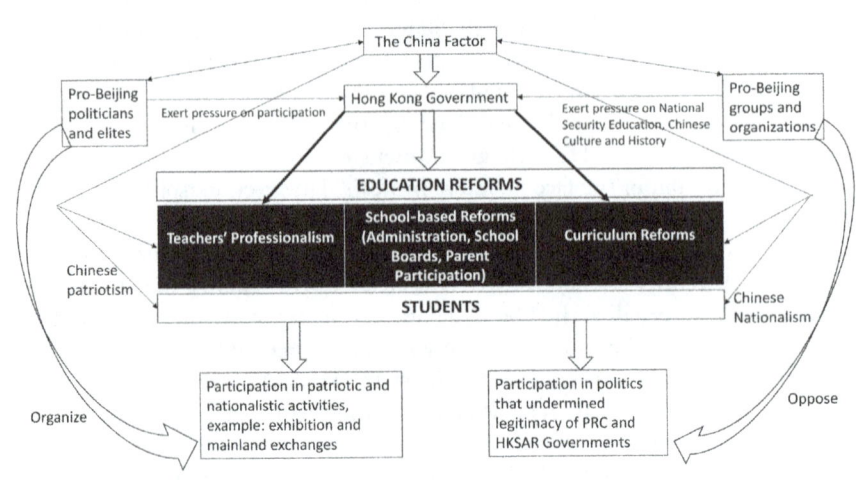

Figure 1.1 An Analytical Framework Understanding the Context and Content of Education Reforms in Hong Kong.

Conclusion

This chapter reviews the literature on Hong Kong's education reform. While the British colonial rulers liberalized and decentralized education reform to the local civil service, the post-1997 government gradually centralized education reform but failed in 2012, when the national education policy was opposed by the civil society. The rise of localism from 2012 to 2019 led to Beijing's decision to centralize education reform in its own hands and, as this book will show, to re-politicize the reform content in a far more nationalistic way than before.

Notes

1 In recent years, PRC officials have no longer mentioned the Sino-British Joint Declaration on Hong Kong, believing that the HKSAR belongs to the domestic affairs of China in which foreign countries should not intervene. While the Basic Law will, legally and technically speaking, end in 2047, it is widely believed that it will likely continue, especially if the PRC cannot and will not settle the question of Taiwan's future in the foreseeable future.
2 Sonny Shiu-Hing Lo, "Ideologies and factionalism in Beijing-Hong Kong relations," *Asian Survey*, vol. 58, no. 3 (June 2018), pp. 392–415.
3 For the details, see Sonny Shiu-Hing Lo, Steven Chung-fun Hung and Jeff Hai-chi Loo, *The Dynamics of Peaceful and Violent Protests in Hong Kong: The Anti-extradition Movement* (London: Palgrave Macmillan, 2021).
4 For the patron-clientelist nature of Hong Kong's political system, see Sonny Shiu-Hing Lo, *The Dynamics of Beijing-Hong Kong Relations: A Model for Taiwan?* (Hong Kong: Hong Kong University Press, 2008), Chapter One.
5 Guohua Zhang, Gordon Boyce and Kamran Ahmed, "Institutional changes in university accounting education in post-revolutionary China: From political orientation to internationalization," *Critical Perspectives on Accounting*, vol. 25 (2014), pp. 819–843.
6 Ibid.
7 Ibid., p. 826.
8 Ibid.
9 Adrian Zenz, "Thoroughly reforming them towards a healthy heart attitude': China's political re-education campaign in Xinjiang," *Central Asian* Survey, vol. 38, no. 1 (2019), pp. 102–128.
10 Ibid.
11 Ibid.
12 Ibid.
13 Ibid.
14 Ibid.
15 Ibid.
16 Ibid.
17 Ibid., p. 113.
18 Ibid.
19 Ibid.
20 Ibid.
21 Ibid.
22 Ibid., p. 124.
23 Raza Zainab, "China's 'political re-education' camps of Xinjiang's Uyghur Muslims," *Asian Affairs*, vol. 50, no. 4 (2019), pp. 488–501.
24 Ibid.

25 *Ibid.*
26 *Ibid.*, p. 489.
27 *Ibid.*
28 Manhong Lai and Leslie N. K. Lo, "Struggling to balance various stakeholders' perceptions: The work life of ideo-political education teachers in China," *High Education*, vol. 62 (2011), pp. 333–349.
29 *Ibid.*, p. 338.
30 *Ibid.*
31 *Ibid.*
32 *Ibid.*
33 The authors' informal discussions with four teachers who were former students, May 28, 2021.
34 Qinghua Wang, "Strengthening and professionalizing political education in China's higher education," *Journal of Contemporary China*, vol. 22, no. 80 (2013), pp. 332–350.
35 *Ibid.*
36 *Ibid.*
37 *Ibid.*, p. 335.
38 *Ibid.*, pp. 335–336.
39 *Ibid.*, p. 335.
40 *Ibid.*
41 *Ibid.*, p. 336.
42 *Ibid.*
43 *Ibid.*
44 *Ibid.*, p. 339.
45 *Ibid.*
46 *Ibid.*, p. 340.
47 *Ibid.*
48 *Ibid.*, p. 341.
49 *Ibid.*
50 *Ibid.*
51 *Ibid.*, p. 346.
52 *Ibid.*
53 *Ibid.*
54 *Ibid.*
55 Gregory P. Fairbrother, "Rethinking hegemony and resistance to political education in Mainland China and Hong Kong," *Comparative Education Review*, vol. 52, no. 3 (2008), pp. 381–412.
56 *Ibid.*
57 *Ibid.*
58 *Ibid.*
59 Quoted from the report of the Curriculum Development Committee in 1985, p. 9, in *Ibid.*, pp. 382–383.
60 *Ibid.*
61 *Ibid.*, p. 404.
62 *Ibid.*
63 *Ibid.*
64 *Ibid.*
65 *Ibid.*, p. 407.
66 Gregory P. Fairbrother, *Toward Critical Patriotism: Student Resistance to Political Education in Hong Kong and China* (Hong Kong: Hong Kong University Press, 2003), pp. 185–186.
67 Lu Jie, "Ideological and political education in China's higher education," *East Asian Policy*, vol. 9 (2017), pp. 78–91.

68 *Ibid.*
69 *Ibid.*, p. 79.
70 *Ibid.*
71 *Ibid.*
72 *Ibid.*, p. 80.
73 *Ibid.*
74 *Ibid.*, p. 90.
75 *Ibid.*
76 *Ibid.*
77 *Ibid.*
78 *Ibid.*
79 *Ibid.*
80 *Wen Wei Po*, July 2, 2021, p. A6.
81 *Ibid.*
82 *Ibid.*
83 *Ibid.*
84 *Ibid.*
85 *Ibid.*
86 *Ibid.*
87 *Ibid.*
88 *Ibid.*
89 *Ibid.*
90 Ray Garland Reed, "Moral and political education in the People's Republic of China: Learning through role models," *Journal of Moral Education*, vol. 24, no. 2 (May 1995), pp. 99–112.
91 *Ibid.*
92 *Ibid.*
93 *Ibid.*
94 *Ibid.*
95 *Ibid.*
96 *Ibid.*
97 Zhu Zhiyong and Deng Meng, "Cultural or political? Origin and development of educational policy of the Tibetan Neidi education in China," *Chinese Education & Society*, vol. 48, no. 5 (2015), pp. 332–340.
98 *Ibid.*
99 *Ibid.*, p. 338.
100 *Ibid.*
101 Li Jun, "Fostering citizenship in China's move from elite to mass higher education: An analysis of students' political socialization and civic participation," *International Journal of Educational Development*, vol. 29 (2009), pp. 382–398.
102 *Ibid.*
103 *Ibid.*
104 *Ibid.*
105 *Ibid.*, p. 393.
106 *Ibid.*, p. 394.
107 *Ibid.*
108 *Ibid.*
109 See Sonny Shiu-Hing Lo, Steven Chung-fun Hung and Jeff Hai-chi Loo, *The Dynamics of Peaceful and Violent Protests in Hong Kong: The Anti-Extradition Movement* (London: Palgrave, 2020).
110 Huang Zhongjing, Wang Ting, and Li Xiaojun, "The political dynamics of educational changes in China," *Policy Futures in Education*, vol. 14, no. 1 (2016), pp. 24–41.
111 *Ibid.*

112 *Ibid.*
113 *Ibid.*
114 *Ibid.*
115 *Ibid.*, p. 31.
116 *Ibid.*
117 *Ibid.*, p. 33.
118 *Ibid.*
119 *Ibid.*
120 *Ibid.*
121 *Ibid.*, p. 35.
122 *Ibid.*
123 *Ibid.*
124 *Ibid.*
125 *Ibid.*, pp. 40–41.
126 Michael Lanford, "Perceptions of higher education reform in Hong Kong: A glocalization perspective," *International Journal of Comparative Education and Development*, vol. 18, no. 3 (2016), pp. 184–204.
127 *Ibid.*
128 Wai-Chi Chee, "Negotiating teacher professionalism: Governmentality and education reform in Hong Kong," *Ethnography and Education*, vol. 7, no. 3 (2012), pp. 327–344.
129 *Ibid.*
130 *Ibid.*
131 Pattie Yuk Yee Luk-Fong and Marie Brennan, "Teachers' experience of secondary education reform in Hong Kong," *International Journal of Educational Reform*, vol. 19, no. 2 (Spring 2010), pp. 128–153.
132 Katherine Forestier, Bob Adamson, Christine Han and Paul Morris, "Referencing and borrowing from other systems: The Hong Kong education reforms," *Educational Research*, vol. 58, no. 2 (2016), pp. 149–165.
133 *Ibid.*
134 *Ibid.*
135 Iris Chui-ping Kam, "Personal identity versus national identity among Hong Kong youths – personal and social education reform after reunification," *Social Identities*, vol. 18, no. 6 (2012), pp. 649–661.
136 *Ibid.*
137 *Ibid.*
138 *Ibid.*, p. 661.
139 For the details of the Mongkok riot, see Sonny Shiu-Hing Lo, *The Politics of Policing in Greater China* (London: Palgrave Macmillan, 2016).
140 Gregory P. Fairbrother and Kerry J. Kennedy, "Civic education curriculum reform in Hong Kong: What should be the direction under Chinese sovereignty?" *Cambridge Journal of Education*, vol. 41, no. 4 (2011), pp. 425–443.
141 *Ibid.*
142 *Ibid.*
143 Eric K. M. Chong, "How does globalization shape the interdisciplinary curriculum development in Hong Kong's education reform," *Curriculum and Teaching*, vol. 35, no. 1 (2020), pp. 23–51.
144 Steven Chung-fun Hung, "Contextual analysis of Hong Kong education policy in 20 Years: The intention of making future citizens in political conflicts," *Contemporary Chinese Political Economy and Strategic Relations: An International Journal*, vol. 3, no. 2 (July/August 2017), pp. 713–745.
145 Shuqin Xu and Wing-Wah Law, "School leadership and citizenship education: The experiences and struggles of school party secretaries in China," *Education Research for Policy and Practice*, vol. 14, no. 1 (February 2015), pp. 33–51.

146 *Ibid.*
147 Chitat Chan, Danping Wang and Kathy Wong, "The representations of youth in Liberal Studies student works in Hong Kong," *The International Journal of the Humanities*, vol. 9, no. 1 (January 2011), pp. 245–256.
148 *Ibid.*
149 Dennis Fung, Wai-Mei Lui, Tim Liang and Angie Su, "The way forward for the development of Liberal Studies: How teachers perceive its introduction and implementation in Hong Kong secondary schools," *Asia Pacific Education Review*, vol. 18 (2017), pp. 123–134.
150 *Ibid.*
151 Robert Spires, "Hong Kong's postcolonial education reform Liberal Studies as a lens," *International Journal of Educational Reform*, vol. 26, no. 2 (Spring 2017), pp. 154–172.
152 Dennis Chun-Lok Fung and Wai-mei Lui, *Education Policy Analysis: Liberal Studies and National Education in Hong Kong* (Singapore: Springer, 2017).
153 Dennis Chun-Lok Fung and Wai-Mei Lui, "Is Liberal Studies a political instrument in the secondary school curriculum? Lessons from the Umbrella Movement in post-colonial Hong Kong," *The Curriculum Journal*, vol. 28, no. 2 (2017), pp. 158–175.
154 *Ibid.*
155 *Ibid.*, p. 175.
156 *Ibid.*
157 *Ibid.*
158 Dennis Fung and Tim Liang, "The legitimacy of curriculum development in post-colonial Hong Kong: Insights from the case of Liberal Studies," *Oxford Review of Education*, vol. 44, no. 2 (2018), pp. 171–189.
159 *Ibid.*
160 *Ibid.*
161 *Ibid.*
162 *Ibid.*
163 *Ibid.*
164 Thomas Kwan-choi Tse, "Remaking Chinese identity: Hegemonic struggles over national education in post-colonial Hong Kong," *International Studies in Sociology of Education*, vol. 17, no. 3 (September 2007), pp. 231–248.
165 *Ibid.*
166 For the role of "organic intellectuals" in Hong Kong's socio-political movement, see Sonny Shiu-Hing Lo, ed., *Interest Groups and the New Democracy Movement in Hong Kong* (London: Routledge, 2018), Introduction and Conclusion.

2 Education Reform in Hong Kong from British Rule to the Post-1997 Period

This chapter traces the development of education reform in Hong Kong from the British colonial era to the post-1997 period. It discusses how education reform has been related to the local political development. The British colonial administration gradually liberalized Hong Kong and its education system. Since July 1, 1997, the Hong Kong Special Administrative Region (HKSAR) government has begun to enhance national education, but a serious setback took place in 2012 when the national education policy was opposed and resisted by the localists, who can be defined as those Hong Kong people who harbor a strong sense of local Hong Kong identity.

The political development of the HKSAR deteriorated rapidly from September to December 2014, when the Occupy Central Movement was launched by the localists to push for democratization, namely the direct election of both the Chief Executive and the entire Legislative Council (LegCo). The movement failed by the end of 2014; nevertheless, the localist movement bounced back again in 2016, when the radicals clashed with the police in Mongkok district in the Lunar Chinese New Year and when two legislators-elect, Baggio Leung and Yau Wai-ching, took their oath in the LegCo in a way "disrespectful" to the PRC. Their provocative remarks and gesture – using the term "Chee-na" to describe China and showing a flag saying "Hong Kong is not China" – alienated Beijing and led to the intervention of the Standing Committee of the National People's Congress (SCNPC), which interpreted Article 106 of the Basic Law on the need for legislators-elect to take their oath solemnly and properly.

The anti-extradition movement of the latter half of 2019 led to the participation of millions of Hongkongers against an extradition bill proposed by the HKSAR government. The movement led to violent confrontations between the localists and police on the one hand, and many students and the police on the other hand. At this juncture, the PRC regime found the situation of the HKSAR as politically intolerable, leading to the imposition of the national security law in late June 2020 as a means of punishing the violent protestors and organizers on the one hand and enforcing national security education in Hong Kong on the other hand.

DOI: 10.4324/9781003147268-2

Education in Hong Kong under British Rule: Legitimization of Colonial Rule

Prior to 1842, when Hong Kong was part of the Qing dynasty, an indigenous tradition of Chinese schooling was deep-rooted. This situation was tolerated after August 1842, when the Treaty of Nanking was signed between the Qing dynasty and the United Kingdom and when the British began to govern the Hong Kong Island. Education was by no means an immediate concern for the British rulers, who treated Hong Kong more as a combined trading, military and diplomatic outpost.[1] Yet, "schools do not exist in a vacuum [because] they are part of the society that surrounds them."[2] Emile Durkheim and Marcel Mauss observed that "education is always the symptom and result of the social transformations in terms of which it is to be explained."[3] If education reflects the societal transformation and its reform responds to political change, Hong Kong under British rule was no exception to this rule.

Socially speaking, the establishment of schools in Hong Kong responded to the societal transformation. The British colonial government provided school grants, a policy parallel to the measures in Britain.[4] While local educational efforts were left largely in the hands of voluntary groups and organizations working in the poorer sections of the community, colonial education demonstrated a pattern of increasing government commitment.[5] The most significant hallmark of the schooling system was its near monopoly on the use of public funds earmarked for education. The way in which schools were organized ensured that there was little competition among them for students. In 1850, the policy of the Education Committee, which was set up by the British colonial administration, was to encourage the study of English for the sake of enhancing the socio-political bond between the Chinese residents and British rulers.[6]

Demographic changes in Hong Kong propelled education reform further. Figure 2.1 shows the increasing population of Hong Kong from 1841 to 2021. The rapid and steady increase in the population from 1841 to 1941 and from 1951 to 1997 necessitated the British administration to take measures to reform the education system in such a way as to meet the increasing demands of students and parents. In 1862, the Central School was established to give English teaching a more prominent place in Hong Kong. The Education Act passed in Britain in 1870 created a compulsory education there, an act that appeared to have an impact on how the British governed Hong Kong's education. In 1872, a grant was offered for the first time to schools belonging to the missions. In 1887, apart from the 94 schools under the Hong Kong government's supervision and examination, there were 110 private schools, including night schools.[7] In 1902, an Education Commission was set up and it recommended that greater attention should be paid to the study of the Chinese language at all schools because the localization of language would better serve the interest and needs of students.[8] Grants were made payable to both English and Chinese schools, while Chinese schools had to be conducted on Western lines.[9] On the other hand, wealthier Chinese attended either the Anglo schools or private Chinese schools, whereas

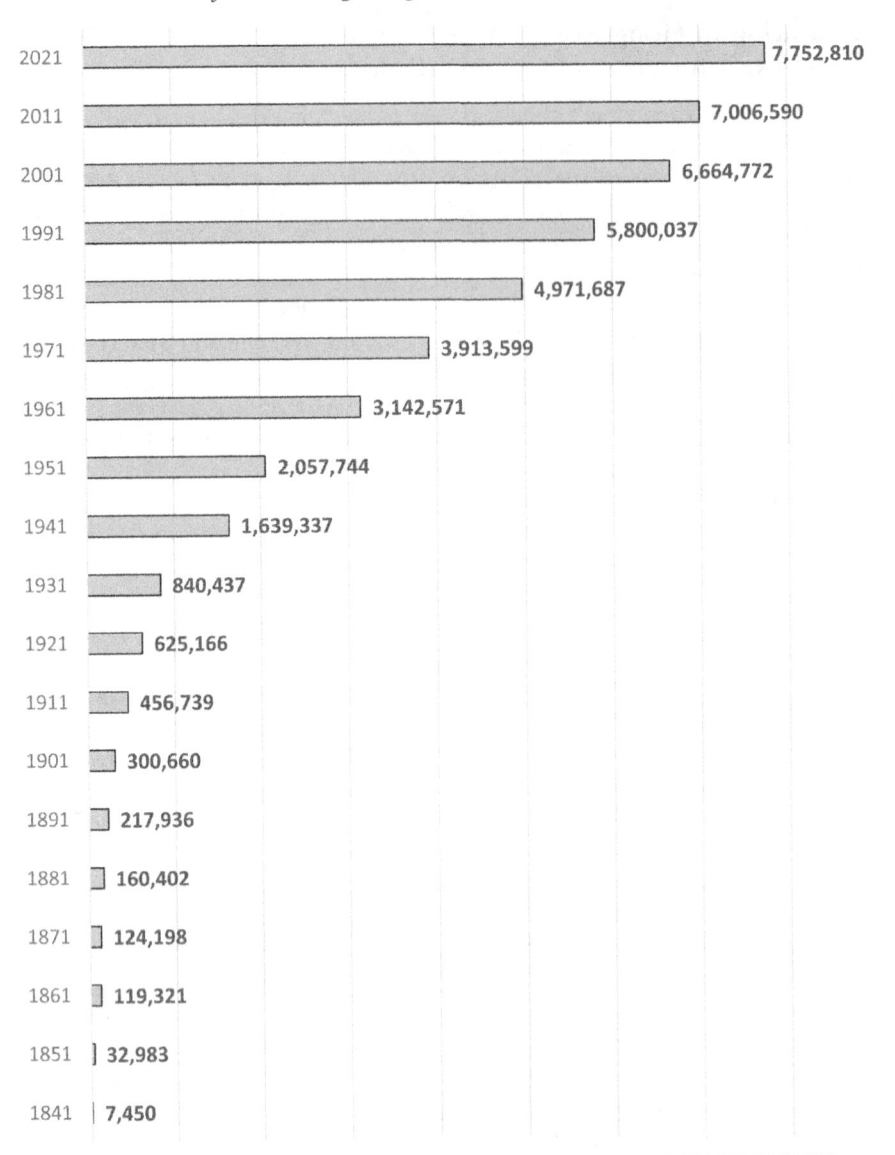

Year	Population
2021	7,752,810
2011	7,006,590
2001	6,664,772
1991	5,800,037
1981	4,971,687
1971	3,913,599
1961	3,142,571
1951	2,057,744
1941	1,639,337
1931	840,437
1921	625,166
1911	456,739
1901	300,660
1891	217,936
1881	160,402
1871	124,198
1861	119,321
1851	32,983
1841	7,450

Figure 2.1 Changing Population of Hong Kong, 1841–2021

Sources: Census Reports on Hong Kong's Population, 1941–2021, in https://www.macrotrends.net/countries/HKG/hong-kong/population, access date: July 1, 2021.

missionary and voluntary schools that taught in Cantonese tended to be less prestigious and to serve the poor pupils.[10]

After the establishment of the University of Hong Kong in 1911, the British administration enacted the first Education Ordinance in 1913, legitimizing the power of inspection on all schools and bringing all private schools under its supervision.[11] The introduction of the Ordinance focused on political control; the Qing dynasty had already been overthrown in 1911. Revolutionary ideas and Chinese nationalistic sentiments were riding high and spreading beyond the mainland border. To prevent the growth of Chinese nationalistic sentiments in local schools, the British administration exercised strict control over the political activities of pupils and teachers. Schools had to provide the Education Department with much information than ever before, including syllabi, class schedules, teachers, class size and the conditions of school premises.[12] As such, the colonial education policy developed as a response to China's political development.

In 1921, the British administration established a Board of Education to oversee education reforms with some degree of flexibility. After strikes and boycotts broke out in Hong Kong from June to October 1925 following a clash between Chinese nationalists and British police in Shanghai in May, it was clear that the Hong Kong Chinese lacked a deep sense of political loyalty to the British rulers. Governor Cecil Clementi (1925–1930) was a Sinophile and a China scholar, establishing a Government Vernacular Middle Chinese School in 1926 (later renamed as Clementi Secondary School in 1951) and the Department of Chinese at the University of Hong Kong in 1927.[13] In 1929, a committee was appointed by the British administration to draw up a syllabus for all private schools to follow the standardization of uniforms of the vernacular schools. The British also curbed the influences of the Kuomintang (KMT or the Nationalist Party) and controlled the textbooks in Hong Kong schools. In 1930, education reforms were implemented in Nationalist China, but Hong Kong under British rule remained minimally reformed. After the Japanese conquest of Manchuria on September 18, 1931, the official relations between Nationalist China and the UK became increasingly friendly, indirectly leaving Hong Kong education relatively unchanged.

In 1935, Edmund Burney, an inspector of schools of the British government, visited Hong Kong and submitted a report. He criticized the Hong Kong government for the low priority given to primary vernacular education and for its one-sided emphasis on the provision of education for upper-class children. He accused the Hong Kong government of neglecting primary education and leaving it excessively in the hands of private schools. He recommended that the Hong Kong administration should pay more attention to Chinese primary education and the enhancement of Chinese education and teachers' training.[14] The Burney report's suggestions were a mixture of enhancing the ability of the local students to master their own Chinese language sufficiently for the needs of thought and expression and their capability of commanding their English language to satisfy vocational demands and needs. From 1935 to 1941, there was a strong demand for an increase in schools. The school population rose from 25,000 to 116,000 – a clear venularization of education in which private education expanded without governmental assistance. The government support of schools was expressed in the form of grant-in-aid, which was available mainly to schools conducted along Western lines.[15]

During the Japanese invasion and occupation of Hong Kong from 1941 to 1945, almost all formal schooling was stopped, with very few students studying in schools. Throughout the Japanese occupation, the school population dropped from the pre-war 1941 total of 120,000, only 3,000 in August 1945. The surrender of Japan in August 1945 was followed by educational reform in Hong Kong, where education remained highly elitist and provided the relatively small sectors of the economy with the bilingual capability of professionals. The number of children enrolled in schools by the end of March 1947 was only 100,000.[16] The schools in Hong Kong were classified as follows:

1. Government Schools which were staffed and maintained by the Education Department;
2. Grant Schools which were schools run by missionary bodies with the assistance of government grants under the provision of the Grant Code;
3. Subsidized Schools which were those schools receiving subsidies from the government under the Subsidy Code;
4. Military Schools which were exempted from the provision of the Education Ordinance in 1913; and
5. Other private schools.

Many subsidized schools were badly housed, understaffed and overcrowded. In 1947, the Education Report stated that "the general policy, therefore, is to improve vernacular education; to build Government vernacular primary and middle schools; to increase the scope and content of teacher training; to give opportunities for local officers to reach the higher grades in the service; to bring the standard of accommodation and staff of all schools to a high level."[17] The post-war years immediately after August 1945 provided a golden opportunity for education reforms in Hong Kong.

Table 2.1 lists the evolution of education policy and reform in post-1945 Hong Kong. The Fisher Report published in 1951 recommended the expansion of primary education. As Hong Kong's economy developed further, there was a shortage of technically educated young people, necessitating education reform. The Education Ordinance of 1952 aimed at prohibiting political indoctrination of schools. It was enacted to empower the Director of Education to inspect schools and to refuse registration to those schools that were considered unsuitable. In 1960, the Education Regulation was amended to impose stricter control on the distribution of teaching materials and the process of instruction without prior approval by the Director of Education.

The 1961 Census indicated that 41 percent of the total population of 3.1 million were under 15 years old, while 16 percent were under 5. There was a shortage of labor in the market, increasing the need for more social services.[18] In 1963, the government focused on the provision of primary and secondary education. But leftist and rightist schools were not given any assistance during the early 1960s when the government tended to subsidize schools that were organized by religious and voluntary groups. In 1965, a White Paper on education policy was published, restructuring primary and secondary education and making the achievement of universal primary education an immediate objective.[19] The

Table 2.1 The Evolution of Education Policy in Hong Kong, 1945–1997

Time	Main event in education
December 1951	A report on the government expenditure on education in Hong Kong was published
January 1963	The government reorganized the structure of primary and secondary education
October 1974	Secondary education was planned for Hong Kong over the next decade
October 1977	Integrating the disabled into the community
October 1978	The development of senior secondary and tertiary education was emphasized
July 1981	Primary education and pre-primary services were expanded
November 1982	An international visiting panel's report on Hong Kong's education system was published
October 1984	The Education Commission's Report No. 1 on Quality School Education was published
August 1986	The Education Commission's Report No. 2 on Quality School Education was published
June 1988	The Education Commission's Report No. 3 on the structure of tertiary education and the future of private schools was published
June 1988	A report by the Council for Recreation and Sport in education was published
May 1989	A Working Group was set up to review language improvement measures
November 1990	The Education Commission's Report No. 4 on the curriculum and behavioral problems in schools was published
March 1991	The School Management Initiative was implemented
June 1992	The Education Commission's Report No. 5 on the teaching profession was published
June 1993	A final report of the Working Group on the support services for schools with Band 5 students was published
January 1994	A report of the advisory committee in the implementation of target-oriented curriculum was published
April 1994	A report of the ad-hoc sub-committee on pre-primary education was published
July 1994	A report of the Working Group on language proficiency was published
December 1995	A report on kindergarten education was published
March 1995	The Education Commission's Report No. 6 on the enhancement of language proficiency was published
May 1996	A report of the sub-committee on special education was published
July 1996	Arts education policy was implemented
October 1996	Higher education in Hong Kong underwent reforms
March 1997	A review of prevocational and secondary technical education was conducted
September 1997	The Education Commission's Report No. 7 on quality school education was published
October 1997	A report on the review of 9-year compulsory education was published

Source: Compiled by the authors based on the historical development of Hong Kong's education policy.

objective of providing compulsory and free primary education was not achieved until 1971. After the 1967 riots in Hong Kong, an improvement in the people's livelihood was emphasized to tackle the social origin of the political unrest. Moreover, the government's management of primary education was decentralized. In 1971, mass compulsory primary education was adopted, while secondary education was expanded further. From the 1970s onward, the provision of education in Hong Kong was led by the public sector, in which most school places were provided at relatively high subsidized rates. The government reformed education in the direction of stimulating the economic and industrial development of Hong Kong. In other words, education was predominantly a utilitarian means of achieving economic and vocational ends.[20] From September 1978 onwards, there was a secondary school place for every primary school leaver. This policy was implemented through a scheme of buying places from private schools. In the 1978 White Paper, namely the *Development of Senior Secondary and Tertiary Education*, vocational education embraced the students' acquisition of their knowledge and skills in reading, writing, mathematics and science in the rapidly changing and highly technically orientated society. However, the leftwing or pro-PRC schools were excluded from governmental support. Still, the leftist schools could survive the financial difficulties and managed to continue.

In the society of Hong Kong, the question of mass education and the cultivation of patriotism were problematic for British colonizers. Given its colonial status, the Hong Kong government could not use the appeals of Chinese patriotism as a means of encouraging the population to accept the laws of the land.[21] The lack of Chinese nationalistic sentiment remained a potential source of social instability in a community where some of the residents were not only skeptical of the colonial government but also critical of its fragile legitimacy. The functions of education in Hong Kong, from the perspective of the British colonizers, were to depoliticize the Chinese, dilute Chinese nationalism and patriotism, provide a channel for the young students to move up the social ladder, and to stabilize and legitimize colonial governance. Schools were organized in such a way as to preserve the political *status quo*. Pro-Beijing schools were under surveillance and under-subsidized, while government schools were financially favored. Students who graduated from local universities, notably the University of Hong Kong, could have the upper hand to join the civil service, where local Chinese played a crucial role as a bridge between the British colonizers and the ruled Chinese. In general, the socialization process within primary and secondary schools helped to legitimize the dominant political institutions, namely the LegCo and the policy-making Executive Council (ExCo). These institutions were portrayed as "consultative" and reflective of public opinion. In a nutshell, education served its politically conservative function by not only reproducing a social structure in which the ruling elites came from subsidized schools and universities but also legitimizing the colonial governance in which Chinese patriotism and nationalism were deemphasized and diluted as far as possible.

To legitimize the education system, the British administration harped on the same theme of seeking to improve education quality. In fact, the emphasis on quality education emerged from the 1980s to 1997. The *Overall Review of Hong Kong's Education System* in 1981 and the *Visiting Panel Report* in 1982 were attempts at streamlining the policy-making process and reforming the education system. Education reforms under the seven reports of the Education Commission from 1984 to 1997 acted as a vehicle of quality improvement. The 1984 Education Commission report made recommendations on quality enhancement, including (1) the improvement in the standards of Chinese and English; (2) the promotion of Chinese as the medium of instruction in schools; (3) the qualitative improvement and quantitative expansion of the teaching services; and (4) the continuation of the existing educational research efforts and the co-ordination of educational research activities for the purpose of planning and formulating educational policies.[22]

In September 1982, when the former British Prime Minister Margaret Thatcher visited Beijing, China under the leadership of Deng Xiaoping decided to resume its sovereignty over Hong Kong on July 1, 1997. After lengthy negotiations from late 1982 to 1984, the Sino-British Joint Declaration was signed in September 1984. Under the Joint Declaration, the education system of Hong Kong would remain unchanged 50 years after 1997. The context of political change in Hong Kong triggered education reforms quickly.

The leftist schools had long been deprived of the opportunity of acquiring subsidies from the existing education system; nevertheless, this situation changed gradually after the signing of the Joint Declaration in September 1984. In November 1984, pro-Beijing secondary schools in Hong Kong lobbied the British administration for receiving government subsidies while maintaining their political allegiance to the PRC. In 1991, the government launched the Direct Subsidy Scheme (DSS) with the intention of giving public grants to schools according to a sliding scale and simultaneously allowing them some autonomy in making curricular choices, changing tuition fees and employing entrance requirements.[23] In September 2006, there were 67 DSS schools, constituting 2.3 percent and 9.5 percent of the total number of primary and secondary schools, respectively.[24] The unique features of DSS schools included the decentralization, marketization and privatization of education in Hong Kong.[25] The DSS scheme created some degree of flexibility in school finance, administration and the provision of a new school choice to parents. Most importantly, the scheme enabled private or aided schools that complied with the government conditions to receive limited but direct and financial assistance. The "patriotic" or leftwing secondary schools were eventually given the formula to be permitted to receive government subsidies while maintaining their political allegiance. Arguably, one of the functions of the DSS was to meet the demand of the leftist schools for governmental assistance without putting them into the mainstream school system. Five leftwing secondary schools –Hon Wah, Heung To, Pui Kiu, Fukien and Mongkok Workers' Children – were targeted as they originally belonged to the non-Bought Places Scheme private schools.[26] Apart from these five leftwing schools, four other international schools were brought into the DSS Scheme in September 1991, namely Chinese (Hon Kee) International

School, French International School, Swiss and German International School, and Hong Kong International School. As Andrew Yung observed, "Quite obviously, these schools felt interested in the offer of government financial subsidy while knowing that they continued to enjoy autonomy in key aspects of school operation."[27] Therefore, education reform in 1991 gradually brought the leftwing schools into the umbrella of governmental subsidies, reversing the previously discriminatory policy against them.

The rapidly changing political development in China did not change the dynamics of education reform in Hong Kong along the line of enhancing quality education. The intense public sentiments provoked by the military crackdown on the pro-democracy movement in China on the Tiananmen Square on June 4, 1989, triggered the development of the local Hong Kong identity in the psyche of many teachers and students. On the other hand, education reforms in Hong Kong persisted in improving education quality, including (1) the official espousal of School-Based Curriculum Development in 1988; (2) the renaming and reorganization of the Curriculum Development Committee, which was set up in 1972 to the Curriculum Development Council (CDC) in 1988; (3) the establishment of the Curriculum Development Institute in 1991 to review textbooks, update syllabi and conduct curriculum planning and research; (4) the introduction of the Direct Subsidy Scheme in 1991; (5) the adoption of the School Management Initiative (SMI) in March 1991; (6) the introduction of Targets and Target-Related Assessment (TTRA) in November 1990 and its later revisions as Target-Oriented Curriculum; and (7) other measures of devolving responsibilities on schools through their management committees.[28] Most of these education reform measures were in line with the global trends in education, especially those in the direction of achieving new managerialism, effective school management and New Right populism.[29] By the end of the British colonial administration in June 1997, the seven Education Commission reports had already made more than 279 recommendations, but few of them could comfortably claim effective implementation. It could be argued that the British Hong Kong administration persisted in education reforms for the sake of legitimizing the educational *status quo* in the name of improving quality education. However, with the establishment of the new HKSAR government, education reforms were destined for more drastic measures to be adopted.

Education Reform in the HKSAR: Increasing Politicization

With the establishment of the HKSAR, education reforms continued but have been increasingly politicized. Article 136 of the Basic Law states that the HKSAR government "shall, on its own, formulate policies on the development and improvement of education, including policies regarding the educational system and its administration, the language of instruction, the allocation of funds, the examination system, the system of academic awards and the recognition of educational qualifications."[30] As we will show in this book, the central government in Beijing has generally allowed the HKSAR government to formulate its policies on the education system and its administration, the language of instruction, the allocation of funds, the examination system, the system of awards and the recognition of educational qualifications. However, since the promulgation of the national security law for the HKSAR in late June 2020, Beijing has been exerting pressure on Hong Kong to deal with the politically "incorrect" areas of education, including public examination questions, the role of the Hong Kong Examinations and Assessment Authority (HKEAA), the proper role of teachers and students, and how national security education should be implemented in the HKSAR. Chapter Four will discuss the Hong Kong style of Cultural Revolution in Hong Kong after the enactment of the national security law in late June 2020.

The Asian financial crisis of 1997–1998 propelled the HKSAR government to restructure its economy and consider whether economic recovery would necessitate education reform.[31] As policymakers in Hong Kong pondered the territory's economic future and compared the education expenditure and achievements with other regional competitors, their concern about the quality of education in Hong Kong emerged. Education reform became an essential policy issue of the HKSAR government under the first Chief Executive Tung Chee-hwa. As early as December 1996, when Tung participated in the first Chief Executive election, he announced his platform in education policies. In September 1997, the HKSAR government published the Education Commission's Report Number 7, focusing on quality school education. Tung's first policy address in October 1997 revealed his education reforms: an increase in recurrent expenditure on basic education by 7.6 percent in 1998; a review of the structure of pre-primary, primary, secondary and tertiary education; an emphasis on innovation in private school system to give parents a greater choice; a review of the examination system; and a request for universities to review their admission criteria for undergraduates to give recognition to student excellence in extra-curricular activities, such as community services, arts and sports.[32] His policy reforms also embraced the language policy of training the teachers; the curriculum review; the improvement in the learning environment of primary and secondary schools; and reforms undertaken at the kindergarten level and special education. However, the occurrence of the Asian financial crisis delayed the implementation of Tung's reforms until November 1998, when Fanny Law was appointed as the Director of Education.

Table 2.2 illustrates the content of education reforms in the HKSAR during the Tung Chee-hwa administration. The reform package contained life-long learning, learning-to-learn reform, education assessment reform, the medium of instruction for secondary schools to switch to the Chinese language, quality education, quality assurance mechanism, school choice reforms, and the teaching profession reform. Although the content of education reforms looked comprehensive, the Asian financial crisis generated an atmosphere of the groom in Hong Kong, where some members of the middle class suffered from negative equity, civil servants complained about civil service reforms targeted at them, and teachers expressed their anger at education reform at the school level. In fact, a few teachers committed suicide due to their work pressure mounting on them. The education reforms proposed and undertaken by the Tung administration created a socially turbulent environment amid the economically pessimistic

Table 2.2 The Content of Education Reform in the HKSAR Soon After July 1, 1997

Life-long learning reform: Reform of the educational system

- *Building HK for a New Era: 1997 Policy Address of the Chief Executive of HKSAR* (October 1997)
- *Review of Academic System: Consultative Document on Education Aims* (Education Commission, January 1999)
- *Learning for Life: Review of Education System: Framework for Education Reform* (Education Commission, September 1999)
- *Excel and Grow: Review of Education System: Reform Proposals* (Chief Executive, May 2000)
- *Learning for Life, Learning through Life: Reform Proposal for the Education System in HK* (Chief Executive, September 2000)
- *Hong Kong Higher Education* (University Grants Council, March 2002)
- *Review of Academic Structure for Senior Secondary Education* (Education and Manpower Bureau, October 2004)

Learning-to-learn reform: Curriculum reforms

- *Learning to Learn: Curriculum Development Roadmap* (Curriculum Development Council, June 2001)
- New senior-secondary curriculum and assessment framework were adopted
- The core subjects: Chinese, English, Mathematics and Liberal Studies
- The elective subjects: Twenty subjects were involved

Education assessment reform

- Abolishment of the Aptitude Test
- Reducing the banding system in Secondary Schools' Place Allocation from five bands to three bands
- Setting up the School Value Added Information System
- Setting up the Territory-Wide System Assessment (TSA)

Medium of Instruction for secondary school

- *Medium of Instruction Guidance for Secondary Schools* (September 1997)
- Implementation of the Guidance in September 1998
- Commissions of two studies on the effects of the implementation of the Guidance, 1999–2001 and 2002–2003
- *The Review of Medium of Instruction for Secondary Schools* (February 2005)
- *Fine-Tuning the Medium of Instruction for Secondary Schools* (June 2009)

Quality-education reform: School management reforms

- *Education Commission Report No. 7*: Quality School Education
- School Performance Indicators for various types of schools (since 1998) with performance evidence (since 2002)

Quality Assurance Mechanism

- Quality Assurance Inspection
- School Self-Evaluation
- External School Review
- 23 Key Performance Measures

(Continued)

Table 2.2 The Content of Education Reform in the HKSAR Soon After July 1, 1997 *(Continued)*

School-choice reform

- Revision of Direct Subsidy School
- The Constitution of Through-Train School
- Discretionary places for Primary One Places and Secondary Schools'
- Place Allocation
- The voucher scheme for kindergarten and their quality

Teaching profession reform

- *The Establishment of a General Teaching Council: Consultation Document* (November 1998)
- Implementation of benchmark assessment for English and *Putonghua* teachers in 2000
- *Towards a Learning Profession: A Teacher Competencies Framework and the Continuing Professional Development of Teachers* (November 2003)

Sources: The authors compiled this Table by using the aforesaid government reports.

atmosphere shortly after the Asian financial crisis, thereby generating considerable public grievances and opposition.

The general thinking within the Education Commission at that time was that there were many means of improving education, but the ends were often forgotten. Many of such means had been recommended for good reasons, but the practical implementation focused on quantitative targets. According to critics, money was spent, and efforts were made, but it was doubtful whether school quality improved. Four areas of school education were covered by the Performance Indicators Framework (Table 2.3). They were (1) management and organization, (2) learning and teaching, (3) student support and school ethos, and (4) student performance.

Although the Tung administration put education policy high on its priority of reform agenda, education expert Paul Morris and political scientist Ian Scott pointed to a "disarticulated" political system with the traditionally top-down fashion of policy implementation that met mobilized opposition in the HKSAR.[33] The executive branch of the government remained fragmented and was constrained by legislators, pressure groups, public opinion and "a destructive political culture."[34] Many education reforms were designed to improve the quality of schooling, but they became more rhetorical than substantive in their impacts on the organizations of schools, leading to a wide gap between policy intentions and outcomes. While this argument advanced by Paul Morris and Ian Scott might explain why many of the education reforms proposed by the Tung administration failed, they perhaps neglected the fact that the political context of education reforms from 1997 to 2003 was characterized by the public reluctance to embrace excessive reforms amid the climate of economic crisis and pessimism. The so-called "destructive" political culture was arguably generated by contextual difficulties, specifically policy missteps and economic downturns.

Table 2.3 Comparing the Examination Subjects in HKCEE and HKDSE

Subject classifications	HKCEE	HKDSE
Language	Chinese Language; Chinese Literature; English Language; French; German (2001); Literature in English; Putonghua	Chinese Literature; English Literature
Science	Additional Mathematics; Biology; Chemistry; Human Biology (2007); Mathematics; Physics	Biology; Chemistry; Physics; Combined Science; Integrated Science
Arts	Buddhist Studies; Chinese History; Economic and Public Affairs; Economics; Geography; Government and Public Affairs; History; Integrated Humanities; Religious Studies; Social Studies	Chinese History; Economics; Geography; History; Ethics and Religious Studies
Technology	Ceramics (2007); Computer and Information Technology; Computer Studies (2005); Information Technology (2005); Design and Technology; Electronics and Electricity; Engineering Science (2007); Metalwork (2004); Science and Technology; Technical Drawing (2007); Technological Studies; Textiles (2007); Woodwork (1992)	Design and Applied Technology; Information and Communication Technology; Technology and Living
Industrial or commercial	Accommodation and Catering Services; Commerce; Fashion and Clothing; Home Economics (Dress and Design); Home Economics (Food, Home and Family); Principles of Accounts; Travel and Tourism; Typewriting (2002); Word Processing and Business Communication	Tourism and Hospitality Studies; Business, Accounting and Financial Studies; Health Management and Social Care
Others	Art (2005); Graphical Communication; Music; Physical Education; Visual Art	Music; Visual Arts; Physical Education

Source: Compiled from curriculum reform documents by the authors.
Note: The year in brackets was the last year of examination.

Interest groups were unwilling to embrace education reform. A good example was the Medium of Instruction (MoI) guidance for secondary schools in 1997.[35] The guidance was deemed as compulsory for all government and government-funded secondary schools from 1998 onwards. This policy was a departure from the colonial era when the choice of MoI was left to schools and parents. The guidance aimed at achieving several objectives: (1) to enable students to be biliterate and trilingual (biliterate in English and modern written Chinese and trilingual in spoken Cantonese, English and Putonghua); (2) to promote mother-tongue teaching; (3) to enable schools and parents to understand the benefits of mother-tongue teaching; (4) to strengthen the teaching and learning of English in schools that used Chinese as MoI; and (5) to monitor the progress of language reform.[36] The new policy had substantial impacts; less than 80 of some 400 schools used Chinese as the MoI in 1997, but some 300 schools had to do so under the new policy.[37] There were strong opposition to the initial government plan of imposing Chinese as MoI on all schools from not only schools but also parents and students. The government made concessions by designating 100 secondary schools that used English as MoI. Yet, such a move infuriated some schools that were left out from the list; 14 schools that appealed eventually were allowed to deliver English as their MoI. The entire language reform proposed by the Tung administration ended in a substantial retreat. It showed how schools that used English as MoI opposed the policy guidance of imposing mother-tongue teaching. Eventually, in response to public demands, the Education Commission report in 2005 had several recommendations, including the continuation of the existing policy toward Chinese as MoI for secondary S1–S3; the modification of the criteria for schools wishing to adopt English as MoI; and the enhancement of English proficiency in schools. The report stepped back from the push for the Chinese language as the MoI while emphasizing the enhancement of the English standard of students.

Interest groups did not often prevail over the government in the politics of education reform in the HKSAR. A typical example was the failure of the Catholic Diocese led by Bishop Joseph Zen to overturn the Education (Amendment) Bill passed by the LegCo in July 2004 to establish in each aided school before 2010 an incorporated management committee that would be composed of elected representatives of teachers, parents, alumni and independent persons to promote school-based management. The Catholic Diocese was concerned about the possibility that it would be disempowered to supervise schools under its sponsorship and be unable to achieve Catholic objectives in education. In the past, the Catholic Diocese could choose its board members like nuns and priests to manage primary and secondary schools, but the new legislation clearly curbed the influence of the church, although it still retained 60 percent of the board membership. The HKSAR government argued that the reform would improve school management by making it more participatory, consultative and "democratic." But the Catholic Church believed that the new law would violate its autonomy, thereby challenging the legislation in the court. In November 2006, the High Court ruled against the Catholic Diocese. In 2010, the Court of Appeal confirmed the ruling of the High Court, saying that schools run by religious institutions were often subject to governmental oversight.[38] Indeed, due to mutual distrust, the power struggle between the HKSAR government and the Catholic Diocese led by Bishop (later Cardinal) Zen could be seen in the tug of war over the controversy over the school management committee. After all, Zen promoted the democratization of the HKSAR along the direction of having a directly elected Chief Executive and an entirely directly elected LegCo. The ideological differences between the HKSAR government, which tends to be far more pro-Beijing than being accountable to the people of Hong Kong, and Zen, who remains supportive of democratic change, were vividly shown in the power struggle over the school management committee.

On the other hand, structural education reforms were implemented in the HKSAR. In 2000, the government endorsed the recommendations of the Education Commission to adopt a 3-year senior secondary and 4-year undergraduate academic system. The new senior secondary school education system was seen by the government as facilitating the implementation of a more flexible, coherent and diversified senior secondary curriculum.[39] As a matter of fact, the new curriculum reduced the subject choices for students by comparing the subjects provided for examinations of the old Hong Kong Certificate of Education Examination (HKCEE) with that of the new Hong Kong Diploma of Secondary Education Examination (HKDSE) (Table 2.3).[40] Schools had to reintegrate their human resources, organizational structure and curriculum orientation for the implementation of the new academic structure as the school years of secondary students were reduced from seven to six years. School resources became the major concern of such reforms.

The reintroduction of 3-year senior secondary and 4-year undergraduate came to the HKSAR without societal disagreement. A three-month consultation in the reform blueprint was launched in October 2004, timing the implementation and financial arrangement of the new academic structure. At this moment, the Tung administration approached its final year as he resigned from his position for personal reasons in March 2005. The government document on the new academic structure for senior secondary education and higher education was published in May 2005. The implementation of the new academic structure was expected to begin in 2009, for the new senior Form 4 students started to study the new curriculum in September during the same year.[41]

In addition to the reform in Chinese, English and Mathematics, Liberal Studies was made a new school compulsory subject for the HKDSE. It was a core subject in the three-year senior secondary curriculum. In addition to the four compulsory subjects that would be examined, students might select one to three more elective subjects for their diploma examinations. The design of Liberal Studies in the three-year senior secondary curriculum aroused public interest.[42] Liberal Studies was first introduced to the school curriculum in Hong Kong in 1992 for the sake of adopting an "issue-enquiry approach to enhance students' social awareness and critical thinking."[43] It was originally proposed as a core subject at the Advanced Supplementary Level (ASL) for Form 6 students by the Working Group on Sixth Form Education; nonetheless, it was later implemented as an elective subject. In 1999, the proposal of making Liberal Studies as a core subject for the senior secondary curriculum was put forward again: a working group on the review of the academic structure of senior secondary education and its interface with higher education accepted this idea in 2003 and recommended Liberal Studies to be integrated as a core subject at the senior secondary level. In November 2003, the CDC and the Hong Kong Examinations and Assessment Authority (HKEAA) set up a committee on Liberal Studies (Senior Secondary) to develop the curriculum and assessment of the subject. The committee membership included principals and teachers at secondary schools, academics and educators from local tertiary institutions, and officials from HKEAA and the Education and Manpower Bureau (now EDB). During the consultation on the adoption of Liberal Studies, over 90 percent of the schools from October 2004 to May 2005 supported the reform.[44] Even the heads of local universities announced their support of the usage of Liberal Studies as an admission criterion in May 2005. At the same time, teachers' education institutes offered their support of Liberal Studies through research and the provision of post-graduate studies. The curriculum was finalized in January 2006 and the curriculum and assessment guide for the subject was published in 2007. In the 2008–2009 academic year, 235 schools offered Liberal Studies, whose design followed the overseas experience in cross-disciplinary studies while considering the Hong Kong context.[45] The government asserted that Liberal Studies "aims to broaden students' knowledge and perspectives, help them connect knowledge and concepts across different disciplines and enhance their social awareness through the study of a wide range of issues that would impact on their lives in the future."[46] Moreover, it "promotes the positive values of students by requiring analysis of relevant issues concerning the well-being of individuals, society, the nation and the world with judgment based on evidence and the understanding of values of their own and others."[47] These issues would be discussed in the context of several modules: (1) personal development and interpersonal relationship, (2) Hong Kong today, (3) modem China, (4) globalization, (5) public health and (6) energy technology and the environment.[48] Textbooks were not recommended for Liberal Studies because "the controversial nature of many issues requires that students have access to a range of materials, and that they are not bound by one or a small number of perspectives as well as static knowledge."[49] The ideology behind the introduction and expansion of Liberal Studies to the senior secondary school system in the HKSAR was liberal, attempting to train and develop students' independent mindset, their critical thinking, and their adaptability to life-long learning capabilities. While students were expected to learn more about Hong Kong and mainland China, they also embraced globalization and were made aware of rapidly developing issues such as public health, energy, technology and the environment.

An unintended consequence of adopting Liberal Studies in the senior secondary school system was that it was introduced at a time when Hong Kong's politicization became more prominent than ever before. The PRC's reluctance to democratize the HKSAR along the Western line in fear of Western influence on Hong Kong's political system meant that there was a constant tension between the assertion of mainland Chinese nationalism and the rise of local Hong Kong identity. The Liberal Studies subject naturally dealt with the rapidly developing issues of Hong Kong, including the movement against the Hong Kong Express Rail Link from mid-2009 to early 2010, the anti-national education movement in the summer of 2012, the Occupy Central Movement from September to December 2014, the Mongkok riot in early 2016, the controversy over the oath-taking behavior of two localist legislators-elect Baggio Leung and Yau Wai-ching, and the anti-extradition bill movement in the latter half of 2019. All these events stimulated classroom discussions between teachers and students in the Liberal Studies subject. As such, the political environment after which Liberal Studies was expanded into the senior secondary school level provided a fertile ground for developing the liberal, independent and critical thinking of students. Naturally, while the pro-democracy and liberal-minded teachers, parents and intellectuals saw Liberal Studies as a successful subject, the pro-establishment and pro-Beijing elites regarded it as a stimulant directly or indirectly fostering anti-governmental sentiments.

One controversy over the Liberal Studies subject was its degree of Chinese nationalism. As early as 2008, the Task Group on National Education of the Commission on Strategic Development reported that Liberal Studies should encourage students to study (1) China's reform and its opening-up process, (2) the Chinese culture and modern life, (3) the relationship of the central government and the HKSAR and (4) the question of identity.[50] However, the pro-establishment elites later found the subject as inadequate in nurturing students' Chinese patriotism but, on the contrary, as a tool of enhancing their civic awareness. Objectively speaking, the Liberal Studies curriculum, pedagogy and examinations helped students build up their consciousness of civil rights rather than encountering patriotic indoctrination. However, starting from the 2014 Occupy Central movement to the period shortly after the promulgation of the national security law for the HKSAR, the pro-government and pro-Beijing media and elites, including intellectuals and legislators, began to target at Liberal Studies and to attack its content, pedagogy and those liberals who supported the subject. Before the imposition of the national security law, the CDC had endorsed the legitimacy of Liberal Studies, which as mentioned before, had been implemented after public consultation, meticulous design and careful deliberation. In September 2020, the Our Hong Kong Foundation published the Liberal Studies Research Report, criticizing its pedagogy and content while exerting pressure on the government to downsize it.[51] Its move was political because the report gave ammunition to the government, which in November 2020 expressed its intention of reforming, diluting and renaming Liberal Studies as a new subject named Citizenship and Social Development, which would begin in April 2021.[52] The rise and fall of Liberal Studies demonstrated the transformation from an era in which liberalism shaped its birth to a new period during which Chinese national security and nationalism have been regarded as of utmost political importance.

Apart from the controversy over Liberal Studies, the HKSAR government conducted various reviews on education. Table 2.4 shows all the recent review activities, including the attempts at deepening student learning at the primary school level in 2014, the efforts at upholding teachers' professional conduct in 2015, the promotion of Science, Technology, Engineering, Mathematics (STEM) in 2016; the improvement of the secondary education's curriculum guide in 2017; the review of the school curriculum in 2020; the optimization of four senior secondary core subjects (including a dilution of the Liberal Studies subject) in 2021; and curriculum reform in accordance with national security education in 2021.

In Table 2.5, education reforms in the HKSAR from July 1, 1997 to late June 2020, when the national security law was promulgated, was characterized by an emphasis on the training of young talents in the Tung Chee-hwa administration, a renewed effort at promoting national education and identity under the Donald Tsang government; a focus on curriculum reform during the C. Y. Leung administration; and the introduction of national security education, an

Education Reform in Hong Kong since British Rule 59

Table 2.4 Recent Education Review, 2014–2021

Date	Items	Major concerns
2014	Basic Education Curriculum Guide – To Sustain, Deepen and Focus on Learning to Learn (Primary 1 to 6)	Reiterating the overall aims of the school curriculum and the framework developed by the CDC in 2001 and providing recommendations on the sustainable development of the whole-school curriculum planning, the learning and teaching strategies, resources and assessment.
October 2015	Report on Review of the Present Framework and Mechanism for Promoting and Upholding Teachers' Professional Conduct	The current government-controlled framework and mechanism would be maintained. The present mechanisms regarding misconduct cases and their investigations of the EDB were satisfactory subject to the provision of clear principles on the handling of misconduct cases and decided cases.
December 2016	Report on Promotion of STEM (Science, Technology, Engineering, Mathematics) Education – Unleashing Potential in Innovation	Integrate and apply the knowledge and skills across different STEM disciplines; nurture their creativity, collaboration and problem-solving skills; and foster their innovation and entrepreneurial spirit.
2017	Secondary Education Curriculum Guide	(1) Strengthening values education (including moral and civic education, and Basic Law education); (2) reinforcing the learning of Chinese history and Chinese culture; (3) extending "Reading to Learn" to "Language across the Curriculum"; (4) promoting STEM education and Information Technology in Education (ITE); (5) fostering an entrepreneurial spirit and diversifying life-wide learning experiences; (6) stepping up gifted education; and (7) enhancing the learning and teaching of Chinese as a second language.
September 2020	Task Force on Review of School Curriculum	(1) Whole-person development; (2) values education and life planning education; (3) creating space and catering for learner diversity; (4) applied learning; (5) university admissions; and (6) STEM education.
April 2021	Optimizing the Four Senior Secondary Core Subjects	Reduced 50 teaching hours each of Chinese, English and Mathematics subjects, and 100 hours of Liberal Studies subject. Schools would have greater flexibility to cater for the diverse learning needs of students through curriculum planning at the school level.
June 2021	Supplementary Notes to the Secondary Education Curriculum Guide	Launched the Curriculum Framework of National Security Education (NSE) in Hong Kong and the NSE curriculum framework of 15 subjects.

Sources: Education Bureau, *Curriculum Development Council, Basic Education Curriculum Guide – To Sustain, Deepen and Focus on Learning to Learn (Primary 1 to 6)* (Hong Kong: Education Bureau, 2014), in https://www.edb.gov.hk/attachment/en/curriculum-development/doc-reports/guide-basic-edu-curriculum/BECG_2014_en.pdf, access date: August 2, 2021; Education Commission, *Working Group on Promoting and Upholding Teachers' Professional Conduct: Report on Review of the Present Framework and Mechanism for Promoting and Upholding Teachers' Professional Conduct* (Hong Kong: Education Commission, October 2015), in Microsoft Word – WGTPC Report (e-c.edu.hk), access date: August 31, 2021; Curriculum Development Council, *Secondary Education Curriculum Guide*, in https://www.edb.gov.hk/en/curriculum-development/renewal/guides_SECG.html, access date: August 2, 2021; *Basic Education Curriculum Guide – To Sustain, Deepen and Focus on Learning to Learn (Primary 1 to 6), 2014*, in https://cd.edb.gov.hk/becg/english/intro.html, access date: August 2, 2021; *Optimizing the Four Senior Secondary Core Subjects*, April 2021, in https://www.edb.gov.hk/en/curriculum-development/renewal/opt_core_subj.html, access date: August 2, 2021; Curriculum Development Council, *Supplementary Notes to the Secondary Education Curriculum Guide* (Hong Kong: Education Bureau, June 2021), in https://www.edb.gov.hk/attachment/en/curriculum-development/renewal/Guides/Supp_notes_SECG_Eng_20210628.pdf, access date: August 2, 2021.

Table 2.5 The Chief Executive's Policy Address, Education Policy and Education Reforms

Chief Executive	Education Policy and Reform
Tung Chee-hwa (July 1997–March 2005)	In 2000: The old education system could not meet the challenges of the new age. Embracing the knowledge-based new economy required a large pool of talent equipped with the right skills and creativity. Rapid advances in science and technology unleashed a series of social and ethical issues, which demanded more critical and analytical thinking by young people. The need to groom a new generation of leaders became more pressing than before. Without sweeping reforms of our education system, the quality of education would not be able to meet the requirements for social development and the community's expectations.
Donald Tsang Yam-kuen (March 2005–June 2012)	In 2008: It was the HKSAR government's policy to promote national education. It would enhance the opportunities for students to join mainland study trips and exchange programs. Teachers would also undergo training. As such, both students and teachers would understand China more than ever before. The quota of subsidizing secondary students to participate in mainland trips would increase annually from 5,000 to 37,000, including junior secondary and upper primary students. The government would adopt a three-pronged approach: Helping students better understand Chinese history and development through curriculum planning; providing students with opportunities to join exchange programs to heighten their sense of national identity; and encouraging students to contribute to China's development. In 2007, the government organized lectures and training programs for teachers and students. Topics included the Beijing 2008 Olympic Games, the staging of the Olympic Equestrian Events in Hong Kong, China's first spacewalk by astronauts in its space mission of Shenzhou-7, the 30th anniversary of China's open-door policy, and disaster relief and reconstruction efforts after the Sichuan earthquake. In 2009: The government continued to promote national education, which was a long-term mission. It would strengthen the elements of China in various key learning areas under the primary and secondary curricula. In 2010: To promote national education, the government would collaborate further with the Committee on the Promotion of Civic Education, District Councils, community organizations, national education organizations and youth groups. More mainland exchange programs, study tours and volunteer activities would be organized. For example, with Shanghai hosting World Expo 2010, the Hong Kong government-sponsored study tours and a volunteer team for our young people to attend this event. More resources would be provided for student teachers to participate in professional study courses in the mainland. In 2011: To strengthen students' sense of national identity and commitment to national development, the government consulted the public on the implementation of the Moral and National Education Curriculum. The government claimed that the education sector generally agreed with the philosophy and importance of introducing the curriculum and that the Curriculum Development Council would submit revised proposals for detailed consideration.
Leung Chun Ying (July 2012–June 2017)	In 2015: The EDB would renew and enrich the curricula and learning activities of Science, Technology and Mathematics and enhance the training of teachers, thereby allowing primary and secondary students to unleash their innovative potential. The EDB would renew the curriculum content of Chinese History and World History and enhance the training of teachers. The objectives were to reinforce students' interest in and understanding of Chinese history and culture and to broaden their global outlook.

(Continued)

Table 2.5 The Chief Executive's Policy Address, Education Policy and Education Reforms (Continued)

Chief Executive	Education Policy and Reform
Carrie Lam Cheng Yuet-ngor (July 2017–June 2023)	In 2017: It was the intrinsic duty of school education to help students to understand the development of the history, culture, economy, technology, political system and law of their country and to cultivate in them a sense of their national identity. The EDB would include Chinese history as an independent compulsory subject for the junior secondary level in the 2018–2019 school year. The EDB would enrich curricular content to promote students' understanding of Chinese history and culture. Basic Law education would be enhanced; professional development programs would be organized for principals and teachers; and sister schools between Hong Kong and the mainland were encouraged to enhance exchange and cooperation. Teachers and students would be arranged to visit cities and provinces relating to the Belt and Road initiative and the innovative and technological enterprises in the Guangdong-Hong Kong-Macau Bay Area.
In 2018: The development of young people should be holistic and should not be limited to academic achievement. An important component in the school curriculum is values education, which includes elements such as moral and civic education, sex education, environmental education, commitment to the community and the development of national identity. The Task Force on Review of School Curriculum deliberated on the school curriculum to create space for schools to deliver values education in a holistic manner and to help young students develop positive values and attitudes.
In 2020: Education is the key to nurturing talents. Carrie Lam's vision for education was to nurture young people into quality citizens with a sense of social responsibility and national identity, an affection for Hong Kong and an international perspective. Education is about building a good character. As such, the cultivation of moral virtues is important. Lam stressed that students must be law-abiding and that they are able to respect different opinions and to become responsible members of civil society. Among the five domains of moral, intellectual, physical, social and aesthetic developments, moral development is regarded as the most important foundation of education. Deepening students' understanding of the Chinese history, culture and developments, and strengthening education on the Chinese constitution and the Basic Law are indispensable for fostering their sense of national identity and awareness of national security.
The government made Chinese History an independent compulsory subject at the junior secondary level, and the new curriculum of the subject was rolled out progressively from Secondary One. The EDB would provide opportunities for students to join mainland study tours and encourage primary and secondary students to learn more about Chinese culture for nurturing their moral character and cultural identity.
Moreover, the EDB would cultivate primary and secondary students' understanding of China's development, the constitution and the Basic Law, the implementation of "one country, two systems" and the importance of national security. Students would be taught to respect and preserve the dignity of the national flag and the national anthem as symbols of our country, to foster positive values, and to develop a sense of identity, belonging and responsibility toward the nation, the Chinese race and our society.

Sources: Adapted from all the annual policy address of the Chief Executive from 1997 to 2020.

emphasis on values education with social responsibility and national identity, and a consolidation of Chinese culture and history in the Carrie Lam era. Clearly, while the Tung administration was relatively softline in education reform, Carrie Lam and her education officials adopted a hardline approach mainly due to the legacy of the 2019 anti-extradition bill movement. Ideologically speaking, the Tung Chee-hwa administration remained conservative in its education reform; the Donald Tsang government gradually became more nationalistic; and the C. Y. Leung government tended to be more pragmatic in its focus on curriculum reform. The most politicized period was led by Chief Executive Carrie Lam, whose education reform increased its thrust of Chinese patriotism and nationalism.

Conclusion

While the British colonial administration reformed the education system due to the necessity of stabilizing the society, consolidating its legitimacy and buttressing its governance, the post-1997 HKSAR government has increasingly politicized and decolonized education reforms through a renewed emphasis on the promotion of Chinese national identity and the stronger awareness of Chinese history and culture. The 2019 anti-extradition bill movement led to the HKSAR government to reform the education system and curricula further along the line of promoting national security education and instilling a stronger sense of law-abiding citizens in the psyche of young students. If liberalism and colonialism marked the features of pre-1997 British Hong Kong, then de-liberalization, decolonization and Chinese nationalism have become the main pillars of education reform in the HKSAR.

Notes

1. Luk Hung-kay, *A History of Education in Hong Kong*: A Report submitted to the Lord Wilson Heritage Fund (York University, 2000), pp. 16–20. G. B. Endacott, *A History of Hong Kong* (New York: Oxford University Press, 1973), pp. 64–71.
2. Gerard A. Postiglione and Wing-on Lee, *Social Change and Educational Development: Mainland China, Taiwan and Hong Kong* (Hong Kong: Centre of Asian Studies, The University of Hong Kong, 1995), pp. 3–12.
3. Emile Durkheim and Marcel Mauss, *Primitive Classification*, translated by Rodney Needham (Chicago: University of Chicago Press, 1969), p. 64.
4. Mark Bray, "Education and Colonial Transition: The Hong Kong Experience in Comparative Perspective," in Mark Bray and Wing-on Lee, eds., *Education and Political Transition: Implications and Hong Kong's Change of Sovereignty* (Hong Kong: Comparative Education Research Centre, The University of Hong Kong, 1997), pp. 11–24.
5. Anthony E. Sweating, "Hong Kong Education within Historical Process," in Gerard A. Postiglione, ed., *Education and Society in Hong Kong: Toward One Country and Two Systems* (Hong Kong: Hong Kong University Press, 1992), pp. 39–82.
6. Endacott, *A History of Hong Kong*, pp. 228–242.
7. Steven Chung-fun Hung, "Financing Schooling Policy of the Hong Kong Government: A Historical Comparative Analysis with the Theories of the State," unpublished PhD thesis, Tarlac State University, 2012, pp. 47–51.

8 The Committee on Education, "Report of the Committee on Education," in *The Hong Kong Government Gazette*, April 11, 1902.
9 Steven Hung, "Financing School Policy of the Hong Kong Government," p. 55.
10 Gail Schaeffer Fu, "Bilingual Education in Hong Kong: A Historical Perspective," a working paper in Language and Language Teaching, The University of Hong Kong, 1979, pp. 1–19.
11 The Hong Kong Government, "Education Ordinance 1913," in *The Hong Kong Government Gazette*, May 22, 1914.
12 Hung Chung Fun Steven, "Financing School Policy of the Hong Kong Government," pp. 58–62.
13 *Ibid.*, pp. 63–66.
14 Edmund Burney, *Report on Education in Hong Kong* (London: Crown Agents for the Colonies, 1935).
15 Hung Chung Fun Steven, "Financing School Policy of the Hong Kong Government," p. 68.
16 Education Department, *Annual Report of the Education Department for the Year 1st May 1946 to 31st March 1947* (Hong Kong: Hong Kong Government, 1947), p. 6.
17 *Ibid.*
18 R. M. Marsh and J. R. Sampson, *Report of the Education Commission* (Hong Kong Government, 1963). Hong Kong Legislative Council, *Official Report Proceedings: Meeting of 20th May 1964*, in https://www.legco.gov.hk/1964/h640520.pdf, access date: August 1, 2021.
19 Hong Kong Government, "Statement on Government's Policy on the Re-Organization of the Structure of Primary and Secondary Education," tabled in Legislative Council on January 23, 1963 (Hong Kong: Government Printer, 1963).
20 Hong Kong Government, *Secondary Education in Hong Kong over the Next Decade* (Hong Kong: The Government Printer, 1974).
21 Eric Ma, "Top-Down Patriotism and Bottom-Up Nationalization in Hong Kong," The Chinese University of Hong Kong, 2003, in https://www.com.cuhk.edu.hk/project/ericsite/academic/top-down.pdf, access date: July 8, 2021.
22 Education Commission, *Education Commission Report Number 1* (Hong Kong: Government Printer, October 1984).
23 Andrew Yung Man-sing, "The Policy of Direct Subsidy Scheme Schools in Hong Kong: Finance and Administration," *Hong Kong Teachers' Centre Journal*, vol. 5 (2006), pp. 94–111.
24 *Ibid.*
25 *Ibid.*, pp. 96–97.
26 *Ibid.*, p. 100.
27 *Ibid.*
28 Anthony Sweeting, *Education in Hong Kong, 1941 to 2001: Visions and Revisions* (Hong Kong; Hong Kong University Press, 2004), pp. 377–378. Also see "Information Paper: Curriculum Development Institute, October 17, 1997," in Panels on Education – Papers 17 Oct 1997 (legco.gov.hk), access date: August 29, 2021. David Wu Tai-wai, "Investigating School-Based Management in Hong Kong to Validate the Prerequisites for Successful Schools Using an Exploratory Sequential Design," unpublished PhD thesis, Hong Kong Institute of Education, October 2015. Also see Veronica Ma Kit-ching, "Implications of School Management Initiative: A Case Study of Teachers' Perspective," unpublished MEd thesis, University of Hong Kong, August 1993. "Handbook on Education Policy in Hong Kong, 1965–1998," Hong Kong Institute of Education, September 1992, in General Introduction to Targets and Target-related Assessment (eduhk.hk), access date: August 29, 2021.
29 Paul Morris and Ian Scott, "Education Reform and Policy Implementation in Hong Kong," in Lok Sang Ho, Paul Morris and Yue-ping Chung, *Education Reform and the Quest for Excellence: The Hong Kong Story* (Hong Kong: Hong Kong University Press, 2005), pp. 83–97.

30 *The Basic Law of the Hong Kong Special Administrative Region of the People's Republic of China*, in Basic Law – Basic Law – Chapter VI (EN), access date: August 29, 2021.
31 Cheng Yin-cheong, "Education Reforms in Hong Kong: Challenges, Strategies, & International Implications," The International Forum on Education Reform: Experiences in Selected Countries, The Office of the National Education Commission, 30 July–2 August 2001, Bangkok, Thailand.
32 Tung Chee-hwa, *Chief Executive's Policy Address* (Hong Kong: the HKSAR Government, 1997), in https://www.policyaddress.gov.hk/pa97/english/paindex.htm, access date: August 1, 2021.
33 Paul Morris and Ian Scott, "Education Reform and Policy Implementation in Hong Kong," *Journal of Education Policy*, vol. 18, no. 1 (2003), pp. 71–84.
34 *Ibid.*
35 Vincent Kan and Bob Adamson, "Language Policies for Hong Kong Schools since 1997," *London Review of Education*, vol. 8. no. 2 (July 2010), pp. 167–176.
36 *Ibid.*, pp. 171–172.
37 *Ibid.*
38 Min Lee, "Hong Kong Catholic Diocese Fails in Schools Appeal," Associated Press, February 3, 2010, in Hong Kong Catholic diocese fails in schools appeal | Taiwan News | 2010-02-03 17:29:48, access date: August 29, 2021.
39 Education and Manpower Bureau, *Review of the Academic Structure of Senior Secondary Education* (Hong Kong: Education and Manpower Bureau, May 2003).
40 HKCEE was a standardized examination between 1974 and 2011 for local students' five-year secondary education.
41 Education and Manpower Bureau, *The New Academic Structure for Senior Secondary Education and Higher Education – Action Plan for Investing in the Future of Hong Kong* (Hong Kong: Education and Manpower Bureau, May 2005).
42 Curriculum Development Council and Hong Kong Examinations and Assessment Authority, *Liberal Studies Curriculum and Assessment Guide* (Hong Kong: Education Bureau, 2007).
43 "Panel on Education: Discussion on Liberal Studies under the New Senior Secondary Curriculum," July 11, 2009, LC Paper No. CB(2)2122/08-09(01), in ed0711cb2-2122-1-e.pdf (legco.gov.hk), access date: August 31, 2021.
44 *Ibid.*
45 *Ibid.*
46 *Ibid.*
47 *Ibid.*
48 *Ibid.*
49 *Ibid.*, pp. 5–6.
50 *The Situation, Challenge and Prospect of implementation of National Education in Hong Kong: Report of Task Group on National Education of the Commission on Strategic Development* (Hong Kong: Task Group on National Education of the Commission on Strategic Development, April 2008).
51 "Our Hong Kong Foundation Launches Liberal Studies Research Report: Cultivating Interdisciplinary Learning, Thinking Skills, and Appreciation of Diversity," Our Hong Kong Foundation, September 7, 2020, in https://www.ourhkfoundation.org.hk/en/media/1264/education-and-youth/our-hong-kong-foundation-launches-liberal-studies-research-report, access date: August 1, 2021.
52 Chan Ho-him and Kathleen Magramo, "Hong Kong's Liberal Studies to be Renamed 'Citizenship and Social Development' as Part of Massive Overhaul," *South China Morning Post*, March 31, 2021, in https://www.scmp.com/news/hong-kong/education/article/3127778/hong-kongs-liberal-studies-expected-be-renamed-citizenship, access date: July 4, 2021.

3 The Mainlandization of Education in Hong Kong

Impacts of the national security law on education reform

This Chapter examines how the PRC authorities have been attempting to mainlandize Hong Kong's education sector. Such process of mainlandization can be seen in several aspects: (1) the emphasis on patriotic education in the Hong Kong Special Administrative Region (HKSAR) and (2) the push for national security education; (3) the reform of Liberal Studies; (4) the expansion of pro-Beijing education-related interest groups, propaganda work and publishing houses, including the monopolization and production of textbooks for schools; and (5) the cooptation of education elites into the PRC's umbrella of united front work. Under these circumstances, the Hong Kong education sector can and will hopefully be mainlandized, trying to strengthen the nationalistic identity of principals, teachers and students in the run-up to 2047.

The origin of China's concern about national security could be traced back to April 2014, when President Xi chaired the central-level National Security Commission and gave a speech on the concept of "comprehensive national security."[1] Due to the rapidly changing international circumstances and the increasing domestic challenges, President Xi emphasized "the people's security as the basic principle; political security as the root; economic security as the foundation; military, cultural and social security as the safeguard; and international security as a reliance."[2] The "Chinese-style national security path" embraces various ingredients, ranging from external to internal security, from territorial to people's security, from traditional to non-conventional security, from development to safety, and from personal to common security. The scope of national security, in the minds of the CCP, is broad: political, territorial, military, economic, cultural, societal, technological, informational, ecological, resource, and nuclear security. Under this comprehensive framework, national security has since April 2014 been shaping the PRC's policy toward the HKSAR.

As early as July 1, 2017, during the 20th anniversary of Hong Kong's return to China, PRC President Xi Jinping remarked that any activity in Hong Kong that undermined the central government's national security would be disallowed and that the HKSAR should implement "patriotic education."[3] Xi's comments could be seen as a reaction to Hong Kong's protests that challenged the authority and legitimacy of the central government, including the 2014 Occupy Central Movement, the early 2016 Mongkok riot, and the oath-taking saga

DOI: 10.4324/9781003147268-3

in October 2016 leading to the SCNPC's interpretation of the Basic Law's stipulation on the proper behavior of legislators-elect in oath-taking.

During the national education conference in Beijing on September 10, 2018, President Xi Jinping said that China's education reform had new thinking, which was characterized by (1) the insistence of the Party's "full leadership in education enterprises," (2) the foundation task of enhancing individual ethics and morality, (3) the upholding of socialism, (4) the emphasis on the people-centered approach, (5) the deepening of education reform, (6) the mission of achieving the Chinese renaissance, and (7) the foundation work of building up a team of teachers.[4] He added that the mainland students needed to be guided on "the long-term ideals of communism and the common ideal of Chinese-style socialism" and that they should shoulder the responsibility of achieving Chinese renaissance.[5] As such, education, according to Xi, should guide students to love the CCP, listen to the Party, and contribute themselves to the Chinese nation. Students must develop, President Xi said, socialist core values, improve the moral conduct, broaden their horizon, enhance their knowledge, cultivate their hard-working spirit, and improve themselves continuously. Finally, education must provide a guiding path for students to work diligently, honestly, innovatively so that they can and will appreciate, respect and understand the beauty and honor of labor.[6] Following President Xi's speech, mainland students were mobilized to be more patriotic and teachers were required to learn the gist of his speech; some students had to copy Xi's remarks to ensure that they memorized his important thinking.[7] If mainlandization of Hong Kong's education was inevitable, teachers and students in the HKSAR would have to learn the importance and content of patriotism, although they might not be mobilized in a way exactly the same as their mainland counterparts.

In September 2019, Beijing's top leaders saw the anti-extradition bill protests in the HKSAR as evidence of the failure of Hong Kong's education.[8] The central leadership's push for the enhancement of patriotism in the local education sector was accompanied by mobilization of elite opinion in the HKSAR. Specifically, the elite opinion in favor of patriotic education was articulated by the Hong Kong members of the Chinese People's Political Consultative Conference (CPPCC). In September 2019, during the anti-extradition bill movement in the HKSAR, Margaret Chan Fung Fu-chun, a member of the CPPCC Standing Committee, said: "Some young Hong Kong people have become more radical than before and this phenomenon stemmed from the schools and education, especially the deficiency in patriotism education."[9] Soon after her remarks, some school principals in the HKSAR suggested that a compulsory subject for Hong Kong's trainee teachers should embrace the teaching practices in the mainland schools.[10]

In October 2019, when the CCP held its Fourth Party Plenum, it sent a strong message to the HKSAR by saying that the legal system and enforcement mechanism of safeguarding national security in Hong Kong and Macau had to be established and improved.[11] At that time, most observers of Hong Kong and Macau did not quite understand the meaning of improving the legal system and enforcement mechanism of protecting the central government's national security in both special administrative regions. However, when news broke out in May 2020 that China would draft a national security law for the HKSAR, it was clear that, with hindsight, the October 2019 Fourth Party Plenum made a politically significant decision in formulating a national security law for Hong Kong.

During the 20th anniversary of Macau's return of its administration to the PRC on December 20, 2019, President Xi Jinping delivered an important speech that directly or indirectly criticized Hong Kong for its failure to observe the "one country, two systems," to implement patriotic education, and to learn from Macau on how external interference had to be eliminated.[12] First, Xi said Hong Kong and Macau belonged to China's internal affairs, which must not be interfered by any foreign country – a remark pointing to the vulnerability of Hong Kong to external influences, especially during the anti-extradition bill movement in the latter half of 2019. Second, President Xi pointed to Macau as a safe city where matters could be discussed with compromise and where social contradictions could be managed harmoniously – an implication that the HKSAR failed to be safe, to make a political compromise and to reduce social contradictions. Third, President Xi praised the proper relations between the executive, legislature and judiciary in Macau, where the three branches fulfilled their duties mutually while respecting the authority of the Chief Executive and maintaining the operation of the executive-led system. He, therefore, indirectly criticized the HKSAR, where the executive-led system was eroded and challenged by a defiant and disobedient legislature where some democrats and radicals confronted the government and pro-Beijing forces without compromise. From the central leaders' perspective, the Hong Kong judiciary challenged the executive branch without fully understanding the meaning of the Basic Law. Fourth, President Xi praised Macau, where Article 23 of the Basic Law had long been legislated in 2009, where a national security commission was established, and where patriotic education was implemented smoothly. By implication, the HKSAR failed to protect China's national security, to enact Article 23 of the Basic Law, and to formulate and implement patriotic education. Fifth, Xi explicitly said that while "the Macau comrades embrace the 'one country, two systems' from their own hearts, it is time for 'one country, two systems' to be the best system maintaining Hong Kong's long-term prosperity and stability."[13] Although *Xinhua* reported Xi's remarks as "maintaining Macau's long-term prosperity and stability," some Hong Kong reporters and observers double-checked that President Xi had actually referred to Hong Kong's long-term prosperity and stability – the discrepancy between the "official" version and Xi's original remark showed how the top PRC leader viewed the HKSAR. Unsurprisingly, the central government decided to impose the national security law onto the HKSAR by late June 2020.

On May 28, 2020, the National People's Congress (NPC) passed the draft national security law for the HKSAR by 2,878 votes, signaling Beijing's intervention in stabilizing the society and politics of Hong Kong.[14] The PRC's increasingly hardline policy toward Hong Kong could be traced back to the publication of the White Paper on the practice of the "one country, two systems" in the HKSAR in June 2014, emphasizing the "overall jurisdiction" of the central authorities over Hong Kong.[15] The origin of this White Paper stemmed from the desire of some Hong Kong democrats to push for democratization in the form of having the right of the Hong Kong people to select their Chief Executive directly through universal suffrage and to elect all Legislative Council members directly in geographical constituencies. The efforts of the three leaders of the Occupy Central Movement – Benny Tai, Chan Kin-man and Chu Yiu-ming – to push for democratic reforms in the HKSAR from early 2013 to mid-2014 triggered the national security concerns of PRC authorities, who had to publish the White Paper to assert the central government's jurisdiction and powers over Hong Kong. In October 2017, when the CCP held its national congress, its Central Committee report emphasized that "we will never allow anyone, any organization, or any political party, at any time or in any form, to separate any part of Chinese territory from China."[16] In October 2019, when the CCP Central Committee held its 19th Fourth Plenum in Beijing, the former director of the Hong Kong Macau Affairs Office, Zhang Xiaoming, emphasized that the "one country, two systems" in the HKSAR was already outdated and that it needed to be improved – a remark showing Beijing's determination to assert its authority and exercise its power over Hong Kong in the midst of rising localism and radical populism.[17] Zhang added that Hong Kong had failed in its education because students lacked national consciousness.[18] As early as 2016, the EDB had to submit the textbooks, examination materials, and information on the management of teachers to the PRC's MoE, which began to oversee how the HKSAR implemented its education policies.[19] Hence, the changing contextual circumstances, including the PRC's adjusted policy toward the HKSAR and the rise of localist challenges to the central authorities, prompted increasing intervention from Beijing in Hong Kong's education system. Of course, Beijing saw such intervention as "positive" and "necessary."

In late June 2017, Christine Choi Yuk-lin was appointed as the Undersecretary for Education to assist the Secretary for Education Kevin Yeung Yun-hung. The appointment could be seen as a watershed because Choi had been the principal of the pro-Beijing Fukien Secondary School from 2013 to June 2017. Supporters of Choi's appointment argued that she had rich experiences in dealing with primary and secondary schools, and that Choi could assist Kevin Yeung, who came from the civil service. In the summer of 2016, Choi participated in the educational functional constituency of the Legislative Council (LegCo) election but was defeated. Most importantly, she had been one of the leaders of the pro-Beijing Federation of Education Workers (FEW) and involved in the production of teaching materials for the 2012 national education curriculum.[20] Her rise in the education leadership of the HKSAR demonstrated Beijing's support, for the central government has to approve the nomination of principal officials, including secretaries and undersecretaries. Furthermore, Choi's relative "redness" meant that she would be responsible for the formulation and implementation of the national education curricula, especially after the promulgation of the national security law in June 2020.

The national security law has stipulations that directly affect the education landscape of the HKSAR, ranging from schools to principals, from teachers to students, and from curricula to teaching and learning activities. Article 1 says that the national security of the central government has to be safeguarded and that it is a criminal offense if anyone is involved in "secession, subversion, organization and perpetration of terrorist activities, and collusion with a foreign country or with external elements to endanger national security in relation to the HKSAR."[21] In the context of Hong Kong's education, Article 1 means that teachers and students must safeguard the central government's national security in the HKSAR. As Article 2 says, "no institution, organization or individual in the region shall contravene these provisions [of the national security law] in exercising their rights and freedoms."[22] In other words, the rights and freedoms of individuals are not unlimited, although their rights are, according to Article 4, protected by the Basic Law and the International Covenant on Civil and Political Rights and the International Covenant on Economic, Social and Cultural Rights as applied to Hong Kong. Article 3 emphasizes that while the central government has the "overarching responsibility for national security affairs relating to the HKSAR," it is the duty of the Hong Kong government to safeguard national security. Article 6 says that the rule of law shall be adhered to in the process of imposing punishment for offenses that endanger national security. Article 6 stresses the "common responsibility" of "all the people of China, including the people of Hong Kong, to safeguard the sovereignty, unification and territorial integrity of the PRC."[23] Most significantly, "any institution, organization or individual in the HKSAR shall abide by this Law and the laws of the region in relation to the safeguarding of national security, and shall not engage in any act or activity which endangers national security."[24] While Article 8 stresses the responsibility of the law enforcement and judicial authorities of Hong Kong to enforce the national security law, Article 9 emphasizes that the HKSAR government "shall take necessary measures to strengthen public communication, guidance, supervision and regulation over matters concerning national security, including those relating to schools, universities, social organizations, the media and the Internet."[25] Most importantly, Article 10 says the HKSAR "shall promote national security education in schools and universities and through social organizations, the media, the Internet and other means to raise the awareness of Hong Kong residents of national security and of the obligation to abide by the law."[26] Hence, the promulgation of the national security law in late June 2020 paved the way for the formulation and implementation of national security education in the HKSAR.

In October 2020, four months after the promulgation of the national security law for the HKSAR, President Xi Jinping visited Shenzhen and delivered his speech not only delineating the special economic zone's achievements and its role as an economic locomotive in South China but also outlining two main areas for Hong Kong to follow up. First, he said that Hong Kong and Macau must "accurately implement the basic principle of "one country, two systems" to promote development mutually with Shenzhen and the mainland.[27] Second,

President Xi added that Shenzhen would have to accelerate the development of Qianhai on the one hand and strengthen its cooperation with Hong Kong's technological development on the other hand. Furthermore, Shenzhen would have to guide the comrades in Hong Kong, Macau and Taiwan to make an investment, while the Greater Bay Area (GBA) should be utilized as a collaborative platform to attract more young people from Hong Kong and Macau to study, work, reside and learn there.[28] Through "comprehensive interactions, full exchange, deep integration," the young people of Guangdong, Hong Kong and Macau would be able to enhance their "centrifugal direction toward their motherland."[29] Xi's speech was interpreted by the Chief Secretary of the HKSAR, Matthew Cheung, as encouraging more Hong Kong youth to study, work and reside in the mainland.[30] Cheung revealed that 16,200 mainland students studied in Hong Kong's tertiary institutions, which had campuses in the mainland as of July 2020 and that the EDB since 2017–2018 academic year had been providing 100,000 exchange positions for Hong Kong's primary and secondary school students to visit the mainland, including cities in the GBA and those related to the Belt and Road initiatives.[31]

The Push for National Security Education

In the minds of PRC President Xi Jinping, education is a key to China's success by grooming young talents, stimulating technological innovation and producing young people with nationalistic identity and fervor.[32] Xi's beliefs have been translated into practice in the HKSAR, where the young people were regarded by PRC authorities as lacking patriotism and nationalistic sentiments. In particular, the HKSAR was viewed by Beijing as a place where foreign countries, especially the United States, participated in shaping the political system in such a way as to make Hong Kong a Trojan Horse for them to "subvert" the PRC.[33] Foreign influence upon the HKSAR, from the PRC's perspective, could be seen in the 2014 Occupy Central Movement and the 2019 anti-extradition movement, while the Hong Kong localists and radicals had their political ideals supportive of Western-style democracy. As such, the PRC authorities have been determined to reverse any attempt at westernizing and democratizing Hong Kong; the assertive civil society in the HKSAR has to be curbed and tamed; groups supportive of democratic change and resistant to the CCP have to be controlled; teachers and students imbued with a strong sense of localism and a weak sense of Chinese nationalism have to be reeducated; and Hong Kong's education system, including curricula and the mentality of teachers and students, has to be reformed urgently.

Shortly after the imposition of the national security law on the HKSAR, Chief Executive Carrie Lam said in an education forum that national security education would have to be formulated and implemented to "raise the level of national consciousness among students."[34] She added that during the anti-extradition protests, 3,000 students from the primary and secondary schools and universities were arrested, a figure occupying 40 percent of all those arrested offenders. Moreover, 45 percent of those arrested were students. Carrie Lam remarked that the confrontation between the police and students at the Chinese University of Hong Kong and Polytechnic University in October and November 2019 was like "a violent hotbed" in which some students formed human chains shouting slogans in support of "Hong Kong independence."[35] She pointed to "a worrying phenomenon" that students' mentality of "resisting the country" and "opposing the government" was entrenched.[36] Another "worrying" trend was that some students had "weak" consciousness of obeying the law and such an attitude ran counter to a diversified society emphasizing peaceful co-existence. Lam explicitly said that the young generation of Hong Kong had problems not mainly because of the education system but more because of the fact that political issues were unresolved and that education was politicized. Ultimately, she added that the young people of Hong Kon did not accurately understand the "one country, two systems" and the principles of "Hong Kong people governing Hong Kong," "a high degree of autonomy" and the maintenance of Hong Kong's long-term stability and prosperity. As such, Lam hoped that the national security law would provide an opportunity for students to turn a new leaf through education.[37] Lam's remarks showed that she had a vague idea of how to formulate and implement national security education just shortly after the enactment of the national security law in late June 2020.

However, at the same forum, the Liaison Office's deputy director Tan Tieniu, articulated a much clearer view of national security education.[38] Tan said that the students of Hong Kong would have to understand the rule of law and national consciousness through the national security law, that the national security education would enable students to understand the rule of law and national consciousness.[39] Moreover, students would be able to understand what is right or wrong through national security education. Finally, Tan added that the national security education would let students understand the inseparable and close relations between Hong Kong and the Chinese nation and that the national security law would enable calmness and stability to the citizens and schools.[40] He called for the need of Hong Kong society to "cut the black hands that extends to the schools," meaning that schools must educate students to understand not only the national security law but also the national anthem.[41] National security education, according to Tan, must be "institutionalized" inside and outside the schools interactively so that Hong Kong would start from a new beginning.[42]

Tan's detailed comments were different from Chief Executive Lam in several aspects. First, the Liaison Office's deputy director emphasized that education reform would be a must. Second, such reform must entail national security education inside and outside the schools. Third, the people of Hong Kong, especially the students, must understand deeply the content of the Basic Law, the national security law, the national anthem and their implications. However, a commonality in the speech delivered by Tan and Lam was that the young students of Hong Kong must be educated to have a much stronger national consciousness and identity. The emphasis on the inculcation of national identity and consciousness into the psyche of Hong Kong students was quickly echoed by the pro-Beijing FEW chairman Wong Kwan-yu, who said that the FEW was concerned about the content of national security education and when it would begin in the HKSAR.[43] The FEW's position was aimed at exerting pressure on the HKSAR government, specifically the Education Department Bureau (EDB), to come up with concrete policy measures to enforce national security education.

As with the FEW, the director of the Ta Kung and Wen Wei Group, Jiang Zaizhong, echoed the remarks of Liaison Office deputy director Tan Tieniu and exerted pressure on the HKSAR government to formulate and implement national security education as soon as possible. Jiang said that the national security law was and would be the "savior" of Hong Kong students and that the root problem of Hong Kong students going toward the path of "distortion" was their lack of national consciousness.[44] He criticized those people who claimed that "achieving justice through illegal acts" were "poisoning the young people" – an implicit criticism of a former law professor Benny Tai who advocated the idea in the 2014 Occupy Central Movement.[45] Jiang added that people who advocated such a view "misled, seduced and incited" the young people to participate in illegal activities.[46] Hence, the introduction of national security education would be conducive to the value change of the young people.

The Secretary for Education, Kevin Yeung Yun-hung, was under the obligation and pressure to undertake education reform. In the same forum, he remarked that national security education and national anthem education were of paramount importance and that it would be necessary to cultivate national consciousness in the psyche of young students when they were children.[47] To show to the audience that the EDB did something to instill national consciousness among the young students, he added that, on July 1, he observed a sense of national pride and civic responsibility among teachers, students and guests in a school event he had attended. Yeung outlined his plan of formulating and implementing the national security education, including the need for schools to explain the importance of national security law and its significance to students, the action of EDB to consult expert opinion on how to come up with detailed guidelines for school management and activities to enforce the national security law and education, and the logistical support that the government would provide for the schools. In response to the pressure on the government to educate the young students on the national anthem, Yeung admitted the importance of the national anthem and flag as symbols of national identity and dignity. As such, school activities would be arranged to impart to students "their necessity of understanding, respecting and loving their country's national flag and anthem."[48] He mentioned that Hong Kong schools would enhance exchange with the mainland counterparts through mutual visits, teachers' networks and learning circles. Finally, Yeung appealed to the need for schools to strengthen the awareness of students in the Chinese constitution, the Basic Law, China's development, Chinese culture, national security and the respect for the national anthem – areas that would be delineated in the guidelines and circulars to be issued by the EDB in the following months.

While Tan's remarks on July 12 implicitly criticized Benny Tai for his mobilization of young students in the 2014 Occupy Central Movement, the pro-Beijing *Ta Kung Pao* on July 13 editorialized and named Tai as a person allegedly "violating the national security law."[49] The editorial criticized Tai for organizing a so-called "primary election" to select the pro-democracy candidates before the September LegCo election, for trying to "overthrow the regime," for raising the idea of occupying more than 35 seats in the 70-member LegCo as an attempt to "manipulate" the election and "usurp" political power.[50] It lambasted Tai and his like-minded democrats for launching a propaganda for the "primary election." Most importantly, the editorial cited Article 22 of the national security law and added that "anyone who organizes, orchestrates, implements or participates in overthrowing the central people's and HKSAR's regime institution, or who seriously disturbs, stops and damages the regime institution of the PRC and HKSAR to enforce their duty is committing an offence."[51] It cited Article 29 of the national security law and said that any action of "manipulating, damaging or likely creating serious impacts on the elections of the HKSAR" is a criminal offence.[52] The editorial also warned that all those people who participated in the "primary election" would have the danger of being disqualified in the future. It concluded the "very serious situation" in the HKSAR where the "faction creating chaos" aimed at taking action to "usurp power."[53] The strongly worded editorial precipitated the action of the government to arrest and prosecute 52 democrats in January 2021 for their "subversive" activities.[54] Eventually, 47 of them were charged with "conspiracy to commit subversion" over legislative primaries. The main target was Benny Tai, a former professor of law at the University of Hong Kong from 1991 until July 2020, when he was dismissed by the university for his conviction of being sentenced to sixteen months' imprisonment for causing a public nuisance and inciting others to cause a public nuisance in the 2014 Occupy Central Movement. If Benny Tai was regarded as a "bad" example of instigating students to participate in the social and political movement, the other side of the coin, from the perspective of PRC authorities, was to implement national security law and education in the HKSAR so that the young people would be able to distinguish what is politically "right" or "wrong."

In August 2020, it was reported that an Administrative Officer To Wing-hang was appointed to be the deputy permanent secretary of the EDB's section dealing with school development and administration.[55] Traditionally, the position was occupied by civil servants working in the EDB. The appointment of To was interpreted as a new move to implant an administrative officer to deal with school development and administration. Such interpretation, however, neglected the likelihood that the personnel reshuffle prepared for the implementation of national security education. Most importantly, as administrative officers are the elite of the civil service, To would take the leadership of propelling the process of education reform in the HKSAR.

On August 11, the SCNPC backed up the HKSAR government's decision in July to postpone the LegCo election due to Covid-19 by deciding that the

LegCo after its term of office on September 30, 2020 would continue for not less than one year.[56] Most importantly, it approved the revised version of the National Flag Law and National Emblem Law, saying that it would be illegal to reverse the raising of the national flag or to handle the national flag in a disrespectful way. Moreover, the national flag cannot be discarded arbitrarily. The National Flag Law and the National Emblem Law were formally integrated into Appendix 3 of the Hong Kong Basic Law on July 1, 1997 and they have been applied in the HKSAR. Amendments were made to the National Flag and National Emblem Ordinance in August 2021. The implication for schools in the HKSAR is that school managers and teachers will have to teach students the proper way of respecting and dealing with the national flag and national anthem.

Curriculum Reform: National Security Education and Renaming of Liberal Studies as Citizenship and Social Development

Table 3.1 sums up the key areas and the scope of national security education as all schools in the HKSAR are now required by law to implement it. The push for national security education was accompanied by a deliberate dilution of the Liberal Studies subject in the HKSAR. In mid-April 2021, the Education Department of the HKSAR government published a detailed lesson plan on how to enhance the ingredient of national security education in eleven subjects in secondary schools. On May 26, the Education Department publicized further how the rest of the four subjects – Chinese history, history, life and society subject and economics – can consolidate the content of Chinese nationalism, national identity and national security.[57]

First, in the subject of Chinese history, curriculum reform in accordance with the national security education is introduced at two levels: junior high and senior high levels. At the junior high level, the reformed pedagogy has to achieve two objectives: (1) let students "comprehensively understand the main events and personalities" in different historical periods, including the need to "understand the importance of political and cultural security and to elevate students' national identity, mission and responsibility;" and (2) allow students to "clearly understand how the nation overcame difficulties amid a foreign invasion, including the British occupation of Hong Kong and China's diligent process of recovering its sovereignty," so that students' sense of national identity, mission and responsibility can be enhanced.[58] At the senior high level, the Chinese history subject needs to "build up the experiences of national independence and autonomy and to help students construct a full and comprehensive sense of the nation" through compulsory topics like foreign invasion, the anti-Japanese war, the open-door policy and foreign relations. Moreover, students need to "appreciate the value of traditional culture, comprehend the evolution of different systems, tolerate different religions" so that "the important foundation of maintaining national stability and development and the solidarity of ethnic minorities can be laid down."[59]

Table 3.1 The Scope of National Security Education

The Curriculum Structure of National Security Education

1 Prelude:

   According to the PRC National Security law, national security refers to the situation under which the national regime, sovereignty, unification, territorial integrity, the people's welfare, the economy and the society can maintain sustainable development and under which other main national interests are neither endangered nor threatened. The Education Bureau drafted the Hong Kong national security education curriculum so that primary and secondary schools can follow.

2 Main Points of the Curriculum Structure:

   a This structure lists the learning elements of Hong Kong's National Security Education, including the national identity and perspective, citizen identification, "one country, two systems," the rule of law, rights and duties, the sense of responsibility, the spirit of shouldering responsibility, and the ideas of respecting others and of have self-discipline.

   b The learning content is going to be integrated into not only different areas and subjects but also the progress of moral, citizenship and national education at the junior primary, senior primary, junior secondary and high secondary levels.

   c Schools can implement national security education through classroom teaching and comprehensive learning activities, thereby enhancing the knowledge of students to understand the rule of law and national development, the importance of protecting national security, the elevation of national identity and consciousness, the new development of the national history and culture, and the constitution and the Basic Law.

3 The Scope

   1 The concept and significance of national security
      - The concept of nation
      - The concept of national security
      - The importance of protecting national security
      - The overall national security perspective
      - Threats and risks
   2 Constitution, Basic Law and National Security
      - Constitution and national security
      - National security as the matter of jurisdiction under the central authorities
      - Basic Law and Hong Kong's local law and stipulations on national security
      - Hong Kong's legislation on national security as an improvement and a supplement for the "one country, two systems"
   3 The legislative intent and principles of Hong Kong's national security law
      - The objectives of the Hong Kong national security legislation
      - Legislative mode: decisions and legislation
      - The scope of effectiveness of Hong Kong's national security law
      - The principles of protecting Hong Kong's national security work
   4 The duties and responsibilities of institutions protecting Hong Kong's national security
      - The constitutional duty of the HKSAR in protecting national security
      - The duties of various departments in the HKSAR
      - The establishment of the organs and institutions protective of national security in the HKSAR

(Continued)

Table 3.1 The Scope of National Security Education *(Continued)*

The Curriculum Structure of National Security Education

5 The basic duty of the central government in protecting national security
    • The duties of the central government in protecting national security
    • The central organs and institutions that are stationed in Hong Kong
6 The criminal behavior of endangering national security
    • The crime of secession
    • The crime of subverting the national regime
    • The crime of terrorist activities
    • The crime of colluding with foreign or external forces that endanger national security
7 The important areas of national security
    • The key areas of national security, their content and their significance
    • The threats and challenges to the nation at present
    • The ways and means of protecting national security
8 The relations between national security, human rights, civil liberties and the rule of law
    • Human rights and civil liberties
    • National security and the protection of the rule of law
    • Constitution and national security
    • Threats and risks

Sources: See https://www.edb.gov.hk/attachment/tc/curriculum-development/kla/pshe/national-security-education/nse_subject_framework_gs.pdf, access date: September 26, 2021.

These two levels of Chinese history subject will, according to the curriculum reform plan, be accompanied by students' activities, such as the appreciation of Chinese culture through an understanding of the life of Tang dynasty's women, the Tang clothing, and the dressing style of people in the Tang dynasty. Other study activities embrace an appreciation of the anti-Japanese war songs, interviews with the old members of the Dongjiang guerillas in South China, oral history interviews with old guerillas, inspections of the anti-Japanese war sites in Hong Kong, and visits to Nanking and the historical sites related to the Opium War and the Treaty of Nanking.

Second, the history subject at the junior high level has to strengthen students' sense of national consciousness and identity by not only emphasizing the historical fact that "Hong Kong from the ancient time has been a part of Chinese territory, but also covering how the Chinese nation recovered its sovereignty over Hong Kong after foreign invasion and the British occupation of the territory."[60] At the senior high level, the history subject needs to let students understand that the Chinese nation in the process of modernization attaches great importance to political, cultural and national security. Students will have to be "responsible citizens" and "Chinese citizens who possess global vision."[61]

Third, the subject of life and society at the junior high level needs to cover the Chinese nation's current development and directions, its constitution, and the constitutional foundation between the Hong Kong Basic Law and the Chinese constitution. In this way, students will be expected to understand the content of national, political, economic, resource and military security and the security of the overseas interest of China.[62]

Fourth, the subject of economics at the senior high level covers the topics of money, banks, international trade and finance and students will be expected to understand the importance of economic security and the people's livelihood.[63] Students will also be expected to comprehend that Hong Kong coexists with the Chinese nation and that Hong Kong has its duty to maintain China's economic security while the nation contributes to the maintenance of Hong Kong's prosperity and stability.[64]

Obviously, the curriculum reform of the four subjects aims at enhancing the Hong Kong students' sense of national identity, their nationalistic sentiment, and their understanding of the historical linkages between Hong Kong and the Chinese nation. A history teacher of the Pui Kiu Secondary School, Muk Ka-chun, responded to the Education Department's efforts at strengthening national security education in the subjects of Chinese history and history in the following way: "China's modern history is like a history of humiliation, and it has a warning function by understanding China's past history of encountering foreign aggression and the foreign scramble for concessions."[65] He added that, by infiltrating the element of national security education into various subjects, students' national identity and national recognition would be enhanced.

Curriculum reform necessitates the teachers of various subjects to select officially recommended textbooks and references and the local textbook writers to enhance the content that can contribute to stronger Chinese nationalism, national identity and national security. In this aspect, the HKSAR government designated reference books written by mainland scholars, notably Wang Zhenmin from Tsinghua University, so that teachers would be able to use them more comfortably in their teaching.[66]

Most interestingly, more pro-Beijing organizations have held activities to strengthen the national identity and consciousness of the Hong Kong people. For instance, Dot News organized a forum on May 26, 2021 during which a Hong Kong member of the NPC, Chan Yong, advocated that the Hong Kong government should resume and repair all the historical sites in Hong Kong during the Second World War, including the sites in Sai Kung where renovation and rebuilding work should be conducted.[67] Moreover, these sites could be turned into local museums with the use of 5G technology to enhance the experiences of visitors. A district council member in the Northern district, Wan Wo-tat, suggested that the government should rebuild the traffic facilities of linking urban areas with a statue commemorating the local heroes who fought against the Japanese army in Sha Tau Kok. During the 2019 anti-extradition movement, the statue in Sha Tau Kok was damaged and defaced, but the repair work was done by social groups. As such, the vice-chairman of the Sai Kung Area Committee, Lee Ka-leung, criticized the Hong Kong government for shirking its responsibility of attaching importance to the history and repairing the historical site.[68]

Apart from curriculum reform and organizational activities of lobbying the government to repair and renovate local historical sites, the Education

Department reconsidered the guidelines for teachers to strengthen their professional ethics and conduct. On May 26, 2021, Kevin Yeung, the Secretary for Education, responded to the remarks from a few LegCo members, who said the 1990 Guideline of the Hong Kong Education Profession was outdated, and he revealed that his department considered the possibility of revising the existing guidelines.[69] Pro-business Liberal Party member and legislator, Tommy Cheung, requested that the government should review the guideline by adding a new stipulation that teachers should be barred from participating in illegal activities, instigating and organizing students to join such illegal activities, publicizing their political views to students, and showing "radical" views through the Internet.[70] Another legislator, Ronick Chan, suggested that the government should issue an official guideline to combine it with the 1990 Guideline of the Hong Kong Education Profession so that schools and teachers would follow the stipulations more easily. Yeung unveiled that, up to April 2021, the Education Department received 269 cases of complaints about teachers' professional and ethical conduct. Three of the teachers had their teaching licenses revoked, while 151 others were scolded, formally warned, advised or verbally persuaded. Obviously, amid the process of conducting curriculum reform, the professional conduct of teachers was under much closer scrutiny than ever before.

After Our Hong Kong Foundation (OHKF) published the Liberal Studies Research Report in September 2020 criticizing its pedagogy and content, the government in November expressed its intention of reforming Liberal Studies as a new subject named Citizenship and Social Development, which would begin in April 2021.[71] The OUHK report appeared to drum up public support for the government to implement education reform. Liberal Studies was diluted to the extent that students would take it as pass or fail basis. The curriculum guideline of a new subject, namely Citizenship and Social Development, shows that Chinese patriotism has already been injected into its content and that Hong Kong teachers and students are increasingly expected to increase their patriotic sentiment. On June 2, 2021, the EDB issued the curriculum and assessment guideline for Citizenship and Social Development.[72] The objective of the guideline is to stress "the respect of multicultural perspectives and views so that students can think carefully and distinguish matters clearly, engage in thinking rationally, reflectively and independently."[73] This objective is different in emphasis from the old objective of Liberal Studies, which originally aimed at not only "respecting multicultural perspectives and views" but also training students to "become critical, reflective and independent thinking persons."[74] While Liberal Studies emphasized the "critical" ability of students, the newly reformed Citizenship and Social Development lay the emphasis on the need for students to think carefully" and "distinguish matters clearly" without just adopting a "critical" attitude.

Table 3.2 sums up the comparisons between the two subjects, showing that Citizenship and Social Development aims at inculcating a stronger sense of Chinese national identity in the psyche of Hong Kong students. Other differences between the new subject, Citizenship and Social Development, and the

Table 3.2 Comparisons of Liberal Studies with Citizenship and Social Development

Liberal Studies	Citizenship and Social Development
Rationale Liberal Studies provides opportunities for students to explore issues relevant to the human condition in a wide range of contexts. Liberal Studies enables students to understand the contemporary world and its pluralistic nature. It enables students to make connections among different disciplines, examines issues from a variety of perspectives and constructs personal knowledge of immediate relevance to themselves in today's world. It will help students develop independent learning capabilities and cross-curricular thinking. Liberal Studies contributes directly to the attainment of the goals of the senior secondary curriculum. In particular, it will help each student to: • acquire a broad knowledge base, and be able to understand contemporary issues that may affect their daily life at personal, community, national and global levels; • be an informed and responsible citizen with a sense of global and national identity; • respect pluralism of cultures and views, and be a critical, reflective and independent thinker; and • acquire information technology (IT) and other skills necessary to life-long learning. Together with the other core subjects and elective subjects, it helps to achieve a balance between breadth and depth in the school curriculum. *Curriculum aims* The aims of Senior Secondary Liberal Studies are: a to enhance students' understanding of themselves, their society, their nation, the human world and the physical environment; b to enable students to develop multiple perspectives on perennial and contemporary issues in different contexts (e.g. cultural, social, economic, political and technological contexts);	*Curriculum Rationale* The curriculum of the renamed subject adheres to the rationale of the existing one. The renamed curriculum places emphases on helping senior secondary students understand the situations of Hong Kong, the nation and the contemporary world, as well as their pluralistic and interdependent nature. Through the learning process, students can connect the knowledge learned in various subjects at the junior and senior secondary levels, broaden their knowledge base, and understand, study and explore different topics from multiple perspectives so as to construct more knowledge relevant to various themes and build up a more solid knowledge base. Furthermore, students can understand the complexities, major considerations and priorities involved in the topics, decision-making process and different solutions to problems. Students can: • acquire a broad knowledge base, and understand contemporary issues that may affect their daily life at personal, community, national and global levels; • become informed and responsible citizens with a sense of national identity and global perspective; • respect pluralism of cultures and views, and become critical, rational, reflective and independent thinkers; and • acquire skills necessary to life-long learning and to be confident in facing future challenges. *Curriculum aims* It aims to help students: i enhance understanding of the complexities and organization of society, the nation, the human world, the physical environment and related knowledge; ii develop multiple perspectives on contemporary mature topics in different contexts (e.g. cultural, social, economic, political and technological contexts);

(Continued)

80 The Mainlandization of Education in Hong Kong

Table 3.2 Comparisons of Liberal Studies with Citizenship and Social Development *(Continued)*

Liberal Studies	Citizenship and Social Development
c to help students become independent thinkers so that they can construct knowledge appropriate to changing personal and social circumstances; d to develop in students a range of skills for life-long learning, including critical thinking skills, creativity, problem-solving skills, communication skills and information technology skills; e to help students appreciate and respect diversity in cultures and views in a pluralistic society and handle conflicting values; and f to help students develop positive values and attitudes toward life so that they can become informed and responsible citizens of society, the country and the world.	iii become independent thinkers; be able to adapt to the ever-changing personal, social, national and external circumstances and construct knowledge; understand the complexities of the topics, and the challenges and processes involved in decision-making for making law-abiding, rational and affective analysis, and learning how to handle conflicting values; iv inherit Chinese culture and heritage in a pluralistic society, deepen understanding and sense of identity of individuals with Chinese nationality and as Chinese citizens, and at the same time appreciate, respect and embrace diversity in cultures and views; v develop skills relevant to life-long learning and strengthen students' ability to integrate and apply knowledge and skills, including critical thinking skills, creativity, problem solving skills, communication skills, collaboration skills, data management skills, self-management skills, self-learning skills and information technology skills; vi develop positive values and attitudes toward life so that they can become informed and responsible citizens of society, the nation and the world.

Broad learning outcomes
By the end of the course, students should be able to:
 	
a develop the capacity to construct knowledge through inquiring into contemporary issues which affect themselves, their society, their nation, the human world and the physical environment so that they
 	
   i understand the personal development process and interpersonal relationships of adolescents with respect to the different challenges and opportunities they face;
  ii evaluate different aspects of life in Hong Kong with respect to the rights and responsibilities of individuals, social groups and the government;
	Broad learning outcomes
	Through studying the subject, students should be able to:
	
	i understand the constitutional basis of the HKSAR, its relationship with the nation, and the latest development of the nation, so as to explore the opportunities and challenges of the interactive development between Hong Kong and the Mainland;
	ii understand the contemporary mature topics related to individuals, the society, the nation, the human world and the physical environment so as to construct knowledge and promote self-directed learning;

(Continued)

Table 3.2 Comparisons of Liberal Studies with Citizenship and Social Development (Continued)

Liberal Studies	Citizenship and Social Development
iii assess the impact of reform and opening-up on the development of modern China and Chinese culture; iv recognize that globalization has many dimensions and that people are affected in different ways and have different responses toward it; v realize how people understand issues on public health and make decisions based on related scientific knowledge and evidence; vi analyze how science and technology interact with the environment in relation to energy resources and sustainable development; b understand the interconnectedness of personal, local, national and global issues, and the interdependence of the physical environment and society, and appraise issues of human concern accordingly; c reflect on the development of their own multiple identities, value systems and worldviews with respect to personal experiences, social and cultural contexts and the impact of developments in science, technology and globalization; d identify the values underlying different views and judgments on personal and social issues, and apply critical thinking skills, creativity and different perspectives in making decisions and judgments on issues and problems at both personal and social levels; e present arguments clearly and demonstrate respect for evidence, open-mindedness and tolerance toward the views and values held by other people; f develop skills related to inquiry learning, including self-management skills, problem-solving skills, communication skills, information processing skills and skills in using information and communication technology; g carry out self-directed learning, which includes the processes of setting goals, making and implementing plans, solving problems, analyzing data, drawing conclusions, reporting findings and conducting evaluations; and h demonstrate an appreciation for the values of their own and other cultures, and for universal values, and be committed to becoming responsible and conscientious citizens.	iii understand the interplay among individuals, society, the nation and the world in relation to environmental, economic and social development through studying the topics of common human concerns covered in the curriculum framework, and based on the above understanding to explore how to resolve difficulties and promote development for reaping mutual benefits; iv develop a sense of national identity with a global perspective, and understand the interconnectedness among areas of economy, science, technology, environmental protection, sustainable development, public health as well as the development of the contemporary world and the related impact; and recognize the roles of Hong Kong, the nation, and the international community and organizations; v identify different views and the values behind various topics; and apply in an integrative manner critical thinking skills, problem solving skills, creativity, data management skills and self-learning skills in examining the background, content, developmental trends and the values of the topics from multiple perspectives, so as to make law-abiding, rational and affective judgments and decisions based on facts and evidence; as well as develop positive values and attitudes; vi present arguments clearly based on facts and evidence, demonstrate objective, fair and empathetic attitudes toward the opinions and views held by other people; vii understand, appreciate and inherit Chinese culture and treat other cultures with respect, receptiveness and appreciation, and be willing to become responsible and committed citizens.

(Continued)

Table 3.2 Comparisons of Liberal Studies with Citizenship and Social Development *(Continued)*

Liberal Studies	Citizenship and Social Development
Curriculum content Module 1: Personal development and interpersonal relationships – understanding oneself, challenges and opportunities, interpersonal factors shaping the transition from adolescence to adulthood Module 2: Hong Kong today – quality of life, rule of law, socio-political participation, rights and responsibilities with respect to the rule of law, and the identities of Hong Kong residents Module 3: Modern China – China's reform, the impacts of opening-up process on the overall development and the people's life, the evolution of the concepts and functions of the family, traditional custom and culture Module 4: Globalization – the impacts of globalization and the responses of different parts of the world to globalization Module 5: Public Health – the people's understanding of public health, the role of science and technology in public health Module 6: Energy Technology and the Environment – the influences of energy technology, the environment and sustainable development	*Curriculum content* 1 Hong Kong under "one country, two systems" – the meaning and implementation of "one country, two systems," the sense of national identity, and characteristics of the cultural diversity of Hong Kong society 2 China since its opening-up reform and the change in people's life – China's latest development, its planning and policies of integrating Hong Kong into national development, its participation in international affairs 3 Interconnectedness and interdependence of the contemporary world – economic globalization, technological development, information literacy, global environmental problems, sustainable development and public health
Independent inquiry studies It contributes to the curriculum aims by: a providing an opportunity for students to learn to become self-directed learners responsible for their own learning; b enhancing students' ability to connect, integrate and apply knowledge, perspectives and skills developed; c helping students develop higher-order thinking skills and communication skills through investigative exploration of issues; and d broadening students' horizons and catering for their interests and inclinations.	*Mainland study tour* The mainland study tour will include the following activities: • Understand the nature of Chinese culture • Online self-learning of articles introducing the special characteristics of traditional Chinese culture • Conservation and inheritance of cultural heritage, including the application of technology in conservation work • Study tour to the Mainland to experience the conservation and inheritance of Chinese culture in society • Detailed planning and reading information before the study tour • Methods of on-site collection of information • Study tour report will be required

Sources: "Liberal Studies Curriculum and Assessment Guide, the Curriculum Development Council and the Hong Kong Examinations and Assessment Authority, 2014," in https://334.edb.hkedcity.net/new/doc/eng/curriculum/LS%20C&A%20Guide_updated_e.pdf, access date: September 6, 2021; and "The Curriculum Development Council and the Hong Kong Examinations and Assessment Authority, Citizenship and Social Development Curriculum and Assessment Guide, the Education Bureau, 2021," in https://ls.edb.hkedcity.net/file/C_and_A_guide/202106/CS_CAG_S4-6_Eng_2021.pdf, access date: September 26, 2021.

old Liberal Studies embrace three aspects. First, while Citizenship and Social Development trains students "to adopt multiple perspectives and angles to ponder contemporary topics "which are already developed in a mature way," Liberal Studies encouraged students to adopt multiple angles to think about "currently emergent topics such as culture, society, economics politics and technology."[75] Obviously, Citizenship and Social Development does not encourage students to deal with those current issues that are evolving politically, whereas Liberal Studies allowed considerable discretion to teachers and students to explore presently developing topics, including political and controversial issues. The new Citizenship and Social Development depoliticizes the curriculum, minimizing the possibility of teachers and students to cover ongoing and politically controversial and sensitive topics.

Second, Citizenship and Social Development aims at training students to "comprehend the complexity of topics, the challenges of decision-making processes so that they can come up with rational and legal analyses and learn to cope with mutually conflicting values."[76] Liberal Studies did not stress the students to "comprehend the complexity of topics and the challenges of decision-making processes." Clearly, the Citizenship and Social Development subject encourages teachers and students to be more "objective" and "holistic" in coping with the governmental decision-making processes and issues that illustrate the clashes of cultural and political values. If Liberal Studies epitomizes a bias in favor of Western liberalism, then Citizenship and Social Development embraces more non-Western ideas and the Chinese perspectives, including an appreciation of the clashes of Chinese and Western civilizations and values.

Third, while Liberal Studies did not emphasize the element of Chinese culture and identity, Citizenship and Social Development explicitly aims at educating students to "simultaneously appreciate, appreciate and accept different cultures and viewpoints and to deepen their individual understanding and identification with the Chinese cultural tradition, Chinese nationality and Chinese national identity."[77] Clearly, education reformers in Hong Kong have believed that Liberal Studies, which trained students to be "critical" without appreciating the Chinese cultural tradition and national identity, was a relatively "unpatriotic" curriculum design that must be rectified.

Kevin Yeung said on June 2, 2021, that the government would give a subsidy of HK$900,000 to each public and directly subsidized secondary school to provide the necessary logistical support for the related pedagogical and learning activities. Such activities would include ten hours of inspection visits to the mainland, the buying of teaching equipment and facilities, the organization of school-based, joint schools and cross-subject activities. Secondary schools are dealing with the new subject of Citizenship and Social Development by redeploying the existing teaching resources and manpower. Moreover, government subsidies to secondary schools include e-learning facilities and activities, reference books, and exchange programs to the mainland. However, the utilization of subsidies cannot be overlapped by asking for the government to subsidize the same project items more than once.

Judging from the guideline on the new curriculum, the ingredient of Chinese patriotism has been enhanced. The topic of Hong Kong under "one country, two systems" needs to stress that Hong Kong from ancient times has remained a Chinese territory, with its sovereignty and administration being possessed by China. For the topic on balance between the national security law on the one hand and the rule of law and human rights on the other, the guideline says that the national security law "has no impact on Hong Kong's rule of law and the rights enjoyed by the Hong Kong residents in accordance with the law."[78] On the topic of the relations between the executive, legislature and judiciary, the guideline stipulates that the three branches have their own duties and positions and that they are complementary to each other. On the topic of interdependence in the contemporary world, the guideline says that China's contributions to the combat against Covid-19 and its production of vaccines must be examined. Finally, on the topic of the Chinese nation after the open-door policy, the mutually economically beneficial relations of the Closer Economic Partnership Arrangement must be supplemented. In short, the inseparable mainland relations with Hong Kong and the important contributions of China to Hong Kong and the world must be taught and emphasized in Citizenship and Social Development.

The EDB sent its guideline to the publishers so that the writers of textbooks and reference books would take into consideration how to come up with appropriate reading materials. It was expected that the textbooks for Form 4 and Form 5 would be published in 2022 so that secondary schools would use these materials in the academic year of 2022–2023. In response to the new guideline of Citizenship and Social Development, the FEW vice-chairman Tang Fei remarked that while Liberal Studies in the past lacked a holistic approach to educating students on mainland China, the new subject can adopt a more comprehensive approach by connecting the "one country, two systems" with the Basic Law, the national development and the relationships between the Chinese nation and the HKSAR. Tang believed that the new subject is "more systematic" and tackling "the whole journey of learning process logically."[79] He suggested that the government should consider either adjusting the annual subsidy to each secondary school upward after one year of implementation or institutionalizing such subsidy in the future.

The vice-chairman of the Hong Kong Liberal Studies Education Society, Lee Wai-hung, said that Liberal Studies, which emphasized too much on the "critical" attitude of students, created lots of problems.[80] Nevertheless, the new subject can strengthen the elements of "law, emotion and reasons."[81] In this way, the new curriculum can teach students on the legal foundation appropriately to avoid not only anyone spreading "the distorted theory of violating the law to achieve justice," but also an arbitrary way of interpreting the "one country, two systems." Lee added that the new subject's guideline correctly reminds teachers of the need to carefully select the Internet sources and media materials. This would avoid some teachers to utilize materials that "distorted the facts." He felt that the mainland visits would be important to students, who in the past had to be persuaded hard by school authorities to visit the mainland to widen their horizon and deepen their understanding of the motherland. Hence, the patriotic education elites in the HKSAR are supportive of the new subject's emphases and remain critical of the "distorted" curriculum design, pedagogy and objectives of Liberal Studies.

On the same day of June 2, China's Ministry of Education published a report on the life and development of language in the GBA. The report advocated that Hong Kong's education system should integrate Putonghua into the examination assessment system. It said that the people of Hong Kong should be knowledgeable about simplified Chinese characters so that more Hong Kong people would be able to "acquire the train ticket to the world and the mainland's fast economic train."[82] As the HKSAR and Macau are incorporated into the Chinese national plan of integration with the GBA, the popularization of Putonghua and its integration into the Hong Kong examination system are only a matter of time.

The replacement of Liberal Studies with Citizenship and Social Development was a significant move by the HKSAR government to start inculcating Chinese patriotism into the psyche of the Hong Kong youth. This Chinese patriotism is made explicit in the curriculum guideline of Citizenship and Social Development. Together with the anticipated and accelerated integration of Putonghua into the Hong Kong examination system, the education system and curriculum of Hong Kong have been undergoing rapid reforms to strengthen the element of Chinese patriotism. By 2047, most people of Hong Kong will likely become far more politically patriotic than the current generation.

Prior to the inception of the school semester in September 2021, pro-Beijing media began to highlight how some schools had successfully reformed Liberal Studies in a rejuvenated manner. For example, in September 2021, *Wen Wei Po* interviewed the pro-Beijing Hon Wah Secondary School and showed how its experienced general education teacher transformed the subject.[83] According to *Wen Wei Po*, the teacher taught students the origin of the Hong Kong question by referring to the unequal treaties signed by the Qing dynasty. Then the teacher delineated the historical processes of how Hong Kong's sovereignty was returned from Britain to the PRC. Moreover, students were taught on China's reform era without the need to memorize all the events but with "quite a lot of space for free development."[84] *Wen Wei Po* depicted the teacher of the Hon Wah Secondary School as educating the students enlighteningly with historical facts, including the emphasis on Hong Kong's sovereignty being possessed by Qing's China, the discussion of the Opium War, the request for students to answer questions on the relations between mainland China and Hong Kong, and the stimulation of students to develop their Chinese national identity.[85] In response to the interview from *Wen Wei Po*, the teacher remarked that Chinese history could be combined with general education so that students did not need to engage in rote learning and that they found Chinese history "fascinating."[86] A student remarked that the revamped Liberal Studies class could make him feel that "I am part of China and can feel honorable and proud of being a Chinese

Hongkonger."[87] *Wen Wei Po* added that without the usage of the textbook during the first year of the reformed Liberal Studies, teachers would have to utilize the designated twelve reference materials provided by the EDB.[88] Clearly, the pro-Beijing *Wen Wei Po* skillfully depicted the teachers and students concerned, emphasizing the success of the reformed Liberal Studies and the enhanced national identity of the Hong Kong people.

On the same day of September 3, *Ta Kung Pao* highlighted the experience of the Hon Wah Secondary School in teaching Citizenship and Social Development.[89] Its reporters sat in a class, witnessing the "happiness" of the teacher and students and getting a student's response that they "learnt real knowledge."[90] Another student interviewed by *Ta Kung Pao* revealed that he had no more pressure to get high marks from Citizenship and Social Development and that he felt relaxed in his studies.[91] A pro-Beijing commentator, To Hoi-ming, wrote on September 3 that Citizenship and Social Development was successfully launched, marking the proper way in which students were and would be "cultivated."[92] If *Wen Wei Po* and *Ta Kung Pao* are propaganda machinery of the PRC government in the HKSAR, their positive portrayal of how Chinese history were taught by pro-Beijing schools constituted a carefully orchestrated political message aimed at winning the hearts and minds of its readers. The message was clear: the "correct" version of Chinese history was integrated into the reformed Liberal Studies curriculum so that teachers and students found their teaching and learning experiences, respectively, enjoyable and meaningful.

In response to the curriculum reform, Kevin Yeung remarked in August 2021 that the new textbooks for Citizenship and Social Development would be available in the academic year of 2022–2023.[93] Together with the designated reference materials, the textbook will provide the instrument through which PRC authorities and their political client, namely the HKSAR government, can and will be able to teach the "correct" version of Chinese history and China's relations with Hong Kong to the students in the HKSAR.

Unlike *Wen Wei Po* and *Ta Kung Pao,* which depicted the immediate success and the "correct" way of teaching students in Citizenship and Social Development, the relatively independent *Ming Pao* interviewed a teacher who taught this new subject in late August.[94] The teacher revealed that, unlike many other teachers who left the profession or emigrated to other countries for fear of the national security law, he opted to stay and to teach students with their autonomy. He cited the remarks from EDB officials, who said that "if we teachers do not distort and yet realize the facts, then suggestions on how to improve the [Chinese] nation and contribute to the country are allowed," and that "this teaching method is safe as with how we taught in the past."[95] Indeed, teachers have their discretion of educating their students with some degree of autonomy and independent thinking; nevertheless, on main historical issues, such as the sovereignty of Hong Kong, the correct version of Chinese history is set down by the textbook and its reference materials. As such, the discretion of teachers to allow students some degree of autonomy can be made within the confines of the political red lines.

National Security Education at the University Level

In late July 2021, *Ta Kung Pao* editorialized that national security education would have to be implemented at the university level because universities in the past had witnessed a "chaotic situation," meaning that many student protestors against the extradition bill initiated by the HKSAR government in 2019 came from local universities. It severely criticized some local universities as providing the "hotbed" and "training camps" for local "terrorists."[96] The battles between the student protestors and the police were fought fiercely at the Chinese University of Hong Kong (CUHK) and the Polytechnic University.[97] The arrests and prosecution of many students at the secondary and university levels mean that, under the national security law, the HKSAR government requires local universities to implement national security education.

At the university level, Hong Kong Baptist University (HKBU) announced in July 2021 that it would list national security education as a compulsory course.[98] Its new Vice-Chancellor Wai Ping-kwong remarked that universities were not political arenas and that time should not be wasted over political questions.[99] The deputy vice-chancellor of the HKBU, Albert Chau, said that the compulsory course would have no credit, but it would have a component of assessment. According to Chau, the content of the national security education course would touch on various dimensions of security, such as environmental, Internet, monetary and financial and public health security, so that students would broaden their knowledge on the concept and scope of national security.[100] In response to the plan of local universities to offer a national security course, Kevin Yeung said that they had the responsibility of implementing national security education.[101] Shortly after the promulgation of the national security law for Hong Kong in late June 2020, Yeung met with the vice-chancellors of the eight government-funded universities, urging them to introduce national security education. The emergence of more concrete plans from universities in July 2021 could be seen as the "full" and accelerated implementation of national security in the HKSAR.

As with the HKBU, Polytechnic University would incorporate national security education into a compulsory course in the first year. Lingnan University announced that it would utilize introduce China's development and national security to students through the core course, seminars and lectures. The Education University of Hong Kong (EdUHK) planned to do the same, including the usage of five to six weeks with two hours of lectures per week to introduce national security law and education to undergraduate students.[102] In September 2021, all three universities announced that national security education would be integrated into their generic courses at the undergraduate level. In October 2021, the EDB wrote to the administrative authorities of all public and private universities, asking them to complete a template on how they implemented national security education, including the details of the national security course and the events in which the PRC national flag would be raised and the PRC national anthem would be sung by students. On November 17, 2021, Secretary for Education Kevin Yeung visited Shenzhen and reported to Xu Yongji, an official from the Office of Hong Kong, Macau and Taiwan Affairs under the Ministry of Education on how national security education was implemented in the HKSAR. Clearly, the implementation of national security education is high on the policy agenda of the HKSAR government's EDB, which remains accountable to the MoE in Beijing.

A controversy erupted over the position of the Hong Kong University Student Union (HKUSU), which issued a statement to "mourn" a man who stabbed a police officer in July 2021 and who committed suicide and died, and whose Council's position aroused the anger of pro-government and pro-Beijing elites. The University of Hong Kong (HKU) refused to recognize the legal status of the HKUSU as an independent and registered society under the university.[103] Although the HKUSU quickly issued an apology over its previous statement of "mourning" the assassin who attempted to kill the police officer, the HKU action to sever all ties with the union and to refuse collecting union fees from students had important implications. First, the Hong Kong police started an investigation into the HKUSU Council's council that appreciated the "sacrifice" of the man who attempted to kill the police – a council action that could be deemed as violating national security.[104] Second, the HKU action of cutting its ties with the student union triggered other local universities to follow suit. A similar action of stopping a traditional act of collecting student union fees from students could be seen in the CUHK, City University of Hong Kong (CityU), Hong Kong Polytechnic University, HKBU and Lingnan University. In other words, the actions and remarks of many student unions no longer represented the position of their universities concerned. After all, many students at local universities came from the mainland and they might be unwilling to support student unions that made remarks and took actions that could be deemed as violating the national security law.

In August 2021, it was reported that the Hang Seng University would introduce national security education, including the provisions of the national security law, as an elective course for students in January 2022.[105] The national security course would be delivered jointly by the departments of general education, accounting, corporate management and law. The Hang Seng University's vice-chancellor, Simon Ho Shun-man, said that the course design was made by the departments concerned rather than discussing with the HKSAR government.[106]

On the other hand, the HKBU decided that the national security law education should be made a compulsory component of the co-curricular learning program, which would be a graduation requirement for students.[107] Its learning objectives are (1) to introduce to students the "one country, two systems" and the constitutional status of the HKSAR with reference to the PRC constitution and the Basic Law; (2) to introduce the importance of the national security law to the HKSAR; (3) to provide an overview of the key provisions of the national security law; and (4) to introduce the fundamental principles of the rule of law.[108] Two credits of the course will be earned by students who take it. Moreover, students will be required to attend a 2-hour face-to-face lecture, complete a 2-hour assigned reading materials, and to obtain a pass in a quiz.[109] The

HKBU published its course on its official website, marking the formal launch of the course and its serious attitude toward the implementation of national security education.

Expansion of Pro-Beijing Education Groups, Propaganda and Publishing Houses

Since 2018, the pro-Beijing education organizations, propaganda and publishing houses have been proliferating for the sake of creating a socio-political environment in which the education of the Hong Kong people, broadly speaking, can and will be far more easily instilled with Chinese nationalistic sentiment than ever before. Conversely, the pro-Western values in the society of Hong Kong can and will hopefully be curbed. This social reengineering process is a long one in which pro-Beijing education elites, interest groups and publishing houses are acting like the PRC's transmission belts to penetrate gradually and deeply into the education sector of the HKSAR. Table 3.3 shows that, from 2018 to 2021, the online media and news agencies stood out as the prominent type of media, while traditional local newspapers and magazines remained significant. Table 3.4 demonstrates the Internet media and their Facebook popularity. The general media websites have been read by many ordinary citizens, while the alternative media emerged as new sources of information after 2012. Since most Hong Kong people read news through the general media websites, pro-Beijing media organizations have been expanding their operation and trying to infiltrate into the society more assertively than before. These pro-Beijing media organizations include, for example, Hong Kong Good News, HKG Pao, Silent Majority, Speak Out Hong Kong, Think Hong Kong and Orange News. Nevertheless, these pro-government and pro-Beijing media websites remain less popular than the general and alternative media websites. As such, it will take some years for the pro-Beijing media to entrench their foothold in the society of Hong Kong. However, so long as the inroads of pro-Beijing media into the society are

Table 3.3 The Number of Media and Organizations in Hong Kong, 2018 and 2021

Type of media	Number of media organizations in 2018	Number of media organizations in 2021
Local newspapers	17	18
Foreign newspapers	9	9
Local TV and radios	8	8
Foreign TV and radios	8	10
Local magazines	16	15
Foreign magazines	6	6
Online media and news agencies	19	21
Non-local news agencies	12	12

Source: Authors' calculation from "Media List" prepared by the Hong Kong Public Relations Professionals' Association, in https://prpa.com.hk/media-list/, access date: August 3, 2021.

90 *The Mainlandization of Education in Hong Kong*

Table 3.4 Internet Media and Their Facebook Popularity

Internet media	Year of birth	Owner and political orientation	Facebook likes and followers		
			February 23, 2019	August 24, 2019	June 27, 2021
1. The general media websites					
HK01.com	2013	Yu Pun-hoi, the former owner of Ming Pao and it is politically moderate, but some observers regard it as relatively pro-Beijing.	577,261/592,790	622,271/647,997	799,020/853,690
The Initium	2015	Zhang Jieping as editor and its investor is Cai Hua, a mainland Chinese who worked in the United States for some years. Its political stance is relatively moderate.	265,950/275,296	288,777/302,392	325,214/347,974
Bastille Post	2013	Lo Wing-hung and it is relatively politically moderate.	1,050,579/1,034,223	1,045,132/1,031,630	1,031,235/1,029,609
South China Morning Post	1903	Jack Ma of the Alibaba Group and it has been increasingly pro-Beijing.	1,427,362/1,716,574	1,744,198/2,254,763	2,488,363/4,423,697
The Standard	1949	The Standard Newspapers Publishing is a part of the Sing Tao News Corporation, and it is politically pro-Beijing. In the pre-1997 era, Sing Tao Newspaper was pro-Taiwan, but it changed gradually to pro-Beijing.	17,637/18,068	22,830/23,591	39,422/41,849
Apple Daily	1995	Jimmy Lai of the Next Digital and it was pro-democracy. Lai was arrested in August 2020 for violating the national security law and is now in prison. The Apple Daily was closed in June 2021.	2,186,499/2,150,132	2,368,972/2,412,629	3,652,255/3,611,048
on.cc (Oriental Daily News)	1969	Ma Ching-kwan and it is pro-Beijing but critical of the HKSAR government and local democrats.	411,124/430,461	462,486/504,160	534,635/769,846
2. The alternative internet media					
Post 852	2013	Yau Ching-yuen of the Freeman Develop Company Limited. It was politically autonomous and critical. After the national security law was promulgated, it was closed.	68,823/67,567	73,457/73,380	Closed
Inmedia HK	2005	Ip Yam-chong and it is politically autonomous and critical.	483,479/461,829	545,761/547,107	615,345/770,139

(*Continued*)

The Mainlandization of Education in Hong Kong 91

Table 3.4 Internet Media and Their Facebook Popularity (*Continued*)

Internet media	Year of birth	Owner and political orientation	Facebook likes and followers			
			February 23, 2019	August 24, 2019	June 27, 2021
The Stand News	2014	Tony Choi and it is politically autonomous and critical. A few reporters of Apple Daily after its collapse joined the Stand News.	239,037/244,773	777,175/880,104	1,274,124/1,717,813
Passion Times	2012	Wong Yeung-tat and it is politically autonomous and critical of both the HKSAR government and Beijing.	403,737/381,097	420,992/405,584	453,057/478,351
Hong Kong Citizen News	2017	Lau Chun-to and it is politically pro-democracy, autonomous and critical.	56,081/60,738	93,723/111,661	241,531/323,048
Hong Kong Free Press	2015	Tom Grundy and Evan Fowler. It is pro-democracy, autonomous and critical.	85,032/87,355	148,763/165,777	249,859/328,212
3. Pro-government Facebook pages						
Hong Kong Good News	Unknown	The late Lau Nai-keung and it is pro-Beijing.	370,467/526,716	395,220/568,833	426,075/607,300
HKG Pao	2015	Robert Chow and pro-government.	128,279/136,941	211,434/271,592	27,842/30,574
Silent Majority 幫港出聲	2013	Robert Chow and pro-government.	178,945/170,792	239,707/266,111	295,983/343,915
Speak Out Hong Kong 港人講地	2013	Tang Yee-bong and pro-Beijing as well as pro-government. It is funded by the Hong Kong United Foundation.	324,050/312,399	386,308/413,197	439,781/513,296
Think Hong Kong	2018	Pro-Beijing and pro-government. It is funded by former Chief Executive Tung Chee-hwa.	107,190/110,245	157,218/161,960	213,765/220,395
Orange News	2014	Cloud Connect Technology Limited, Sino United Publishing (Holdings) Limited.	240,618/242,454	243,334/245,686	251,487/257,322
Wakeuphk people	2018	Unknown and pro-government.	16,295/16,559	30,948/32,837	Closed

Sources: See all the following Facebook pages: https://www.facebook.com/hk01wemedia/, https://www.facebook.com/theinitium/, https://www.facebook.com/Bastillepost/, https://www.facebook.com/standnewshk/, https://www.facebook.com/passiontimes/, https://www.facebook.com/hkgpaocom/, https://www.facebook.com/silentmajorityhk/, https://www.facebook.com/speakouthk/, https://www.facebook.com/thinkhongkong/, https://www.facebook.com/wakeuphkpeople, https://www.facebook.com/hkorangenews, https://www.facebook.com/HongKongGoodNews/.

Notes

The numbers of likes and follows were seen on their websites and Facebook pages on 23 February 2019, 24 August 2019 and 27 June 2021. Post852 and Wakeuphk no longer exist due to various reasons. The Apple Daily is now operating in Taiwan. See https://www.facebook.com/appledaily.tw/, access date: September 6, 2021.

slow, many young people develop their own views of Hong Kong and mainland China by having various autonomous news sources.

Understanding the limitations of penetrating into every corner of the mass media in the HKSAR, PRC authorities have been utilizing the Sino United Publishing (Holdings) Limited since its formation in 1988 to act as a united front agent that attempts at monopolizing the local publishing industry. In 1988, the Sino United Publishing Limited (SUPL) integrated other publishing agencies, such as the Commercial Press, the Chung Hwa Hong Kong, Hong Kong Joint Publishing and the Joint Printing Limited.[110] Most importantly, the SUPL is now engaging in not only publishing and printing operations but also other sectors, such as wholesaling, retailing, and becoming the dealer of calligraphy and art. As of 2021, the SUPL had 34 members of companies in different places of the world, including Taiwan, Singapore, Malaysia, the United States, Canada, United Kingdom, France and Australia. Furthermore, the SUPL is now operating under the Bauhinia Culture Holding Limited, a large pro-Beijing cultural organization that assists the SUPL to act as monopolizing machinery in the Chinese publishing sector.

The educational impacts of the SUPL are tremendous. Firstly, the Joint Publishing Company Limited controls at least seven publishing houses: Chi Nang Education Publishing, Tin Kin Publisher, Southern Guangdong Publisher, Kwang Yu Publisher, Sing Chun Publisher, China Books and Magazines Publisher, and Chiu Yang Publisher.[111] Secondly, the Commercial Press controls many other publishers, including Commercial Press Electronic Commerce and Trade, Hong Kong Education Publishing Company, Tai Ping Books, Chin Chun (formerly Kam Ling) Publisher, Bloomsbury Books, Commercial Press Internet Bookstore, Oriental Think Tank Information Technology Company, Sino United Electronic Publisher, and Shantou City United Books Publisher.[112] Thirdly, the Chung Hwa Bookstore controls the distribution, marketing and selling of Chinese books in the HKSAR. In recent years, most of its books in the Chung Wah Bookstores are either published in the mainland or being screened out for political sensitivity and correctness. As such, the SUPL is like an umbrella publishing house that monopolizes the publication, marketing and sale of most Chinese books in the HKSAR.

An important research conducted by Tommy Cheung Sau-yin in June 2018 found that the Liaison Office, China's representative office in the HKSAR, had been expanding its tentacles to the media and publishing industry quickly.[113] The Liaison Office controls not only 99.9 percent of the SUPL ownership but also the ownership of two other cultural enterprises, namely the Guangdong New Culture Enterprise Development and the New Culture Enterprise (Hong Kong) Development.[114] As early as 2015, the *Next Magazine* found that the Guangdong New Culture Enterprise's headquarters was located at a military district in Guangzhou, implying the likelihood of having a military background.[115] The two pro-Beijing newspapers – *Wen Wei Po* and *Ta Kung Pao* – are under the 88.44 percent and 99.9 percent of the Liaison Office's ownership. In terms of the publishing houses, the SUPL controls Wan Li Publishing

Institution, Sun Ya Culture Enterprise, Hong Kong Education Publisher and the Hong Kong Open Page Publishing. In total, the Liaison Office owned 30 out of 53 large bookstores in Hong Kong and it is acting as the political patron of the SUPL, exerting a considerable degree of influence on the Chinese publishing industry in the HKSAR. When asked whether the Liaison Office undermined the "one country, two systems" in Hong Kong's publishing sector, Chief Executive Carrie Lam said that if this phenomenon took place in accordance with the law, then the government should not intervene.[116] As the Chief Executive is accountable to the central government in Beijing, it was natural for Carrie Lam to be evasive in her answer; nevertheless, the inroads made by the Liaison Office into the local publishing industry were politically significant. In September 2018, when Carrie Lam attended the 30th-anniversary banquet of the SUPL, she congratulated its business success and expressed her hope that it would expand its publication venture into the GBA.[117] Politically, the publishing market in the GBA requires books, journals and magazines in the HKSAR to undergo vetting processes, implying that the SUPL has to ensure the political correctness of its Chinese publications if the GBA is a new market of expansion.

The monopolization of the SUPL in the publishing industry of the HKSAR has implications for the survival space of small publishing houses and bookstores. Small bookstores have to rent places at the second or third floor of some buildings in less busy districts. Some of the bookstores that sold politically sensitive books, notably the Causeway Bay Bookstore, suffered a severe setback from October to December 2015, when five of its publishers and co-workers disappeared in Hong Kong, Thailand and the mainland one by one.[118] The bookstore was eventually closed down and its fate signaled the difficulties of other smaller bookstores to survive in the HKSAR, where the monopolistic market in the publishing industry has driven out independent publishers and bookstores that published and sold politically sensitive books. After the imposition of the national security law in late June 2020, politically sensitive books are currently possessed by individual citizens. Previous sensitive books on topics like the 1989 Tiananmen massacre and its related democracy movement have almost disappeared in all bookstores; they are now possessed privately by individual citizens. Public libraries have already censored those books written by localists, notably Joshua Wong, while libraries at some secondary schools have followed suit.[119] The imposition of the national security law in June 2020 has brought about self-censorship on the part of public and school libraries, except for libraries at universities that, at the time of writing, remain relatively autonomous in their storage of politically sensitive works. Above all, the publication of school textbooks is now monopolized by pro-Beijing publishers in the market, resulting in the phenomenon that students and parents have little choices but to adopt all these increasingly government-screened textbooks. The dominance of pro-Beijing publishers creates a political environment conducive to the gradual expansion of Chinese nationalism and patriotism through the usage of official textbooks and references.

The Emergence of Pro-Beijing Schools, Teachers' Unions and Education Groups

The rapid mainlandization of the HKSAR can be seen in the emergence of the pro-Beijing schools. Table 3.5 shows the rise of many pro-Beijing schools after 1997, including the prominent cases of Heung To Middle School, Pui Kiu Middle School, Pui Kiu College, and the schools under the Fukien community's organization. Although these pro-Beijing schools belong to a minority of all the schools in the HKSAR, their rise represented the change of political wind from pro-British before July 1, 1997 to pro-Beijing after the transfer of sovereignty.

Table 3.6 shows the major teachers' unions in Hong Kong. The pro-Beijing teachers' union was weak with only the Education Employees General Union. Yet, the imposition of the national security law onto Hong Kong in late June 2020 resulted in the disbandment of the Professional Teachers' Union (PTU) in

Table 3.5 The Transformation of Pro-Beijing Schools in Hong Kong after 1997

School	Establishment	Development
Workers' Children Secondary School	1946	Participated in the Direct Subsidy Scheme in 1991
Heung To Middle School	1946	Participated in the Direct Subsidy Scheme in 1991
Tin Shui Wai Heung To Middle School	2001	Under the Direct Subsidy Scheme
Tseng Kwan O Heung To Middle School	2003	Under the Direct Subsidy Scheme
Pui Kiu Middle School	1946	Participated in Direct Subsidy Scheme in 1991
Pui Kiu Primary School	2000	Government-aided School
Pui Kiu College	2005	Under the Direct Subsidy Scheme
Hon Wah College (cum Primary Section)	1945	Participated in the Direct Subsidy Scheme in 1991 and it moved to Siu Sai Wan in 2000
Fukien Secondary School	1951	Participated in Direct Subsidy Scheme in 1991 and it moved to Kwun Tong in 2002
Siu Sai Wan Fukien Secondary School	1997	Government-aided (secondary) school
Fukien Secondary School Affiliated School	2009	Took over the Pegasus Philip Wong Kin Hang Christian Primary School cum Junior Secondary School[120]
Chung Sang Middle School	1954	It was closed in 1993 because it did not have a formal school site beside the Silvery Theater although its branch was located at the Wan Hon Street in Kwun Tong
Hong Kong Federation of Education Workers (HKFEW) Wong Cho Bau School	2001	Government-aided (primary) school
HKFEW Wong Cho Bau Secondary School	2001	Government-aided (secondary) school

Sources: The authors constructed this table by using the information of the websites of all these schools and through personal discussions with several teachers and principals.

Table 3.6 Major Teachers' Unions in Hong Kong

Name of the union	Year of registration	Declared membership	Political affiliates
Hong Kong Teachers' Association	1949	663	Independent
Education Bureau, Government, Grant-in-aid, Subsidized and Private Schools Junior Staff Union	1966	917	Federation of Hong Kong and Kowloon Labor Unions
Government Educational Staff Union	1973	401	Independent
Hong Kong Professional Teachers' Union	1973	98,304	Pro-Democracy Confederation of Trade Unions
Association of Inspectors, Education Bureau	1975	193	Independent
Union of Government Primary School Headmasters and Headmistresses	1976	192	Independent
Union of Government School Teachers	1979	283	Independent
Association of Principal, Senior, Assistant and Certificated Masters and Mistresses of Education Bureau	1979	50	Independent
Association of Professional Teachers in English Foundation Schools	1980	342	Independent
Association of Principals of Government Secondary Schools	1982	31	Independent
Hong Kong Aided Primary School Heads Association	1983	370	Independent
Sheng Kung Hui Primary Schools Council School Principals Association	1986	50	Independent
Hong Kong Aided School Teachers' Association	1986	–	Stopped functioning
Association of Assistant Principals of Government Secondary Schools	1993	61	Independent
Association of Curriculum Officers, Education Bureau	1994	69	Independent
Social Welfare Department Teachers' Union	1996	11	Independent
Diocesan Boys' School Teachers' Association	2003	94	Independent
Education Employees General Union	2005	1,045	Pro-Beijing Federation of Trade Unions
The Association of Deputy Heads of Government Primary Schools	2011	56	Independent

Sources: Registry of Trade Unions, *Annual Statistical Report of Trade Unions in Hong Kong* (Hong Kong: Registry of Trade Unions, Labor Department of the Hong Kong Government, 2017 and 2018).

August 2021, when its demise favored the reorganization and rise of pro-Beijing teachers' unions.

Table 3.7 illustrates that the PTU continued to be strong in its membership from 1973 to 2019. However, the pro-Beijing Education Employees General Union (EEGU) was no match with the PTU from 1973 to 2017. The core leaders of the EEGU come from pro-Beijing schools, such as Hon Wah, Pui Kiu,

Table 3.7 Membership of Education Unions, 1955–2019

	HKTA	GESU	HKPTU	HKASTA	EEGU	EGSP
Establish	1934	1973	1973	1986	2006	1966
1955	2,099					
1956	6,003					
1957	5,887					
1958	5,812					
1959	5,593					
1960	5,007					
1961	4,572					
1962	4,454					
1963	3,869					
1964	3,854					
1965	3,680					81
1966	5,182					365
1967	2,887					377
1968	3,552					401
1969	3,546					420
1970	3,777					422
1971	2,894					427
1972	2,761					473
1973	2,032	2,092	8,112			595
1974	2,241	1,951	9,552			668
1975	1,889	1,968	12,697			851
1976	1,676	2,023	15,721			1,126
1977	2,027	1,871	17,480			1,374
1978	2,113	1,824	18,592			1,966
1979	2,203	1,532	19,888			1,698
1980	2,150	1,565	22,272			1,837
1981	2,083	1,544	23,573			2,016
1982	2,136	1,753	26,289			1,996
1983	1,790	1,791	27,586			1,972
1984	1,686	1,805	30,719			1,864
1985	1,561	1,685	31,750			1,972
1986	1,604	1,621	32,748	40		1,929
1987	1,528	1,556	35,828	988		1,846
1988	1,346	1,532	40,912	1,051		1,728
1989	1,018	1,469	44,089	1,051		1,613
1990	1,019	1,474	47,009	1,127		1,474
1991	939	1,334	50,045	1,131		1,334
1992	948	1,360	53,427	1,313		1,360
1993	904	1,356	56,498	1,314		1,356
1994	919	865	58,620	1,312		1,263
1995	911	761	61,416	1,312		1,249
1996	958	1,225	64,196	1,313		1,193
1997	911	562	67,631	255		1,194
1998	998	663	71,007	101		1,223
1999	947	694	74,096	54		1,186
2000	950	611	75,754	20		1,112
2001	933	748	78,221	20		1,128
2002	750	656	79,551	20		1,020

(Continued)

Table 3.7 Membership of Education Unions, 1955–2019 (Continued)

	HKTA	GESU	HKPTU	HKASTA	EEGU	EGSP
Establish	1934	1973	1973	1986	2006	1966
2003	744	794	78,447	20		967
2004	733	801	76,887	20		907
2005	737	680	77,495	20	246	922
2006	737	637	78,423	20	2,143	921
2007	717	595	78,974	20	3,696	925
2008	722	542	79,988	20	4,535	917
2009	742	563	82,206	20	4,854	917
2010	736	575	84,616	20	5,748	934
2011	734	594	88,261	20	4,367	928
2012	717	610	90,551	–	3,048	928
2013	652	443	93,170	–	2,213	930
2014	659	443	93,996	–	1,728	920
2015	653	412	95,685	–	1,445	917
2016	659	384	95,981	–	1,189	917
2017	663	401	98,304	–	1,045	917
2018	679	433	99,332	–	1,058	920
2019	682	457	96,670	–	1,066	916

Sources: Annual Statistical Report of Trade Unions in Hong Kong, 1954–2019.

Notes

The shaded areas mean that there were no data for those years, for the unions did not exist at that time. HKTA: Hong Kong Teachers' Association; GESU: Government Educational Staff Union, formerly the Government School Non-Graduate Teachers' Union. HKPTU: Hong Kong PTU; HKASTA: Hong Kong Aided School Teachers' Association; EEGU: Education Employees General Union; EGSP: Education Bureau, Government, Grant-in-Aid, Subsidized and Private Schools Junior Staff Union.

Heung To and Fukien. With the PTU's disbandment in 2021, it remains to be seen how the pro-Beijing EEGU would develop gradually with the support of PRC authorities in the HKSAR.

The inroads made by pro-Beijing forces into the education sector remain relatively slow and limited. While pro-Beijing teachers' unions remain relatively small and weak, there are some educational interest groups without being registered as teachers' unions. Table 3.8 shows the Hong Kong FEW was set up in 1975 and it remains pro-Beijing. However, its membership is unknown. With the PTU's disbandment, the FEW would likely tap into the former members of the PTU and try to recruit more members. It remains to be seen whether the FEW would be successful in its expansion, exploiting the political vacuum left by the PTU.

The PRC authorities have directly or indirectly coopted many leaders of Hong Kong's public and private universities. A good example was the responses of some vice-chancellors of publicly funded universities to the protestors' occupation of the LegCo on July 1, 2019, during which many secondary school and university students participated. The vice-chancellors who reprimanded the students' and protestors' occupation of LegCo included Zhang Xiang from the

Table 3.8 Educational Interest Groups that Are Not Registered as Teachers' Unions

Educational groups	Year of establishment	Membership
Hong Kong Federation of Education Workers	1975 and pro-Beijing	Unknown
Hong Kong Subsidized Secondary Schools Council	1971	345*
Hong Kong Association of the Heads of Secondary Schools	1964	356**
Education Convergence	1994	Unknown
New Territories School Master Association	2006	932
Hong Kong Women Teachers' Organization	2006	2,000
Hong Kong Senior Education Workers' Association	1997	Unknown

Sources: See the websites of these organizations, such as http://www.ntsha.org.hk/index.php?option=com_content&task=view&id=1&Itemid=2, access date: August 2, 2021. Also see *Apple Daily*, June 13, 2014.

Notes

*For its member schools, see https://www.hksssc.edu.hk/schools.php, access date: August 2, 2021.

** The figure refers to the number of principals as their membership includes principals, vice principals and affiliated as well as life members. There are also overlapping memberships between the Hong Kong Subsidized Secondary Schools Council and the Hong Kong Association of the Head of Secondary Schools.

HKU, Shyy Wei from the Hong Kong University of Science and Technology (HKUST) Leonard Cheng from Lingnan University, and Stephen Cheung from the EdUHK. Teng Ginguang of Hong Kong Polytechnic University did not scold the protestors, but he appealed to the public for the need to maintain non-violence in the resolution of the political dispute; he understood the societal mood at that time.[121] Similarly, the private Heng Sang University's vice-chancellor Simon Ho Shun-man did not reprimand the protestors but questioned why such a tragic event took place.[122] Objectively speaking, it was not easy for the leaders of local public and private universities to deal with the 2019 anti-extradition bill movement, for many protestors involved students from universities. On the one hand, vice-chancellors had to support the maintenance of law and order, but on the other hand, they had to deal with the grievances and anger of many students, who found the extradition bill as politically unacceptable.

In March 2021, the NPC redesigned, changed and approved a new political system for Hong Kong where the 90-member LegCo would be composed of 40 members returned from a 1,500-member Election Committee, 30 members returned from functional constituencies, and only 20 directly elected by citizens in geographical constituencies. This new electoral system has empowered the pro-Beijing educational groups and curbed the influence of the pro-democracy counterparts, especially as the PTU disbanded itself in August 2021. Table 3.9 shows the new composition of the 30 Election Committee members of which 16 are the ex-officio members and 14 are elected. Of the 16 ex-officio members, 11 are vice-chancellors of universities or the members of the Board of Directors of these universities, while 5 comes from the statutory bodies, consultative bodies

Table 3.9 Elites from the Thirty Members of Education Section in the Election Committee

Election method	Number	Details
Ex-officio members	16	Specified office: Vice-Chancellor/Presidents of Universities: 1 the Vice-Chancellor of The University of Hong Kong 2 the Vice-Chancellor of The Chinese University of Hong Kong 3 the President of The Hong Kong University of Science and Technology 4 the President of the City University of Hong Kong 5 the President of The Hong Kong Polytechnic University 6 the President of The Education University of Hong Kong 7 the President and Vice-Chancellor of the Hong Kong Baptist University 8 the President of Lingnan University 9 the President of The Open University of Hong Kong 10 the President of the Hong Kong Shue Yan University 11 the President of The Hang Seng University of Hong Kong Sponsoring bodies that operate secondary schools, primary schools and kindergarten that receive recurrent funding from the Government, and the total number of schools managed by the school sponsoring bodies are among the top five of all school sponsoring bodies: 12 the office specified by the Roman Catholic Diocese of Hong Kong 13 the office specified by the Po Leung Kuk 14 the office specified by the Hong Kong Sheng Kung Hui 15 the office specified by the Tung Wah Group of Hospitals 16 the office specified by The Hong Kong Council of the Church of Christ in China
Elected members	14	a institutions of higher education funded through the University Grants Committee; b post-secondary colleges registered under the Post-Secondary Colleges Ordinance; c The Open University of Hong Kong; d The Hong Kong Academy for Performing Arts; e the Vocational Training Council; f The Hong Kong Examinations and Assessment Authority; g the Hong Kong Council for Accreditation of Academic and Vocational Qualifications; h schools registered under section 13 of the Education Ordinance; or i schools entirely maintained and controlled by the Government

Source: "Sector 24 of the Election Committee: The Education Sector," 2021, in 24. 教育界 (cmab.gov.hk), access date: September 4, 2021.

and related educational organizations. Almost all the educational elites who are ex-officio members or elected come from education institutions subsidized by the HKSAR government. If financial dependence on the government is the hallmark of all these education institutes, their leaders and elites representing these organizations are necessarily pro-establishment. They have the right to select not only 40 LegCo members but also the candidates running for the Chief Executive election in March 2022.

It was reported that the vice-chancellors at the HKU, HKUST and CityU (Zhang Xiang, Shyy Wei, and Way Kuo, respectively) did not meet the requirements of being ex-officio members, who have to be registered electors, who are permanent residents and who ordinarily reside in the HKSAR.[123] As a result, the chairpersons of the Board of Directors of these three universities become the representatives who are qualified to be the ex-officio members.

The disbandment of the PTU and the emergence of the new electoral system provided a golden opportunity for pro-Beijing educators and groups to replace the PTU immediately in the summer of 2021. A new pro-Beijing education group, namely the Education Professional Alliance (EPA), was born in April 2021 and it is composed of 13 "patriotic" educators, such as Ho Hon-kuen from Education Convergence, Wong Kam-leung from the FEW, Chiu Cheung-kay from the Direct Subsidy Scheme Schools Council, and Fong Chung-lun from the Hong Kong Island School Heads Association (Table 3.10).[124] The pro-Beijing media hailed the EPA's emergence as a break away from the PTU's previous "monopoly" of the membership of the Election Committee.[125] However, the EPA comprises all the school principals and leaders of the pro-establishment education groups without involving any frontline teachers – a criticism reflective of the elite cooptation in the way in which the 1,500-member Election Committee was formed.[126] Politically, the EPA advances the agenda of national education as its platform proclaims to implement "one country, two systems" and to strengthen Chinese history and national education.[127]

All the thirteen members of the EPA are obviously pro-establishment and pro-Beijing school principals. Some of them openly supported the HKSAR government during the 2014 Occupy Central movement and the 2019 anti-extradition bill movement. They are also the education activists; some are coopted by the PRC government into various consultative committees in the mainland. Overall, the downfall of the pro-democracy PTU in the summer of 2021 provided a fertile ground for the pro-Beijing education elites to fill in the electoral vacuum for the new election of the members of the 1,500-member Election Committee that would select the legislators and the Chief Executive.

In September 2021, shortly after the PTU's disbandment, the FEW grasped the chance of having a political vacuum to set up a new union, namely Hong Kong Education Workers Union (HKEWU), whose chairman Wong Kin-ho comes from The Yuen Yuen Institute Nei Ming Chan Lui Chung Tak Memorial College, and whose vice-chairman Ng Chi-hui is a teacher from the Hong Kong Chinese Women's Club College. The honorary chairpersons of the HKEWU are Yeung You-chung and Wong Kwan-yu, the honorary president and president

Table 3.10 Composition of the Education Professional Alliance, 2021

School Principals	Background and details of public service
Chiu Cheung-kay	Principal of Chan Shu Kui Memorial School; the vice chairman of the Hong Kong Direct Subsidy Schools Council; chairman of the Cantonese Correct Pronunciation Promotion Association; a member of the Board of Directors of the Education University; an advisor of the Lingnan University's Chinese Department; a member of management committee of the Center of School Partnership at the Chinese University of Hong Kong; a board member of the Center of Comparative Politics Study between the Shanghai Fudan University and the Chan Shu Kui School; a member of the consultative committee of the education development fund under the Education Bureau of the HKSAR government; and a member of the Grantham Scholarship Fund under the Home Affairs Department of the HKSAR government.
Ho Hon-kuen	Principal of the Chinese History Education Centre; chairman of the Education Convergence; chairman of the University of Hong Kong's Master of Chinese History Alumni Center; chairman of the Chinese History and Cultural Awards Foundation; and a member in the supplementary list of the National People's Congress.
Wong Kam-leung	Chairman of the Federation of Education Workers (FEW) from 2017 to 2022; vice-chairman of EWF from 2011 to 2016; currently Principal of Wong Chor Bau School. Wong is also a member of Guizhou CPPCC; a member of the Outlying Islands Fight Crime Committee; a member of the Education Commission; a member of the Hong Kong Technology and Innovation Education Alliance; a deputy director of the coordination and professional committee of the Hong Kong members of the Provincial-Level CPPCC; a deputy chair of the Hong Kong Guizhou Cultural Exchange Foundation; an executive committee member of the Shaanxi Province's Overseas Friendship Association; and an executive member of the Wuhan Overseas Friendship Association. Wong was conferred with the HKSAR Bronze Bauhinia Medal in the year 2021.
Poon Suk-han	Principal of the Christian and Missionary Alliance Sun Kei Secondary School; the chairperson of the Hong Kong Subsidized Secondary Schools Council; a member of the Board of Directors of the University of Hong Kong; a member of the Board of Directors of the City University; a member of the Education Commission; a member of the Chief Executive Outstanding Teaching Awards Supervisory Committee; and a member of the Education Development Fund Consultative Committee under the Education Bureau.
Cheung Yung-bong	Honorary chairman of the Hong Kong Aided Primary School Heads Association; former chair of the Hong Kong Aided Primary School Association; former chair of the Hong Kong Primary School Education Leadership Association; advisor to the Aided Primary Schools Council; and currently principal of the S. K. H. St. James' Primary School.

(Continued)

Table 3.10 Composition of the Education Professional Alliance, 2021 *(Continued)*

School Principals	Background and details of public service
So Ping-fai	Advisor of the Aided Primary Schools Council; and currently principal of the Tin Shui Wai Methodist Primary School.
Fong Chung-lun	Chairman of the Hong Kong Island Principals Federation; principal of the Kiangsu-Chekiang College.
Mok Chung-fai	Chairman of the Kowloon District Principals Federation; formerly appointed member of the Wong Tai Sin District Council; a member of the Basic Law Promotion Supervisory Committee; and chair of the Hong Kong Youth Development Federation; and he signed his name to oppose the 2014 Occupy Central Movement.
Yau Siu-hung	Former principal of the Hong Kong Teachers' Association Lee Heng Kwei Secondary School; currently principal of the Yan Chai Hospital Wong Wha San Secondary School; chair of the New Territories Principals Association; chair of the Hong Kong Teachers' Association; chair of the Sai Kung Principals Association; and a member of the Appeal Committee that handles teachers' appeals.
Leung Wing-hung	Chair of the Hong Kong Special Schools Council; principal of the TWGHs Kwan Fong Kai Chi School; and a member of the Appeal Committee that handles teachers' appeals.
Hung Mei-kay	A member of the Board of Directors of the Victoria Shanghai Academy; an advisor of the Hong Kong Kindergarten Education Professional Exchange Association; and the chief principal of the Victoria Education Organization.
Liu Fung-heung	Vice-chair of the Association of Hong Kong Kindergarten Education Professional Exchange; chairwoman of the Hong Kong Kindergarten Federation; and principal of the Choice English School and Kindergarten.
Lam Chui-ling	A member of the Executive Committee of the Association of Hong Kong Kindergarten Education Professional Exchange; vie-chair of the Federation of Education Workers from 2014 to 2022; founding principal of the Tsuen Wan Trade Association Chu Cheong Kindergarten from 1994 to the present; a former founder of the Kwai Tsing District Kindergarten Principals; and a former appointed member of the Kwai Tsing District Council from 2008 to 2019.

Sources: Compiled from various newspapers and websites of the schools concerned by the authors, September 2021.

of the FEW, respectively.[128] Two legal advisers of the HKEWU are Maggi Chan Man-ki, a Hong Kong member of the NPC, and Lau Ngai, the vice-chairman of the youth group of the pro-Beijing Democratic Alliance for Betterment and Progress of Hong Kong (DAB). During the inauguration press conference of the HKEWU, the FEW chairman Wong Kam-leung said teachers should "put aside the idea of making politics in command."[129] Clearly, under the new political landscape of the HKSAR, pro-Beijing teachers' unions have much room for their maneuvers and expansion.

Conclusion

The deepening and accelerated process of the mainlandization of Hong Kong's education system can be seen immediately after the imposition of the national security law, which requires local schools and universities to implement national security education. Although pro-Beijing educational interest groups and teachers' unions remain relatively weak, they are expanding to assist the HKSAR government to implement national security education, and to promote a deeper understanding of the Chinese culture and history in the psyche of Hong Kong students.

Notes

1. "National Security Extended to Hong Kong," April 19, 2021, in 國安教育延伸至香港分析:強迫全民參與的文革升級版 (voacantonese.com), access date: August 22, 2021.
2. "Xi Jinping first talks about the comprehensive national security perspective," April 16, 2014, in 圖解: 習近平首提"總體國家安全觀"－獨家稿件-人民網 (people.com.cn), access date: August 22, 2021.
3. "Xi Jinping warns Hong Kong that students need patriotic education," July 2, 2017, in 习近平警告香港: 学生需要爱国教育 (voachinese.com), access date: August 14, 2021.
4. "Xi Jinping delivers important speech during the national education conference," September 10, 2018, in 習近平出席全國教育大會併發表重要講話_滾動新聞_中國政府網 (www.gov.cn), access date: August 15, 2021.
5. *Ibid.*
6. *Ibid.*
7. *Apple Daily*, September 3, 2019.
8. *Ibid.*
9. *Ibid.*
10. *Ibid.*
11. Ben Westcott, "China's top political body met in secret and issued an ominous message to Hong Kong," CNN, November 1, 2019, in China's top political body met in secret and issued an ominous message to Hong Kong – CNN, access date: August 16, 2021.
12. "Xi Jinping uses Macau to say something to Hong Kong: Article 23, Patriotic Education and the Maintenance of the Center's Power," December 20, 2019, in 习近平借澳门向香港喊话: 23 条、爱国教育、维护中央权力 – BBC News 中文, access date: August 15, 2021.
13. *Ibid.*
14. "Lui Ping-kuen interprets and dissects the blueprint of the central government on Hong Kong's governance," June 2, 2020, in https://www.businesstimes.com.hk/articles/127288/呂秉權-一國兩制-習近平-浸會大學-新聞系, access date: August 15, 2021.
15. "The Practice of 'One Country, Two Systems' in the Hong Kong Special Administrative Region," June 10, 2014, in 《"一国两制"在香港特别行政区的实践》白皮书(英文) (scio.gov.cn), access date: August 21, 2021.
16. "Full Text of Resolution on CCP Central Committee Report," October 24, 2017, in Full text of resolution on CPC Central Committee report (www.gov.cn), access date: August 21, 2021.
17. For the rise of localism and radical populism in the HKSAR, see Sonny Shiu-Hing Lo, "Ideologies and Factionalism in Beijing-Hong Kong Relations," *Asian Survey*, vol. 58, no. 3 (June 2018), pp. 392–415.

18. "Lui Ping-kuen interprets and dissects the blueprint of the central government on Hong Kong's governance," see footnote 12 above.
19. *Ibid.*
20. "Board chairman Lo Man-shui confirms Christine Choi resigns from her position of principal: She is not very leftwing," August 1, 2017, in 【副局政助任命】校董盧文端證蔡若蓮辭任校長：她也不是很左 | 香港01 | 社會新聞 (hk01.com), access date: August 21, 2021.
21. "The law of the People's Republic of China on Safeguarding National Security in the Hong Kong special administrative region," June 30, 2020, in The Law of the People's Republic of China on Safeguarding National Security in the Hong Kong Special Administrative Region (elegislation.gov.hk), access date: August 21, 2021.
22. *Ibid.*
23. *Ibid.*
24. *Ibid.*
25. *Ibid.*
26. *Ibid.*
27. "Xi Jinping's speech in the celebration meeting of the 40th anniversary of the Shenzhen special economic zone," Xinhua, October 14, 2020, in （受权发布）习近平：在深圳经济特区建立40周年庆祝大会上的讲话-新华网 (xinhuanet.com), access date: August 22, 2021.
28. *Ibid.*
29. *Ibid.*
30. "Matthew Cheung: Hong Kong has the responsibility of propelling national education and doing well in national anthem and national security education," October 18, 2020, in 指習近平重要講話對港有特殊意義 張建宗：港校推國教應有之責，望做好國歌及國安教育 | 立場報道 | 立場新聞 (thestandnews.com), access date: August 22, 2021.
31. *Ibid.*
32. For Xi's view on how education can make China successful and strong, see "Xi Jinping says Chinese education can produce great experts," May 29, 2021, in 習近平稱中國教育能夠培養出大師 (rfi.fr), access date: August 22, 2021.
33. For this Trojan Horse argument, see Sonny Shiu-hing Lo, *Hong Kong's Indigenous Democracy* (London: Palgrave, 2015).
34. *Ta Kung Pao*, July 12, 2020, p. A6.
35. *Ibid.*
36. *Ibid.*
37. *Ibid.*
38. *Wen Wei Po*, July 12, 2020, p. A2.
39. *Ibid.*
40. *Ibid.*
41. *Ibid.*
42. *Ibid.*
43. *Ibid.*
44. *Ibid.*
45. *Ibid.*
46. *Ibid.*
47. *Ibid.*
48. *Ibid.*
49. Editorial, "Clear Evidence of Benny Tai violating the national security law," *Ta Kung Pao*, July 13, 2020, p. A4.
50. *Ibid.*
51. *Ibid.*
52. *Ibid.*
53. *Ibid.*

54 Christy Leung, "National security law: 52 former lawmakers, activists arrested in January told to report to police on Sunday – more than a month early – with some expecting charges," *South China Morning Post*, February 26, 2021, in National security law: 52 former lawmakers, activists arrested in January told to report to police on Sunday – more than a month early – with some expecting charges | South China Morning Post (scmp.com), access date: July 22, 2021.
55 *Oriental Daily*, August 11, 2020, p. A10.
56 *Ta Kung Pao*, August 12, 2020, p. A1.
57 Education Bureau Circular, No. 6/2021, "National Security Education in School Curriculum – Additional Curriculum Documents and Learning and Teaching Resources," May 26, 2021, in EDBC21006E, access date: September 5, 2021.
58 "Curriculum Framework of Chinese History's National Security Education," May 2021, in nse_subject_framework_chinese_history (edb.gov.hk), access date: September 5, 2021.
59 *Ibid*.
60 "Curriculum Framework of History's National Security Education," May 2021, in nse_subject_framework_history (edb.gov.hk), access date: September 5, 2021.
61 *Ibid*., p. 12.
62 "Curriculum Framework of Life and Society's (Form 1 to Form 3) National Security Education," May 2021, in nse_subject_framework_life_and_society (edb.gov.hk), access date: September 5, 2021.
63 "Curriculum Framework of Economics Subject's (Form 4 to Form 6) National Security Education," May 2021, in nse_subject_framework_economics (edb.gov.hk), access date: September 5, 2021.
64 *Ibid*.
65 *Wen Wei Po*, May 27, 2021, p. A6.
66 Wang Zhenmin et al., *The Reading Materials of the National Security Law for the HKSAR* (in Chinese) (Hong Kong: Joint Publishing, March 2021).
67 *Ta Kung Pao*, May 27, 2021, p. A6.
68 *Ibid*.
69 *Wen Wei Po*, May 27, 2021, p. A12.
70 *Ibid*.
71 Chan Ho-him and Kathleen Magramo, "Hong Kong's liberal studies to be renamed 'citizenship and social development' as part of massive overhaul," *South China Morning Post*, March 31, 2021, in https://www.scmp.com/news/hong-kong/education/article/3127778/hong-kongs-liberal-studies-expected-be-renamed-citizenship, access date: September 6, 2021.
72 "Citizenship and Social Development: Curriculum and Assessment Guide (Secondary 4–6)," EDB, 2021, in CS_CAG_S4-6_Eng_2021 (edb.gov.hk), access date: September 6, 2021.
73 *Wen Wei Po*, June 3, 2021, p. A6.
74 "Liberal Studies: Curriculum and Assessment Guide (Secondary 4–6)," EDB, 2007 (updated in January 2014), in Liberal Studies (hkedcity.net), access date: September 6, 2021.
75 Citizenship and Social Development: Curriculum and Assessment Guide (Secondary 4–6)."
76 *Ibid*.
77 *Ibid*.
78 *Ibid*.
79 *Wen Wei Po*, June 3, 2021, p. A6.
80 *Ibid*.
81 *Ibid*.
82 *Ibid*.
83 *Wen Wei Po*, September 3, 2021, p. A2.

84 *Ibid.*
85 *Ibid.*
86 *Ibid.*
87 *Ibid.*
88 *Ibid.*
89 *Ta Kung Pao,* September 3, 2021, p. A1.
90 *Ibid.*
91 *Ibid.*
92 To Hoi-ming, "Citizenship and Social Development studies was successfully opened, and this is a new turning point in education reform," *Ta Kung Pao,* September 3, 2021, p. A5.
93 *Ta Kung Pao,* August 26, 2021, p. A7.
94 *Ming Pao,* August 30, 2021, p. A6.
95 *Ibid.*
96 "National Security Education, Universities Cannot be Neglected," *Ta Kung Pao,* July 27, 2021, p. A5.
97 For details, see Sonny Shiu-hing Lo, Steven Chung-fun Hung and Jeff Hai-chi Loo, *The Dynamics of Peaceful and Violent Protests in Hong Kong: The Anti-extradition Movement* (London: Palgrave Macmillan, 2021).
98 *Ta Kung Pao,* July 27, 2021, p. A7.
99 *Ibid.*
100 *Ibid.*
101 *Wen Wei Po,* July 27, 2021, p. A17.
102 The authors' information from academics at the EdUHK, July 2021.
103 *Ta Kung Pao,* July 27, 2021, p. A7.
104 Chan Ho-him, "National security classes to be compulsory in at least 3 Hong Kong universities," *South China Morning Post,* July 27, 2021, p. A3.
105 *Oriental Daily,* August 24, 2021, p. A11.
106 *Ibid.*
107 "National Security Education," August 2021, in National Security Law Education (NSLE0001) – NSLE0001 – Co-curricular Learning – Office of Student Affairs, Hong Kong Baptist University (hkbu.edu.hk), access date: September 5, 2021.
108 *Ibid.*
109 *Ibid.*
110 For details, see the SUPL website, in 聯合出版集團 (sup.com.hk), access date: August 22, 2021.
111 *Ibid.*
112 *Ibid.*
113 Tommy Cheung, "A Small Story Behind SUPL," June 2, 2018, in 聯合出版集團背後小故事. 最近大家都講三中商, 其實《壹周刊》都一早已經踢爆左, 三中商背後既聯合出版集團, 就... | by 張秀賢 Tommy Cheung | Medium, access date: August 22, 2021.
114 *Ibid.*
115 "Next Magazine: Liaison Office violates the constitution by monopolizing the publishing industry," April 9, 2015, in 壹週刊: 滅聲行動升級 中聯辦違憲壟斷出版市場. 書展期間, 該重讀這篇 | by Kaykku | Jul, 2021 | Medium, access date: August 22, 2021.
116 *Ming Pao,* May 29, 2018.
117 "Chief Executive's speech during the 30th anniversary banquet of the SUPL," September 19, 2016, in 行政長官出席聯合出版集團成立三十周年酒會致辭全文 (只有中文) (附圖／短片) (info.gov.hk), access date: August 22, 2021.
118 Ilaria Maria Sala, "Hong Kong bookshops pull politically sensitive titles after publishers vanish," *The Guardian,* January 7, 2016, in Hong Kong bookshops pull politically sensitive titles after publishers vanish | Hong Kong | The Guardian, access date: August 22, 2021. Also see Sonny Shiu-hing Lo, *The Politics of Policing in Greater China* (London: Palgrave, 2016).

119 Information provided by one former student, May 28, 2021.
120 Result announced for takeover of school sponsorship, http://www.info.gov.hk/gia/general/200907/10/P200907100130.htm; July 10, 2009, access date: September 2, 2021.
121 "Polytechnic University vice-chancellor: Understand the social mood but violence is not the solution," July 3, 2019, in 【佔領立法會】無謂責示威者　理大校長: 明白社會情緒　但暴力非解決方法 | 立場報道 | 立場新聞 (thestandnews.com), access date: August 31, 2021.
122 *Ibid.*
123 "Zhang Xiang, Shyy Wei and Way Kuo are not eligible to be ex-officio members and change is made to the chairpersons of the Board of Directors," August 26, 2021, in 眾新聞 – 張翔史維郭位不符資格　改由校董會主席任當然選委 (hkcnews.com), access date: September 4, 2021.
124 Cho Kai-lok, "Election Committee election in the education sector is full of changing possibilities," *Hong Kong Economic Journal*, April 28, 2021, p. A6.
125 "Ho Hon-kuen forms a group to compete in the education sector and Wong Kam-leung from the Education Workers Federation says it breaks the PTU monopoly," August 9, 2021, in 選委會 | 何漢權等13人組隊戰教育界　教聯會黃錦良: 打破教協壟斷 | 香港01 | 政情 (hk01.com), access date: September 4, 2021.
126 *Ming Pao*, August 10, 2021.
127 *The Sky Post*, August 10, 2021.
128 *Ming Pao*, September 13, 2021, p. A11.
129 *Ibid.*

4 A Hong Kong-Style of Cultural Revolution in the Education Sector

The promulgation of the national security law in late June 2020 had profound implications for the education sector in the HKSAR. The most important impact is the launch of a Hong Kong-style of "Cultural Revolution" in the education sector.[1] This Cultural Revolution in the HKSAR has been evolving since the inception of the national security law on June 30, 2020. It is composed of at least four components of transformation: (1) teachers; (2) the Professional Teachers Union (PTU); (3) the struggle over a politically "incorrect" public examination question and "yellow" officers of the Examination Authority and (4) students and student unions. This chapter is going to focus on how some "yellow" or politically liberal-minded teachers were targeted, how the PTU was "struggled," how the HKEAA underwent a personnel reshuffle after a controversial examination question and how students who participated in opposition to the extradition bill in the latter half of 2019 were tackled. Unlike the PRC's Cultural Revolution that entailed bloodshed and affected many ordinary citizens, the Hong Kong-style of Cultural Revolution after the promulgation of the national security law in late June 2020 has been comparatively conducted in a more peaceful manner. It has also been influencing a relatively fewer number of people and focusing on the core activists in the HKSAR. However, the common features of the two revolutionary movements were that they were led by highly nationalistic Chinese and triggered by a desire to transform not only the political culture but also the education of targeted citizens. The impact of initiating and conducting the Hong Kong style of Cultural Revolution was significant, namely the migration of teachers and students from Hong Kong to other places. Of course, many teachers and students who cannot afford to migrate, and whose political values are more pragmatic and less idealistic, prefer to stay in the HKSAR.

Targeting "Yellow Teachers" and Teachers Who Taught "Incorrectly"

The political struggle against some liberal-minded, or "yellow teachers," could be traced back to the anti-national education campaign in the summer of 2012 and, the Occupy Central movement from September to December 2014, when the two events witnessed the political participation of some teachers. The case

DOI: 10.4324/9781003147268-4

of Ng Mai-lan, a teacher originally teaching at the Belilios Public School, could illustrate how a politically "yellow" teacher was gradually struggled by her political opponents and leading to her "defeat." In May 2010, when the former Chief Secretary Henry Tang visited Belilios Public School, Ng was an outspoken teacher raising a banner that said, "I have the right to elect the Chief Executive."[2] In the summer of 2010, when she saw the Democratic Party leaders going into the Liaison Office to negotiate with PRC officials over the scope and pace of democratic reforms in the LegCo, she was angry and decided to run for LegCo's functional constituency election against Cheung Man-kwong of the Democratic Party. However, she could not run easily because of her status as a civil servant in the government-funded public school. Ng had a deep conviction of being a "conscientious teacher."[3] She opposed the national education policy of the HKSAR government in 2012, believing that the EDB tried to "brainwash" the students. Her liberal political outlook attracted criticisms from pro-Beijing media, such as *Wen Wei Po*, but Ng said she was not afraid of being "bombarded."[4] Ng taught English and Liberal Studies, using the examples of Aung San Suu Kyi, Barack Obama and Julian Assange to teach students about human rights advocates. She championed the rights of the poor and the needy, showing to her middle-class students the lives of those poor Hongkongers who resided in cage homes. Born in a poor family, Ng understood the predicament of the poor and the needy. Ideologically, she is a liberal and social democrat shaped by her mother, who told her about the negative aspects of the CCP's policies, notably the hunger of the Chinese people in the Maoist era and the June 4th incident in 1989.[5] In 2012, two years after her encounter with Henry Tang, she was rotated to teach ethnic minority students in another school. Ng admitted that her rotation did not exclude the possibility of being hindered in the process of promotion in the Belilios Public School.[6] Later, she joined the Progressive Teachers' Alliance (PTA), an interest group critical of such government policy as penalizing a few teachers who were allegedly violating the national security law.[7] In early July, shortly after the PTU had its working relationship terminated formally by the HKSAR government, the PTA announced that it had ceased operation.[8] The PTA belonged to one of the radical but influential groups in the PTU. In the PTU's executive committee election in 2014, the PTA occupied 6 of the 19 seats, including Hon Lian-shan, a retired teacher, and Ng Mei-lan. The termination of the PTA's operation meant that its executive committee members had to adapt to the rapidly changing political atmosphere in the HKSAR.

If some teachers are politically liberal, they could become a target of political struggle from the opposing pro-government and politically conservative groups. The case of Lam See-wai, a teacher critical of the way in which the police handled a dispute between the members of Falun Fong and members of the pro-Beijing Hong Kong Youth Concern and Care Association in Mongkok district July 2013. Lam was so critical of the police that she used foul language to confront her political enemies – an action that prompted considerable criticism as she was a teacher expected to behave morally and properly. Two police unions – the Police Inspectors Association and the Junior Police Officers' Association – publicly expressed their anger at Lam's remarks and behavior.[9] The pro-Beijing supporters uploaded videos of Lam's behavior onto the Internet, triggering a protest initiated by Lam's supporters, who included members of the political groups such as the People Power and Civic Passion on August 4.[10] Later, Chief Executive C. Y. Leung asked the EDB to investigate the Lam incident. In February 2014, the EDB submitted a report to the Chief Executive. The Secretary for Education, Eddie Ng Hak-kim, expressed his hope that the dispute over Lam could be solved and that the school concerned would return to normal operation. Supporters of Lam said that she had only expressed her anger, whereas critics pointed to her "inappropriate" behavior. In July 2017, four years after the Lam incident occurred, the EDB ruled that the complaint against Lam's violation of teachers' ethical conduct was established, and that Lam should maintain her professional ethics.[11] After the ruling was released, Lam criticized the CCP on social media, adding that she would not sing the national anthem, that the education system was "rotten," and that she decided to resign from her school.[12] In response to Lam's provocative comments on social media, her school wrote to her and pointed to her "inappropriate" remarks that would have "negative impacts on the students and public."[13] Unlike Ng Mei-lan whose actions and remarks were pro-democracy and liberal, Lam's action on the street and her remarks on social media appeared to be politically provocative. However, the two politically liberal teachers encountered the same fate: their original teaching position was endangered, leading to the outcome that Ng was sent to work in another school while Lam was so depressed as to resign.

The anti-extradition protests in 2019 highlighted the politically sensitive role of teachers, who were expected to be politically neutral and who might have their own political views and choice of participating in politics. In July 2019, a teacher named Colin Lai Tak-chung at the Sacred Heart Canossian College resigned from his position as the chair of the Liberal Studies committee at the HKEAA and the chair of the Liberal Studies Teachers Association after he publicly apologized for his remarks saying that "the families of black cops die" in his Facebook.[14] Although two Form 5 students whom he taught said Lai was often "objective" in his teaching, Lai's remarks in the social media prompted the EDB investigation and criticisms from pro-Beijing elites. His school said that it would seriously investigate Lai's case. After the incident, Lai adopted a low-profile approach.[15] His reckless public comments sparked an outcry from pro-government and pro-Beijing media and elites. He acted swiftly to apologize for his remarks, while his school emphasized the importance of impartiality in teaching and supported him softly, thereby appeasing the anger of the pro-government camp in the short run. In August 2021, it was reported that the Sacred Heart Canossian College decided to discontinue hiring Lai.[16] The case of Colin Lai showed that careless public remarks made by a teacher could incur political costs, especially at a time when the PRC was determined to enforce its national security policy over the HKSAR.

In September 2019, a teacher in the Po Leung Kuk Ho Yam Tong Secondary School inappropriately set a fill-in-the-blanks question in which the police were described as having "a conspiracy with triads without caring about the life and death of citizens."[17] The EDB contacted the school concerned as such behavior was unacceptable. The Po Leung Kuk said that its schools were politically neutral and that it demanded teachers to maintain their neutrality and impartiality in teaching.[18] The cases of Colin Lai and Po Leung Kuk showed that if teachers were reckless in their public remarks and teaching pedagogy, especially their view toward the police, they could easily be a target of criticisms. Their experiences demonstrated the deeply divided society of Hong Kong, where many citizens had different views toward how the police handled a series of peaceful and violent protests in the anti-extradition bill movement in the latter half of 2019.

In June 2020, a music teacher in the pro-Beijing Heung To Middle School did not have her contract renewed because she had allowed some students to sing "Glory to Hong Kong" – a popular song sung by supporters of the anti-extradition bill movement in 2019.[19] The school issued a statement saying that its Board of Directors handled the contract of the teacher concerned in accordance with proper procedures, including whether the teacher's beliefs diverged from the school's mission and philosophy.[20] No student was disciplined in the case. However, the teacher whose contract was not renewed claimed that she had reminded students of the need to select songs carefully to sing in the class, and that the school did not have guidelines on the banning of some songs.[21] She revealed that the school board regarded her political position as different from the school. Some students said that the principal admitted the incident of not offering another contract with the teacher concerned. The principal also said that he implemented the decision of the Board of Directors, but some students who interacted with the media pointed to the phenomenon that the teacher had seldom talked about politics. Hence, the incident unveiled the sensitivity of the school's Board of Directors to the song, "Glory to Hong Kong," allowed by the music teacher in the class. In support of the teacher, about 100 students in four schools in Kowloon Tong formed their human chains, but their activities of forming human chains outside their schools were not stopped by their schools.[22] Since the student action of forming human chains was outside the campuses of the schools, the schools could not interfere with their activity.[23] They shouted slogans such as "Cultural Revolution 2.0," "purging the education sector," and "opposing suppression and killing the freedom of speech."[24] One of the alumni of Heung To Middle School criticized the school administration for being compliant toward the CCP since the 1970s, adding that the Long March of the CCP was actually like a massive escape of refugees, while other students expressed their regret of victimizing the teacher concerned because of the song.[25] Another student from a nearby school asked: "Are we now breathing the air of the CCP?"[26] Thirty police officers arrived at the scene and said that students violated the rule of forbidding citizens to group together during the Covid-19 outbreak – an announcement that made students flee immediately. According to the music teacher, the school's letter sent to her mentioned the need to "maintain the same political line rather than adopting a neutral position."[27] The action of the music teacher who tolerated her students to sing the political song, "Glory to Hong

Kong," eventually led to the school board's decision not to offer her another contract – an indication that a teacher's decision of dealing with the political song entailed the risk of being "discontinued."

With the implementation of the national security law in late June 2020, a few teachers had their licenses revoked by the EDB for violating the law. A controversy erupted in September 2019, when the Internet showed the teaching plan and materials of a teacher at the Alliance Primary School.[28] Students were required to watch a video showing the content of "Hong Kong independence" as espoused by Andy Chan Ho-tin, a former leader of the banned Hong Kong National Party, in September 2018.[29] Then the teacher planned to allow students to discuss the reasons for advocating "Hong Kong independence." Students were asked about their views toward "the results of having no freedom of speech."[30] The EDB, which received complaints against 247 teachers from June to August 2020, investigated 204 cases in which 73 complaints were not established.[31] However, 21 of the teachers were reprimanded, while 12 others received warning letters. The EDB did not go into the details of all the cases, which might include the involvement of teachers in the 2019 anti-extradition protests, and which might embrace inappropriate teaching materials and pedagogy. On October 5, 2020, the EDB announced that since the teacher planned to spread the idea of "Hong Kong independence," and that since such idea did not conform to the status of the HKSAR under the Basic Law, his license was revoked. Moreover, the vice-principal of the Alliance Primary School was reprimanded by the EDB for failing to supervise the teacher sufficiently.[32] The case of the teacher at the Alliance Primary School was straightforward because any teacher who spread the idea of "Hong Kong independence" naturally violated the national security law, which was promulgated in late June 2020. Under the circumstances that teachers are required to uphold the national security law, the annulment of the license of the teacher at the Alliance Primary School was natural and understandable.[33]

In November 2020, another teacher at the Ho Lap Primary School had his license revoked by the EDB because he was criticized for teaching the Opium War wrongly. He taught his students that the Opium War originated from the desire of Britain to "eliminate opium," for Britain found that "it was a serious situation for the Chinese to smoke opium."[34] He was an English teacher but was deployed by the school to teach a class of the General Studies subject. Someone leaked out a video of his teaching in the class on April 28, 2020, and some parents complained about his teaching content, leading to the EDB investigation. The teacher concerned acquired the teaching qualification in 2019. Although he apologized to the public and the school after the video lecture delivered by him triggered complaints, the school also apologized to the parents and terminated his teaching on April 29. On May 4, the Board of Directors of the Ho Lap Primary School set up a committee to investigate the teacher's teaching content.[35] On June 22, the EDB sent the teacher a letter saying that he violated professional ethics and conduct. On July 31, the school issued a warning letter to him, although the letter said he did not have the motive of deliberately misleading his students. On August 31, both the teacher and the school did not discuss the renewal of his contract, which expired on the following day. On September 21, the EDB sent a formal letter to the teacher, saying that it intended to exercise the power of revoking his license, and that the teacher could reply formally on or before October 6. On November 9, the EDB issued a letter to inform the teacher that his license was revoked on the same day. On November 12, the EDB made this announcement in public. According to Ip Kin-yuen, the PTU chairman who helped the teacher to appeal against the EDB decision, the normal process of disciplining a teacher included exhortation, warning, rotation, demotion and dismissal, but the Ho Lap teacher's license was revoked.[36] The seriousness of the case reflected the EDB's concern about the reactions from PRC authorities, which had already exerted pressure on the HKSAR government to implement national security education and enhance the education of Chinese history and culture. Most importantly, on a topic about the Opium War, political correctness was a principle adopted by the EDB to deal with the teacher whose teaching material was inaccurate and misleading. As such, it was understandable why the EDB chose the most serious disciplinary measure, namely revoking the license of the teacher. The EDB also sent a warning letter to reprimand another teacher who was the director of the General Studies subject at Ho Lap Primary School for being negligent and failing to help and supervise the teacher who was redeployed to teach Opium War.[37] Strictly speaking, the entire case of Ho Lap Primary School demonstrated professional negligence and errors rather than a deliberate punishment of any politically "yellow" teacher.

In May 2021, a teacher at the Lung Cheung Government Secondary School had his license being revoked by the EDB, which criticized him for not only utilizing a large amount of one-sided material to teach his students, but also instigating the strong feelings of students toward the Chinese nation and people and undermining their national identity.[38] A student in the school said that the teacher taught students the reasons for the anti-extradition bill movement, the police-citizens relations and the June 4th incident in China in 1989.[39] One of his students in the lower form complained to the authorities about his teaching. The EDB admitted that the origin of the complaint came from students, that it investigated the case comprehensively, and that the teacher concerned did not use a balanced approach and lacked evidence in his teaching content. One student felt that the teacher was quite balanced in his teaching pedagogy, and that the teacher did not really encourage students to participate in the annual June 4th candlelight vigil. Another student revealed that the teacher used health reasons to leave the school, while a student criticized the EDB for "framing" the teacher who taught both positive and negative sides of the topics.[40] Overall, under the prevailing atmosphere of observing the national security law and abiding by the correct political line, the EDB tended to adopt a hardline approach in coping with teachers who were the target of complaints from either parents or students.

In November 2020, the Secretary for Education Kevin Yeung revealed that the government might revise the existing law to allow those teachers who appealed successfully against disciplinary action to retain their teaching license after a fixed period, or to have their salaried being deducted temporarily.[41] This measure aimed at dealing with those teachers who appealed successfully to the disciplinary action taken by the EDB. However, if teachers do commit mistakes in the major issues that impinge on the national security law, such as the cases of the teachers at the Alliance Primary School and Ho Lap Primary School, the teachers concerned must be punished legally, especially in a political environment under which Chinese legalism has been adopted by Beijing and the HKSAR government to penalize the law breakers. The other cases, such as Ng Mei-lan and the teacher at the Lung Cheung Government Secondary School, appeared to be politically targeted because of their relatively "liberal" political orientation. The Lam Wai-see case was concerned about her moral integrity, leading to her resignation from the school. Overall, there were cases in which teachers were inexperienced and politically naïve, but there were also incidents in which the politically "yellow" teachers were vulnerable, targeted and penalized.

In May 2021, a visual arts teacher whose comics in Facebook contained political satires during his leisure time was criticized by the EDB for making "unreasonable accusations" against the government and the police and "lacking professional ethics."[42] In early 2020, someone complained about the teacher's comics to the authorities. Then in mid-2020, his school, namely SKH Bishop Mok Sau Tseng Secondary School, used the reason of lacking financial resources to discontinue the working relations with him.[43] He left the school and drew and sold his political comics to ordinary citizens. His case demonstrated the Hong Kong-style of Cultural Revolution in which some "yellow" teachers became the easy target of political complaints and reprisals. Although the EDB claimed that it could not comment on individual case, the visual art teacher used his leisure time to draw political comics and posted his comics on Facebook – an act of arguably exercising his freedom of expression. However, due to complaints against the visual arts teacher, the EDB took action to investigate him, directly leading to the school's refusal to renew the appointment with him. Again, politically liberal teachers are vulnerable to being disciplined in an era during which Hong Kong's education sector has been suffering from a revolution of political attacks and personnel purges.

On June 17, 2021, one week before the announcement made by the pro-democracy *Apple Daily* that it would be closed mainly due to the government's arrests and prosecution of its top executives for alleged violation of the national security law, a primary school teacher in Tin Shui Wai district had bought a pile of *Apple Daily* and distributed the newspapers to other teachers. However, his teaching colleague complained to the school – a complaint that led to the school's decision to collect all the distributed newspapers, to ask the teacher who bought *Apple Daily* to write up a report and to temporarily stop some of his teaching.[44] When asked why the school took such action, the school authorities said that "the school organization does not talk about politics and it stipulates that politics cannot be brought into the school."[45] The school criticized the teacher who distributed *Apple Daily* for having "bad motive," asking him to collect all the newspapers back, but the teacher refused.[46] His colleagues returned the newspapers to him. The PTU chairman, Ip Kin-yuen, criticized the school management for "making a mountain out of a molehill," because the teacher's behavior did not really affect the interests of other teachers and students.[47] Ip cited the code of conduct for professional teachers, saying that they should not be discriminated against on the basis of their status, position, gender, race, color, nationality, religion and political views.[48] He appealed to the school to stop discriminating against the teacher concerned. On June 23, Ho Chun-yin, a member of the pro-government and pro-Beijing political party the Democratic Alliance for Betterment and Progress of Hong Kong (DAB), asked the government how it could identify those teachers with "invisible political viruses," Kevin Yeung replied that the government could not comment on individual cases that were handled by the schools.[49]

The case of the teacher distributing *Apple Daily* was problematic in several aspects. First, as the PTU chairman Ip Kin-yuen argued, if the teacher's action of distributing the newspapers to other teachers did not really affect students, it was questionable why the teacher was asked not to teach some classes temporarily – a decision reflecting the problematic decision of the school. Second, the school authorities themselves appeared to be ignorant of the meaning of politics. If the school authorities exercised arbitrary decision to "punish" the teacher who distributed a politically liberal newspaper, its decision was already political. Third, did the school really have guidelines for teachers to follow in dealing with the distribution of newspapers? The act of asking the teacher to collect back all the newspapers was controversial, implying that only the politically "correct" newspapers were allowed. Fourth, if a few teachers complained about the action of the teacher to distribute *Apple Daily*, the case could have been handled more informally rather than "penalizing" the teacher, whose action was arguably not targeting the students. The whole case reflected the school management's unskillful handling of the teacher's distribution of *Apple Daily*. Finally, some pro-Beijing and pro-government legislators kept on exerting pressure on the HKSAR administration, showing that once the national security law was in place, the political clients loyal to the PRC demonstrated their politically "correct" behavior. The result is that teachers at the secondary and primary school levels have been encountering tremendous pressure.

In fact, pro-Beijing legislators have been exerting tremendous pressure on the HKSAR government since the promulgation of the national security law in late June 2020. In January 2021, Tommy Cheung Yu-yan of the pro-business Liberal Party advocated that video cameras should be installed in classrooms so that teachers' remarks and actions could be scrutinized, and that the teachers who were defamed would be able to use the videos to defend themselves.[50] In June 2021, Cheung asked Kevin Yeung further on the reasons behind the annulment of teachers' licenses. Yeung replied that there were six and seven licenses of teachers being revoked in 2019 and 2020, respectively, involving various reasons such as "improper relations between teachers and students."[51] Yeung added that the government would strengthen the training of teachers, especially in the areas of enhancing their knowledge of China's development and Hong Kong's national security law. The HKSAR government planned to introduce a four-day mainland visit for all new teachers from the school semester in 2021–2022. Yeung elaborated that all teachers would undergo professional training of 150 hours once every 3 years. While the national security law requires Hong Kong's schools and universities to conduct national security education, the suggestion of installing video cameras in classrooms at the primary and secondary schools appeared to be intimidating to some schoolteachers, even though Cheung had the good intention of allowing teachers who were the target of complaints to defend their behavior and remarks by using video evidence.

Target at the Professional Teachers Union: Its Eventual Dissolution in August 2021

One year after the implementation of the national security law in the HKSAR, the pro-CCP news agency, *Xinhua*, carried a commentary without any author's name, severely criticizing the PTU for its actions.[52] This commentary was officially shown on the official website of the Liaison Office, meaning that its arguments represented the PRC government's perception of the PTU. The commentary made the following assertions on the PTU, symbolizing open and written attacks on the union and precipitating the action of the HKSAR government to derecognize the largest trade union representing the teachers in Hong Kong.

First, it criticized the PTU's decision of withdrawing from both the Civil Human Rights Front (CHRF) and the Hong Kong Alliance in Support of Patriotic Democratic Movements of China (HKASPDMC). While the CHRF traditionally organized the annual July 1 protests from 2003 to 2019, the HKASPDMC was established on May 21, 1989 and had an explicit platform of calling for the release of mainland political dissidents, the "rehabilitation" of the official verdict on the pro-democracy movement in the PRC in 1989, the demand for "accountability of the June 4th massacre," the end of "one-party dictatorship," and the building of "a democratic China."[53] In view of the implementation of the national security law, the HKASPDMC reduced the number of its executive members. Nevertheless, the pro-Beijing media in Hong Kong severely criticized its actions of mobilizing Hongkongers to protest against government policies and of collaborating with the CHRF to engage in "anti-China" and "anti-governmental" activities. The *Xinhua* commentary on July 31, 2021, pointed to the triangular alliance and "leadership" between the PTU, CHRF and the HKASPDMC, accusing the PTU of engaging in allegedly "illegal activities," "stirring up protests and chaos," and "shouldering the responsibility of undermining Hong Kong and making it disastrous."[54] It criticized the CHRF and the HKASPDMC for being the "frontline soldiers before the horses," "openly slandering the nation's social system and the center's policies toward Hong Kong," "maliciously spreading the distorted discourse of defaming the 'one country, two systems,'" "seditiously instigating all kinds of rallies and protests," and "becoming the main enemies of threatening the foundation of 'one country, two systems' and endangering the security of the nation and Hong

Kong as well as undermining Hong Kong's prosperity and stability."[55] The PTU was allegedly an "accomplice" of the CHRF and the HKASPDMC. The CHRF disbanded itself in August 2021, whereas the HKASPDMC followed suit in September as both were perceived as politically "subversive."

Second, the commentary argued that the PTU deviated from its professional objectives and had "complex relations" with the CHRF and HKASPDMC in terms of personnel, organization, capital and interests.[56] It criticized the PTU for mobilizing young people to oppose the HKSAR government policy of implementing national education in 2012, participating in the 2014 Occupy Central movement, encouraging teachers and students at the primary and secondary levels to boycott classes in the early phase of the anti-extradition bill movement in 2019, "pushing the immature students to become ashes of cannons on the streets," and "propelling the tide and assisting the trend of making Hong Kong chaotic."[57]

Third, the commentary held the PTU responsible for the politicization of Hong Kong students and campuses. It criticized the union for raising the banner of the teachers' union, allowing "poisonous ideas and thinking" to spread in Hong Kong campuses in the name of protecting "the freedom of speech" and "academic freedom," protecting the "poisonous teachers" to assist the "violent elements" arbitrarily, organizing and writing up the Liberal Studies subject's teaching materials to attack the "one country, two systems," "brainwashing the students," "persistently defaming the national education that should be taken for granted," and "maliciously stopping the process of decolonizing Hong Kong's education."[58] Obviously, the PRC government regarded the PTU as the main culprit in opposing and delaying the implementation of the national education in 2012, politicizing teachers and students, participating in the liberalization of the liberal studies subject and refusing to reform Hong Kong's education system and curricula in a nationalistic manner.

Fourth, the commentary argued that, at a time when the Hong Kong police were investigating the CHRF and the HKASPDMC, the action of the PTU in withdrawing from the two pro-democracy organizations was "self-deceptive" and could not hide the fact of its "dirty records without regrets."[59] The tone of the commentary was clear: the HKSAR government should pursue its investigation of the PTU further because the union remained as the "protective umbrella of the yellow teachers."[60]

In response to the New China News Agency's open criticisms of the PTU and explicit pressure, the HKSAR government, in the late afternoon on July 31, stated that the EDB decided to terminate all its working relationships with the PTU. The EDB spokesman said that the PTU's remarks and actions were like a political organization.[61] He repeated the *Xinhua* criticisms of the PTU, saying that the union actively participated in the activities of the CHRF and HKASPDMC, that it mobilized teachers to boycott classes, that it politicized the school campuses and that it sacrificed the students' welfare by encouraging teachers to join "violent and illegal activities."[62]

The EDB's formal termination of its relations with the PTU involved several aspects. First, the department would not hold any formal or informal meetings with PTU members. Second, the department would temporarily not handle the requests and cases from the PTU. Third, the EDB's advisory committees would terminate the members from PTU and refuse their participation in the committee work. Fourth, the EDB would no longer recognize the classes and training sessions held by the PTU. As such, teachers who participated in the PTU classes would not have their training recognized by the government. The EDB spokesman finally reiterated the *Xinhua* commentary's arguments, emphasizing that the PTU used its professional nature as a disguise to mislead both teachers and students, to produce teaching materials in support of the 2014 Occupy Central Movement and to participate in the civil disobedience movement.[63] The EDB's political move and gesture were timed to respond to the PRC's official criticisms of the PTU, demonstrating that the HKSAR government implemented Beijing's central directive of implementing the national security law and education wholeheartedly.

On August 1, 2021, two pro-Beijing newspapers in the HKSAR, *Wen Wei Po* and *Ta Kung Pao* launched severe attacks on the PTU. The cover page of *Wen Wei Po* elaborated on the "major crimes" committed by the PTU, including (1) the provision of subsidies for teachers to lead students in the class boycott during the 2012 anti-national education campaign; (2) the production of teaching materials and transport subsidies for teachers to encourage students to participate in the 2014 Occupy Central movement; (3) the publication of remarks of PTU executive members in the 2016 Olympics to denigrate the PRC's national sports team and the toleration of students to show their "disrespect" of the Chinese national flag; (4) the establishment of assistance funds to provide legal aid for teachers arrested in the 2019 anti-extradition bill movement and the usage of "white terror" to refer to those students and teachers who were penalized for violent political participation; (5) the penetration of PTU members into the HKEAA to shape the setting of examination questions and the utilization of Liberal Studies to resist the government's policy of implementing education reforms and (6) the secret meetings with the CHRF and HKASPDMC were accompanied by the PTU's open opposition to the national security law and the March 2021 revamp of the electoral system as well as the PTU chairman Ip Kin-yuen's plot of resigning from the LegCo with other legislators.[64]

To add fuel to the fire of bombarding the PTU with criticisms, *Wen Wei Po* interviewed some pro-Beijing political elites to call for the HKSAR government to replace the PTU, which was "an organization generating chaos to Hong Kong."[65] The chairman of the pro-Beijing FEW, Wong Kwan-yu, hoped that the EDB's action of terminating its relations with the PTU was only the first step to be followed by other necessary actions undertaken by the HKSAR government. The executive member of the Hong Kong Future Education Society, Lee Hiu-ying, remarked that it was a timely action for the government to give warnings to other education organizations through its decisive action against the PTU before the school semester would begin in September.[66] The chairman of the Education Policy Concern Group, Mervyn Cheung, said that if the PTU did not repent and if it continued to play politics, the union should be subsequently punished.[67] A member of the National Security Education Center, Or Chiu-fai, added that the police and the national security officials should see whether the PTU engaged in illegal activities and whether the union should have its asset frozen and status formally revoked.[68] Clearly, pro-Beijing elites and interest group leaders were mobilized by the pro-PRC media to exert pressure on the HKSAR government to take appropriate action against the PTU.

The sister newspaper of *Wen Wei Po*, namely *Ta Kung Pao*, used its cover page to attack the PTU on August 1, 2021 – a phenomenon showing the division of labor and coordinated action between the two newspapers under the leadership of the Liaison Office. *Ta Kung Pao* emphasized the need to "eliminate the poisonous fester of the PTU," echoing the *Xinhua* commentary.[69] It showed the pictures drawn for the PTU chairman, Fung Wai-wah, and its vice-chairman, Ip Kin-yuen.[70] Most importantly, *Ta Kung Pao* criticized the PTU position and issued a rebuttal to each of the four points by elaborating on the "crimes" of the union.[71]

First, in response to the PTU's claim that it promoted professional development and protected the rights and interests of teachers, *Ta Kung Pao* said that the PTU not only provided financial support for the violent teachers who were arrested but also continued to criticize the EDB for revoking the license of a teacher from the Alliance Primary School for using teaching materials that supported "Hong Kong independence."[72] The EDB deregistered this teacher for his lack of "professional ethics" in October 2020, saying that it had already listened to the explanation from the teacher concerned.[73] The EDB said that the teacher unnecessarily indoctrinated students with the ideas of "Hong Kong independence" and a video of the banned Hong Kong National Party.[74] The department had investigated the incident in September 2019, an action followed up by the school's own investigation in April 2020. The EDB's action of revoking the license of the teacher prompted the PTU to conduct an opinion survey of 125 principals of primary and secondary schools. The survey results showed that 70 percent of the respondents believed that the EDB's action of revoking the teacher's license was "unreasonable."[75] Moreover, 80 percent of the respondents found that the EDB's action of reprimanding the principal and deputy principal of the school concerned was "unreasonable." These findings were, according to *Ta Kung Pao*, a political move made by the PTU to "blacken the image of the EDB."[76]

Second, *Ta Kung Pao* said that, as with *Wen Wei Po*, the PTU was by no means concerned about teachers' and students' well-being. It cited the PTU action of supporting the 2014 Occupy Central Movement led by law professor Benny Tai and making teaching materials in Liberal Studies to encourage student participation in the movement.[77] Moreover, the pro-Beijing newspaper criticized the PTU for mobilizing teachers to boycott classes together with students in the anti-extradition movement in 2019.

Third, *Ta Kung Pao* saw the PTU as a political machine "instigating students to participate in protests."[78] As with *Wen Wei Po*, *Ta Kung Pao* referred to the PTU's action of cooperating with Joshua Wong of Scholarism to mobilize students to oppose the national education policy in 2012, and of providing transport subsidies to both teachers and students in their protest activities. Furthermore, in 2014, the PTU was criticized for producing a lot of yellow ribbons for teachers and students to participate in the Occupy Central movement.

Fourth, *Ta Kung Pao* was criticized by the PTU for opposing the development of the Chinese nation and supporting "Hong Kong independence."[79] In March 2015, the PTU organized an activity for secondary school students to read a list of 60 "good books" in which Horace Chin Wan's book on Hong Kong's city-state theory was regarded by *Ta Kung Pao* as "pro-independence."[80] Although some scholars have labeled Horace Chin Wan as the "father" of Hong Kong nationalism, a careful reading of Chin's work showed that he actually advocated the idea that *Huaxia* values should ideally be developed in the mainland based on the core values of Hong Kong.[81] His arguments were supportive of the idea of building up a Greater Hong Kong, but it remains debatable whether he really supported "Hong Kong independence." Furthermore, *Ta Kung Pao* criticized the PTU bookstore for selling some books that could be seen as supportive of "confrontations."[82]

Finally, *Ta Kung Pao* listed eight members of the PTU, who were also the members of the HKSAR government's advisory committees, including Fung Wai-wah, who was a member of the Education Commission.[83] As with *Wen Wei Po*, *Ta Kung Pao* reporters interviewed several pro-Beijing elites, who were all in supportive of the tougher action of the HKSAR government to replace the PTU. These elites included former Chief Secretary C. Y. Leung, Executive Council member Regina Ip, Hong Kong member of the NPC Cai Yi, legislators Holden Chow and Chan Hak-kan, legal expert Fu Kin-chi and deputy president of the Hong Kong and Macau Study Association Lau Siu-kai.[84] They all came to a consensus that the PTU's "damages" were "tremendous."[85]

Hence, the pattern of the PRC's attacks on the PTU was as follows: (1) the commentary from the New China News Agency triggered the official PRC criticisms, (2) the publication of the commentary in the official website of the Liaison Office, (3) the immediate response from the HKSAR government to terminate its relations with the PTU, (4) the coordinated work of *Wen Wei Po* and *Ta Kung Pao* to launch attacks on the PTU and (5) the mobilization of the pro-Beijing elites to express their views against the PTU and in support of further action taken by the HKSAR government. The entire saga illustrated the political struggle initiated by PRC authorities in the Hong Kong style of Cultural Revolution.

In response to the government's termination of its relations with PTU and the criticisms from *Xinhua*, the union responded in its press release on July 31. First, the PTU stressed that, according to the existing education and employment ordinances, it had to manage and enquire into the complaints from teachers.[86] If the EDB refused to deal with the cases transferred by the PTU, this action would affect the interest and welfare of teachers. Moreover, the PTU played a "positive role" in the protection of employees' rights and the improvement of government policies. If the HKSAR government terminated its working relations with the PTU, it would be a loss to the whole educational profession.[87] The

PTU appealed to the government to understand that it was a representative body whose communication and interaction with officials were necessary. In response to *Xinhua*'s criticisms, the PTU stressed that it was an organization promoting, protecting and developing the interests of teachers, that it was concerned about the well-being of teachers and students, that it attached importance to students' safety, that it did not instigate students to participate in protests, that it was concerned about the Chinese nation's development, that it opposed "Hong Kong independence," and that it would continue to listen to the opinions of the society for the sake of performing well in its professional work.[88] Apparently, the PTU was on the defensive, reiterating its positive role as an interest group in the advancement of the interests of teachers and students.

On August 1, *Wen Wei Po* and *Ta Kung Pao* continued to launch their fierce attacks on the PTU. The front page of *Wen Wei Po* criticized the PTU's 100-word reaction as containing six lies.[89] First, it said the PTU mobilized students to boycott classes on June 13 and 14, 2019, while encouraging teachers to explain to students on the implications of the extradition bill. Second, it criticized the PTU for shirking its responsibility by informing teachers to remind students of their risks if students participated in the class boycott and political activities. Third, *Wen Wei Po* criticized the PTU for assisting "yellow" teachers to participate in the government's advisory committees, and yet these "yellow" teachers expressed their "extreme political views" to influence the students.[90] Fourth, the PTU had never mentioned the 14th five-year plan and the Greater Bay Area (GBA) blueprint of the PRC government, and its former deputy chairman Cheung Yui-fai portrayed the young people of the GBA as "confrontational" to "international social citizenship."[91] Hence, the PTU was regarded as "opposing" China's national plan and development. Fifth, the PTU "blackened" the image of the HKSAR government by rejecting the "fact" that Liberal Studies "alienated" students, and it also opposed the government's efforts at inspecting the textbooks of the subject. Furthermore, the PTU "opposed" the implementation of the new Citizenship and Social Development curriculum. Sixth, the PTU tolerated not only some radical students to engage in "pro-independence" activities in 2016, but also a teacher to reserve 50 minutes in his class plan to introduce the platform of the banned Hong Kong National Party (HKNP) and prepare 35 minutes for students to discuss topics related to the HKNP, Tibetan, Xinjiang and Taiwan "independence" in 2020.[92] *Wen Wei Po* editorialized on the same day to call for the HKSAR government to analyze the issues deeply, to lead educational organizations and the school managers to realize the "real face" of the PTU, and to ensure that teachers' interests would not be affected in the process of terminating the relations with the PTU.[93]

Established in 1973, the PTU had a track record of fighting for the interests of teachers. It also became a hotbed of producing pro-democracy elites in Hong Kong's political arena. The late chairman, Szeto Wah (1974–1990), was a highly respected pro-democracy leader who opposed the referendum movement launched by some radical democrats in 2009.[94] After Szeto Wah gradually faded away from the political scene, the PTU was led by Cheung Man-kwong from 1990 to 2010. Cheung went to the Liaison Office in the summer of 2010 to negotiate with PRC officials over an acceptable model of political reform. However, with the election of the new chairman, Fung Wai-wah in 2010, Hong Kong's political landscape gradually shifted to the dominance of localism and radicalism, while Beijing's officials responsible for Hong Kong matters also shifted to more conservatively nationalistic than ever before.[95] As a result, the deteriorating relations between the PTU and the HKSAR government on the one hand, and the PTU and PRC officials on the other hand, made the break with the PTU inevitable, especially after the promulgation of the national security law in June 2020.

On August 3, *Ta Kung Pao* published reports and commentaries supportive of the HKSAR government to take action to revoke the PTU's license. A commentary written by Lau Yung-fei pointed to the political nature of the PTU in opposing the HKSAR government's education reform in 2000, rejecting the proposed legislation on Article 23 of the Basic Law in 2003, mobilizing people to participate in the 2014 Occupy Central movement and participating in the parade against the extradition bill in 2019.[96] It called for the Registry of Trade Unions to revoke the PTU's license because Article 34 of the Trade Union Ordinance's says that a union's expenditure should not be used for political purposes.[97] However, the fact that the PTU assisted four teachers whose licenses were revoked because of their participation in the anti-extradition bill movement in 2019 showed the union's political action. As such, the police, according to Lau, should investigate the PTU and take necessary action. Furthermore, Lau cited Article 7 of the Trade Union Ordinance and said that the Registrar of trade unions could exercise the decision to reject the registration of a union that did not abide by the Ordinance. The argument of Lau's commentary marked an unofficial view that constituted a lobbying effort at the government to take strong action against the PTU. To give more weight to Lau's arguments, *Ta Kung Pao* referred to Article 10 of the Trade Union Ordinance, which empowered the Registrar of Trade Unions to revoke the license of a union whose expenditure might be used for "illegal" purposes.[98] The pro-Beijing newspaper interviewed two legal experts, Fu Kin-chi and Kung Ching-yee, who concurred that the PTU allegedly breached the Trade Union Ordinance by establishing an "arbitration and urgent assistance fund" to help teachers whose licenses were revoked because of their involvement in the violent protests in 2019.[99] It highlighted a new interest group, namely the Post-PTU Era, which sent three representatives to the PTU headquarters and to reprimand the union for "allowing politics to hijack education" and "misleading the education sector to move on a deviated path."[100] Combining elite interviews with reports, commentaries and interest group activity, *Ta Kung Pao* skillfully orchestrated the demand for the PTU to be investigated and penalized by the government authorities.

When asked by the media on whether the PTU's license would be revoked, Chief Executive Carrie Lam remarked that such an action would require a solid legal foundation and evidence.[101] She could not comment on whether the government was really investigating the PTU, but Lam stressed that the bottom line of the national security law could not be touched.[102] The Chief Executive mentioned the PTU's phenomenon of letting politics "hijack the entire educational sector."[103] Lam said that although she had attended the PTU's 45th-anniversary banquet in May 2018, the PTU later deviated from its objectives and "violated its professionalism," especially during the 2019 disturbances.[104] When asked whether the government's termination of its relations with the PTU would affect the education sector, Carrie Lam stressed that her administration would continue to communicate with other education groups and organizations. By implication, even if the government terminated the relations with PTU and might consider revoking its license, the government's consultation with other stakeholders in the education sector would not be affected.

On August 6, the pro-Beijing *Wen Wei Po* and *Ta Kung Pao* continued to launch fierce attacks on the PTU. An "experienced commentator," named Fong Ching-chi, said that the reform of Hong Kong's education system, including the PTU, needed a "thunderbolt" approach instead of a "softline" and "pardoned" approach as advocated by some "open-minded people."[105] It said that students in the campuses of secondary schools and universities became "violent protestors" in the anti-extradition movement in the latter half of 2019, and as such, they should not be "spoiled" and should be punished in accordance with the law.[106] The commentary concluded that the liberal-minded advocates of a soft-line approach made a mistake because, for Hong Kong to return to political and social normalcy, it was necessary to govern Hong Kong by adopting a punitive approach.[107] Given the tendency of *Ta Kung Pao* to delineate its official position through various commentaries, Fong's advocacy of adopting the hardline measure to punish the PTU was reflective of the PRC's official belief. On the same day, an editorial of *Wen Wei Po* echoed the hardline approach advocated by *Ta Kung Pao*. The editorial criticized the PTU's move of setting up a center for teachers and students to learn Chinese history and culture was merely a political show "deceiving" its critics.[108] It called for the HKSAR government to investigate the PTU by using the Trade Unions Ordinance and the Societies Ordinance. Clearly, the pro-Beijing media continued to exert tremendous pressure on the HKSAR government to take action against the PTU.

On August 10, the PTU executive committee announced that it would dissolve the entire union amidst tremendous pressure (Table 4.1). Its chairman Fung Wai-wah said that its 200 staff members would be dismissed with a compensation payment, that the PTU would sell its assets to fund the dismissal payment, that it would stop the legal litigation fund that was criticized by the pro-Beijing media, that the union would expedite the process of helping those teachers whose licenses were revoked by the EDB and that it would stop handling applicants for membership.[109] Operating since 1973, the PTU eventually failed to tackle the prospects of having its license revoked by the government and the pressure of stopping its anti-governmental activities.

On August 11, *Xinhua* carried a commentary that pushed the HKSAR government to continue investigating the PTU for its "illegal" activities, notably its relationships with the CHRF and HKASPDMC.[110] As with the previous

Table 4.1 Events Leading to the Dissolution of the Professional Teachers Union

Time	Events
March 14	PTU announced that "due to the recent political circumstances, it decides to stop participating in the work and operation of the Civil Human Rights Front, and that this announcement was effective immediately.
June	PTU withdrew from the Alliance in Support of Patriotic and Democratic Movement in China.
July 31	*Xinhua* and *People's Daily* criticized the PTU severely as a "political organization" and a "poisonous fester" that should be eliminated. The EDB terminated its relationship with the PTU and no longer recognized it as an educational professional organization. PTU expressed its disappointment and regret toward the EDB decision, saying that as an organization with 95,000 members, it did have representativeness. As such, terminating relations with the PTU would be a loss to the whole educational profession.
August 1	EDB said PTU chairman Fung Wai-wah's position in the Education Commission was not reappointed after June.
August 2	Chief Executive Carrie Lam criticized the PTU for having its political position "hijack" the whole educational profession, bringing anti-governmental and anti-central government sentiments into schools, hijacking the entire educational sector and being unfair to teachers. The PTU's executive committee held a meeting to discuss its future affairs.
August 3	The Secretary for Education Kevin Yeung criticized the PTU for not appealing to teachers and students to abide by the law, and for encouraging teachers and students to violate the law and deviating from the behavior of the educational profession. Tam Yiu-chung, a Hong Kong member of the SCNPC, supported the government's move and he hoped that the PTU would return to the correct path rather than having close relations with organizations that are "anti-China and making Hong Kong chaotic." PTU sent a letter to all members, saying that it would focus on the educational profession and the work on their rights. It would continue to serve members and work as a union. It reiterated that the union supported peace, rationality and non-violence.
August 4	PTU announced that it withdrew from the independent Confederation of Trade Unions. The PTU's litigation and emergency support fund would focus on the employers–employees disputes and rights-related issues.
August 5	PTU announced that it would withdraw from the Education International and that it would set up a Chinese History and Culture Work Group whose adviser would be the former chairman Cheung Man-kwong.
August 6	PTU put down all its textbooks and reference materials supportive of the 2014 Occupy Central and civil disobedience movement. The bookstore had already been closed in June and it was changed to a reception desk and staff office.
August 10	PTU announced that it was dissolved.
September 11	PTU held a general meeting of its members. Only 140 attended and 95 percent of them voted for the PTU's dissolution.

Source: "PTU press conference: announcing its dissolution, chair Fung Wai-wah says many solutions cannot tackle the crisis," August 10, 2021, in 教協記者會｜宣布解散　會長馮偉華：多個方案都難解當前危機｜香港01｜社會新聞 (hk01.com), access date: August 10, 2021. Also see *Wen Wei Po*, August 11, 2021, p. A2 and *Ta Kung Pao*, September 12, 2021.

commentary in *Xinhua*, this commentary criticized the PTU for supporting teachers and students in the 2019 violent protests, for being "unpatriotic" and "anti-China," and for politicizing the operation of teachers' union. On August 12, *Ta Kung Pao* used its front page to highlight the PTU's swift move of deleting "the evidence of crime" on its website, including the union's criticisms of the court ruling on the leaders and activists of the 2014 Occupy Central Movement in April 2019, its mobilization of teachers to support the class boycott in June 2019 against the extradition bill, its criticisms of the HKSAR government for "exercising political censorship" in the process of using new textbooks for Citizenship and Social Development, its denunciation of the community quarantine measures during Covid-19 pandemic in September 2020 for exerting pressure on teachers and students, and its condemnation of the EDB for politicizing education by reforming Liberal Studies in November 2020.[111] Like *Ta Kung Pao*, *Wen Wei Po* on August 12 highlighted the PTU's malpractices, including its decision to disband the union without the approval of its members and its move to set up a special fund for staff members without any approval from the meeting of ordinary members.[112] The *Xinhua* commentary and the coverage in *Ta Kung Pao* and *Wen Wei Po* had one thing in common: they all exerted pressure on the HKSAR government to investigate the "illegal" moves of the PTU.

While many teachers and members of the PTU flocked to its headquarters in Mongkok to buy daily necessities from its supermarket, *Wen Wei Po* and *Tai Kung Pao* highlighted the importance of other teachers' groups, notably the FEW and the Education Professional Alliance, to replace the PTU and continued to work for the interests of teachers.[113] The message of the two pro-Beijing dailies was clear: the PTU was replaceable while exerting continuous pressure on the HKSAR government to investigate and pursue its "illegal" activities. Pro-Beijing legislator Mok Pui-fan wrote so far as to appeal to the HKSAR authorities to "bring the leaders of PTU to justice."[114] The new politics of the HKSAR was characterized by the politically assertive role of *Ta Kung Pao* and *Wen Wei Po* to attack the PRC's political enemies in the HKSAR by working side by side with the mainland mass media, by highlighting the PTU's "illegal" moves, and by grasping the political opportunities to promote the new political clients loyal to Beijing.

The PTU's fate was indirectly undermined by the CHRF, which had become the main target of suppression by the PRC and Hong Kong national security authorities after the promulgation of the national security law in late June 2020. The CHRF was found to be an unregistered company according to the Societies Ordinance, meaning that its financial sources and information on the organization of the annual July 1 rallies were problematic and became the targets of police investigation.[115] As a result, many groups affiliated with the CHRF had to withdraw for the sake of protecting themselves, including the PTU, the Kaifong and Neighborhood Friends Association (KNFA), the Association for Democracy and People's Livelihood, the Democratic Party, the Civic Party, the already dissolved Neo-Democrats, the already disbanded Power for Democracy, the Chinese Democracy University and the Justice and Peace Commission of the Hong Kong Catholic Diocese (JPCHKCD).[116] The pro-Beijing media reported that a number of protests organized by the CHRF were "instigating violence," including the protests on July 1, 2019; August 31, 2019; September 15, 2019; October 1, 2019; October 20, 2019; July 1, 2020; and the rally on October 1, 2020.[117] Most importantly, the public donations raised by the CHRF on the streets during its annual and open rallies were subject to police investigation, including its accounts which according to *Wen Wei Po* belonged to the KNFA and JPCHKCD. The CHRF was involved in the organization of a "612 Humanitarian Support Fund," which was utilized to support the protestors in 2019.[118] If the PTU was involved in the activities of the CHRF, it naturally became one of the main targets of investigation and severe criticisms. As critics of the PTU argued, if it remained a pure trade union without involving in the activities of other pro-democracy organizations, such as CHRF, its fate might have been different. However, from another perspective, since the PTU belonged to one of the flagships of the pan-democracy camp, its involvement in pro-democracy activities and organizations was ironically inevitable, making it vulnerable under the national security law.

The most lethal blow to the PTU was that its activities were deemed as anti-PRC, anti-HKSAR government and anti-CCP. Its support of the teachers who participated in the 2019 protests and class boycott, and young teachers whose licenses were revoked by the HKSAR government after the implementation of the national security law, and its critique of education reforms carried out by the EDB along the direction of replacing Liberal Studies with Citizenship and Social Development Studies were all seen by national security officials of the mainland and Hong Kong as politically "subversive." The PTU became a core enemy of the mainland Chinese state and the HKSAR administration, a political foe that had to be eliminated, as the mainland media emphasized.

Controversy over History Examination Question and Personnel Politics of Examination Authority

A huge controversy erupted in May 2020 over the content of a question in the history subject paper at the Hong Kong Diploma of Secondary Education (DSE) Examination. The question was set as follows: "From 1900 to 1945, Japan brought about more advantages than disadvantages to China. Do you agree with this statement?" The question then used the materials saying that a university principal in Japan agreed with an idea from an educator in the Qing dynasty that the Japanese Law and Political University set up a school for the Chinese students to shorten the period of finishing their studies in Japan from several years to one year. Another material used by the examination question was a letter written by Wang Xing, who represented the provisional government of the Republic of China in 1912 to a Japanese elderly statesman, requesting that the Japanese stateman's company could make donations for the nationalists to overthrow the Qing dynasty and set up a new government. The person who set the examination question was not revealed because of the confidentiality principle in the Hong Kong Examinations and Assessment Authority (HKEAA), which established an examination committee concerned to set the examination questions for the history subject.

On May 13, a pro-government and pro-Beijing news media, Orange News, reported that a manager responsible for history in the HKEAA's assessment development office, Hans Yeung Wing-yu, had been exposed for his remarks in his social media for saying that "without the Japanese invasion of China, how could we have the new China?"[119] On May 14, the history subject examination was held in the morning. Interestingly, the pro-government and pro-Beijing FEW criticized the question for "one-sidedly saying that Japan promoted China's modernization and for "leading students to be 'traitors.'"[120] Coincidentally, the Office of the Commissioner of the Ministry of Foreign Affairs (OCMFA) of the PRC in the HKSAR made an unprecedented move by announcing that it suspected the senior staff of the HKEAA holding a political position that influenced the way in which the question had been set. In response to the criticism, the EDB, on the same night of May 14, made a declaration reprimanding the question and believing that it was "misleading" and "seriously hurting the feeling and dignity of the national citizens who suffered greatly in the Japanese invasion of China."[121] The EDB requested that the HKEAA should follow up with the incident. It appeared that, under the influence of the OCMFA's unprecedented political posture, the EDB had to respond to the criticism, especially if the OCMFA represented the official line of the central government in Beijing.

On the morning of May 15, the HKEAA formally replied that it would seriously manage the issue, but it could not comment on the examination question because of the need to avoid affecting not only the fairness of marking but also the interest of students. It added that the history subject had formed a committee scrutinizing the question, which was acceptable to most of the committee members. The committee had a review mechanism. Nevertheless, the Secretary for Education Kevin Yeung said that the answer had no room for discussion and that it only entailed disadvantages rather than advantages.[122] Yeung announced that he had requested the HKEAA cancel the controversial question for the sake of ensuring fairness to students. The HKEAA, however, said on the same night that the cancelation of the question would deeply affect the examination results of students. On the same day, *Xinhua* criticized the question for "beautifying" the Japanese violent behavior in China, and it said that if the "poisonous" question was not repealed, it would be difficult to appease the anger of the Chinese people.[123] *Xinhua* explicitly asked the HKSAR government to "correct the mistake" and to establish a new education system to adapt to the "one country, two systems."

From the reactions of the stakeholders, several observations can be made. First, objectively speaking, the examination question allowed room for students to agree or disagree with the statement, although the time period of the question concerned touched on a long period from 1900 to 1945, which could be historically divided into at least two stages: the Japanese "assistance" in the modernization of the Republic of China and also its territorial ambition over China from 1900 to 1936, and the formal military invasion and the sufferings of the Chinese people from 1937 to 1945. The materials provided in the question did not really touch on the second stage, opening the door to easy criticisms.

Second, the statement asking whether Japan's invasion did more advantages than disadvantages was academically debatable. Some political historians, like Chalmers Johnson, argued that the Japanese invasion of China created a military vacuum in North China, opened the door for the CCP and its military to be active and acquire considerable Japanese weaponry in 1945, and to defeat the Kuomintang army from 1946 to 1949.[124] If the academic debate were allowed and tolerated, the controversial question could have survived. However, the question setter and the committee members assumed that secondary students were so sophisticated in their knowledge of Chinese history that they could answer such a question covering 45 years in a short period of 20 minutes' answering time. In a nutshell, the examination question was not well set, albeit it was academically defensible and debatable.

Third, even if the question was not asked skillfully, the fact that it allowed students to disagree with the statement and that it was academically defensible meant that the intervention from the OCMFA and *Xinhua* was ultimately political. Political correctness was the principle adopted by both the OCMFA and *Xinhua*, forcing the EDB to follow the same political line. Most importantly, Orange News is pro-Beijing, so as *Wen Wei Po* and *Ta Kung Pao*. The fact that Orange News led the attacks on the HKEAA's managers dealing with the examination question and that this was followed up by the open attacks from *Wen Wei Po* and *Ta Kung Pao* demonstrated the politicization of the controversy over the examination question and the relatively liberal-minded managers working in the HKEAA. Arguably, a Hong Kong style of Cultural Revolution could be seen in the dispute over the controversial examination question, because within two weeks, the attacks from the pro-Beijing media on the HKEAA managers could lead to the resignation of three managers, including Keith Lo, Yeung Chi-yim and finally Hans Yeung Wing-yu.

Fourth, under the heavily politicized circumstances, the HKEAA was under tremendous pressure to repeal the question, even though its public statements were issued with student interest in its mind. Judging from the way in which the HKEAA emphasized the importance of student interest and fairness, its initial reaction was far more politically neutral and professional than the critics assumed. However, on a major controversy tainted with the element of political "correctness," it was understandable that the HKEAA's general secretary, So Kwok-sang, decided to step down at the end of his contract in March 2021 due to "personal reasons."[125] However, PTU chairman Ip Kin-yuen speculated that So's departure was related to the controversy over the examination question in the History subject.[126] Interestingly, So's successor, Wei Xiangdong, was an academic at Lingnan University but was once a member of the Shenzhen CPPCC.[127] Given that CPPCC is a mainland political institution co-opting the people of Hong Kong, Macau and some overseas Chinese, Wei's political background was undoubtedly questioned by the media. The fact that Wei, as a mainland-born academic replacing the Hong Kong-born So Kwok-sang, was arguably a watershed in the leadership of the HKEAA, whose examination questions would need more scrutiny after the controversy over the history examination question in May 2020. Immediately after Wei's appointment as the HKEAA's general secretary, the EDB appointed an ex-officio member to join the HKEAA's examination scrutiny committee – a prominent move by the EDB to ensure more control over how examination questions would be set.[128] Although Wei openly said that the examination scrutiny committee has five members, one of whom is an ex-officio member nominated by the EDB, the image of deliberately enhancing governmental supervision over examination questions could not be avoided.

Fifth, the fact that the FEW criticized the examination question illustrated that it became a pro-Beijing political tool of exerting pressure on the HKSAR government and the HKEAA on the one hand and creating public opinion in support of the cancelation of the controversial question on the other. Together with the pro-Beijing media, such as Orange News, *Wen Wei Po* and *Ta Kung Pao*, the pro-CCP organizations played a crucial role in politicizing the controversy over the problematic examination question, exerting pressure on the HKSAR government and HKEAA to take action.

The controversy over the examination question witnessed a power struggle between pro-Beijing forces and the liberal camp. On May 16, the pro-Beijing official mouthpiece, *People's Daily*, published a commentary pointing to the "poisonous" nature of the Hong Kong education system, which was shown in a "ridiculous" examination question.[129] It severely criticized the HKEAA for its failure to nurture students with a "historical" and "national" identity. The commentary appealed to the HKSAR government to intervene, rectify the situation and ensure the "healthy growth" of the young people. This commentary was timed to exert pressure on the HKSAR government and HKEAA to rectify the "error" of having a politically "incorrect" examination question.

In the face of pressure from PRC authorities and pro-Beijing media, the HKEAA on May 18 held a special meeting to discuss whether the question concerned should be canceled and what kinds of arrangements should be made if it was repealed. At the same time, two pro-student and liberal-minded interest groups – the Secondary School Students Preparatory Platform (SSSPP) and Demosisto – petitioned the HKEAA and presented 60,000 signatures, including the signatures from 1,200 students sitting for the Chinese history examination, against the cancelation of the examination question.

In response to the pressure from PRC authorities, the EDB indicated on May 18 that, according to Article 13 of the Hong Kong Examinations and Assessment Authority Ordinance, the Chief Executive could issue direct instructions to the HKEAA based on "issues that had impacts on public interest."[130] At this juncture, it was clear that the HKSAR government stood firmly on the side of PRC authorities, while the HKEAA was like a political sandwich facing not only the pressure from the government and PRC authorities but also the complaints from student interest groups.

On May 19, Chief Executive Carrie Lam remarked that the incident demonstrated "professional error," that it was highly problematic if the HKEAA did not accept the government's view, that the government did not have any political interference and that she would not shy away from exercising her power in accordance with the ordinance concerned.[131] At this moment, the HKSAR government had to follow the political stance of the central authorities, whose position was firstly clarified by the OCMFA and then reiterated by official agencies like *Xinhua* and the *People's Daily* (Table 4.2).

On May 21, the PTU publicized its opinion poll showing that 97 percent of the 268 front-line teachers opposed any move to repeal the examination question. Yet, such opinion survey result could not alter the political decision already made by the HKSAR government, namely the controversial examination question would have to be scrapped by the HKEAA. On May 22, the HKEAA backed down from political pressure, announcing that the examination question "deviated" from the objective of student learning and assessment, that it was repealed, and that other questions would be counted in the student performance. Three days later, the HKEAA's general secretary, So Kwok-sang, revealed that 51 percent of the students answered the question saying that Japan's invasion of China had more disadvantages than advantages, 38 percent pointing to more advantages than disadvantages and 17 percent just talking about the advantages. The HKEAA appeared to be open in disclosing the assessment result, but it had already made a concession in the face of political pressure from PRC authorities and the HKSAR government.

On June 3, the SSSPP lodged a complaint to the court, trying to stop the HKEAA from repealing the examination question. However, on July 3, the High Court ruled its appeal as a failure, because the court judge said that the entire issue did not show procedural impropriety, and that the decision of repealing the examination question was made after detailed deliberation by the HKEAA.[132] Objectively speaking, the HKEAA had the right of repealing the examination question, but academically speaking, the controversial question was defensible. Most significantly, if the examination question was canceled after the criticisms leveled by PRC authorities and the support from the HKSAR government, the HKEAA was clearly a pawn in the entire political game. One student who attended the court hearing said: "My marks are not the most important matter; I am more concerned about the erosion of academic freedom."[133] At least some students believed that the examination question was academically defensible and debatable, and that its cancelation represented political interference with "academic freedom."

An interesting phenomenon in the entire saga was a revelation in March 2021 that, among the seven members of the history subject committee, two of them came from the EDB – a situation different from the past when there was only one government official sitting in the committee.[134] The PTU vice-president, Ip Kin-yuen pointed out that there was a likelihood of the leakage of the content of the examination question by some members of the committee.[135] A complaint to the Standnews revealed that four of the seven members were actually

Table 4.2 Chronology of the Controversy over the History Examination Question, May–June 2020

Date	Detailed events and development
May 13	Orange News reported that the HKEAA manager (history) Hans Yeung was revealed in his social media that he remarked that "without Japan's invasion of China, how could there be a new China?"
May 14	The DSE History examination was held on the morning of May 14. An examination question, which asked students on whether Japan facilitated China's modernization, was criticized by the Hong Kong Federation of Workers as encouraging students to be "traitors." The OCMFA made a statement and suspected that the HKEAA officers had a political stance that affected the setting of the examination question. It reprimanded the "misleading" examination question, which "seriously hurt the feelings and the dignity of the nationals who suffered tremendously during Japan's invasion of China. The OCMFA requested that the HKEAA should follow up on the issue seriously.
May 15	The HKEAA responded on the morning of May 15 that it would seriously deal with the issue, but for the sake of avoiding the fairness of marking and affecting the interest of examination candidates, it did not comment on the controversy. It also pointed out that the History subject had a committee overseeing the design of examination questions, which were finalized after the consensus of the committee members. Moreover, a review mechanism was also set up. The Secretary for Education, Kevin Yeung, reiterated that the answer to the examination question was clear, meaning that Japan's invasion into China merely had disadvantages. He announced that the EDB had requested the HKEAA to cancel the examination question to ensure equal treatment to all candidates. On the same night of May 15, the HKEAA said that the cancelation of the examination question would affect the results of candidates in the examination with profound implications. On the same day, *Xinhua* criticized the examination question and said that if the "poisonous" question was not repealed, it would be difficult to appease the anger of the sons and daughters of the Chinese peoples. *Xinhua* also called for the HKSAR government to "correct the mistake and establish a new education system suitable for the 'one country, two systems.'"
May 16	A former secretary general of the HKEAA, Choi Chi-cheong, wrote a commentary saying that any cancelation of the public examination question was a serious matter. He urged the government to reconsider the interest of students. Choi wrote: "It is necessary to make decisions based on science and the opinions of scientific expert. In the event that professionalism was abandoned, the consequences would be serious." On the same day, the *People's Daily* said that the education system in the HKSAR must be "cleaned in its bones and poison," that the textbooks concerned must be corrected in their "poisonous content," and that "those people who deliberately spread the poison" must be under investigation.

(Continued)

Table 4.2 Chronology of the Controversy over the History Examination Question, May–June 2020 (Continued)

Date	Detailed events and development
May 18	The EDB sent officers to probe the HKEAA's mechanisms of designing and scrutinizing public examination questions. The HKEAA's executive committee held a special meeting to discuss whether the controversial examination question would be repealed and what kinds of arrangements should be adopted if the question was canceled. Two student interest groups, Secondary School Students Preparatory Platform and Scholarism, collected 60,000 signatures to oppose the cancelation of the examination question and they presented the signatures to the HKEAA. On the other hand, the EDB pointed out that the Chief Executive could invoke Article 13 of the HKEAA Ordinance to issue direct instructions on matters affecting the public interest.
May 19	Chief Executive Carrie Lam regarded the incident as "a professional error," adding that it would be a big problem if the HKEAA did not accept the government's view, and that there was no political interference. However, to protect education and students, she would not avoid exercising the power conferred to her by the related ordinance.
May 21	A survey conducted by the PTU showed that 97 percent of the 268 frontline teachers opposed the cancelation of the examination question.
May 22	The HKEAA announced the cancelation of the examination question, which deviated from the objective of learning and assessment. It would cancel the examination question from the database of examination questions and recalculate the marks obtained by candidates based on their answers to the rest of the questions in the history subject paper.
May 25	The HKEAA secretary general So Kwok-sang revealed that, for the answers to the controversial examination question, 57.1 percent of the candidates said that Japan's invasion into China "had more harm than good," and 38 percent argued that there were "more good than harm." Moreover, 78 percent of the candidates pointed out the harmful aspects, while 17 percent mentioned only the good aspects.
June 3	A student from the Secondary School Students Preparatory Platform filed an appeal to the court for judicial review of the cancelation of the examination question.
June 10	EDB said it would set up a special committee including representatives from the education sector and the HKEAA. It added that the HKEAA would be required to conduct an internal investigation and to submit a report to the special committee for scrutiny and follow-up action.
June 12	The Liaison Office's spokesman pointed out that the controversial examination question misled students to be "anti-China," "anti-police" and to "hurt the national feelings openly." It is believed that the situation reflected the "chaos" in Hong Kong's education system in which young students "seriously lack their national identity and national identification."

Source: Fung Cheuk-yiu, "From an examination question seeing history class: A timeline of the controversy over DSE History subject's examination question," June 30, 2020, in DSE 歷史科試題風波時間線 -教育- 明周文化 (mpweekly.com), access date: August 6, 2021.

Cultural Revolution in the Education Sector 133

pro-EDB.[136] In short, critics of the entire saga argued that there was a coordinated plot to reveal and criticize the examination question, including the criticisms from PRC authorities and the cooperation from the HKSAR government.

The history subject committee, which was responsible for setting and scrutinizing the examination questions, was politicized in the controversy. On May 16, 2020, two examination managers, including Keith Lo and Leung Chi-yim, resigned. Lo and another manager, Hans Yeung Wing-yu, were suddenly attacked by pro-Beijing media and groups for harboring explicit political views on their Facebook.[137] Lo was criticized by the pro-Beijing media for saying that Chief Executive Carrie Lam should leave her position on his Facebook.[138] He was exposed for being politically "dark yellow" or very liberal because of his open appreciation of Chan Kin-man, one of the three organizers of the 2014 Occupy Central movement.[139] Critics of Lo said that the examination questions tended to be political – a reflection of the political orientation of HKEAA officers.[140] Lo was accused of having "bias" in the appointment of politically liberal teachers, notably Cheung Yui-fai, as a chairman of the examination paper committee and a supervisor of the Liberal Studies projects.[141] Hans Yeung was also personally attacked by pro-Beijing media for asking people to buy the British Hong Kong flag.[142] Both were openly labeled as the so-called "black hands" behind the controversial examination question.[143] The *Xinhua* criticized the HKEAA officers for being "anti-China and creating chaos to Hong Kong."[144] In March 2021, the EDB appointed some officials into the HKEAA's committee dealing with the history subject's examination questions.[145] It was natural that, after the saga over the examination question concerned, the EDB would like to appoint its politically "correct" officers into the HKEAA's examination scrutiny committee dealing with the history questions for the sake of stabilizing the situation and avoiding another similar incident. However, the entire saga leading to the resignation of three HKEAA managers – Keith Lo, Leung Chi-yim and Hans Yeung – proved to be highly political, openly targeted (especially Lo and Yeung) and swiftly pressured. Ip Kin-yuen, the PTU chairman, said that the resignation of Lo and Leung illustrated the occurrence of "white terror."[146] With regard to the resignation of Hans Yeung, the HKEAA stated that it did not pressure him to resign.[147] If the politics of education reform entail a purge of political enemies, the three officers' resignation was a matter of time.

In November 2020, HKEAA manager Hans Yeung, who dealt with the Chinese history subject, eventually left after he had resigned in July. He revealed that the EDB was like "a sleeping lion" that intervened when an incident took place.[148] Yeung defended the examination question, which to him did not have problems in its design and content. However, he said that on May 13, when Orange News criticized his remarks on Facebook, the pro-Beijing *Wen Wei Po* and *Ta Kung Pao* followed up and interviewed him, escalating the entire incident further. When *Ta Kung Pao* on May 14 questioned two examination managers for their political neutrality, it was clear to Yeung that the pro-Beijing media took the initiative in the struggle against liberal-minded managers in the HKEAA. On the night of May 14, legislator Holden Chow from the pro-Beijing

DAB and the FEW leveled criticisms at the HKEAA – a move followed by the OCMFA's statement on the same night that Hong Kong's education system could not be uncontrolled. Yeung revealed that an examination question setter later wrote a report to the senior management of the EDB and the report said that the question concerned was "neither suitable for educational purpose nor suitable for a public examination that aims at differentiating students' abilities objectively."[149] According to Yeung, his liberal political views prompted the Liaison Office to notice him and "open his file" as early as 2017, because of two examination questions in 2017 – one asking students to express their views on whether China envisaged changes in the leadership principles after the CCP had come to power in the mainland in 1949, and another asking students on the worries of the people of Hong Kong about the city's development after 1997.[150] He claimed that the HKEAA was already infiltrated with pro-Beijing supporters, thereby undermining its neutrality and politicizing its operation. Yeung added that the decision of the 17-member Council of the HKEAA to cancel the examination question in May 2020 proved that the Council was by no means politically neutral.[151] The PTU chairman, Ip Kin-yuen, remarked that the cancelation of the examination question demonstrated not only the "supremacy of politics over education" but also the emergence of a Cultural Revolution in the HKSAR.[152] The politicization of the HKEAA came from both inside and outside.

Objectively speaking, one of the two examination questions that Yeung mentioned in the 2017 DSE on history was politically provocative and sensitive but academically defensible and debatable. One question asked students how they reacted to the report from Chairman Mao Zedong to the Seventh NPC meeting prior to the war with Japan in 1945.[153] Mao said that the one-party dictatorship of the Kuomintang (KMT) collapsed, that the KMT, CCP and independent parties should set up a coalition government, that "a really democratically elected government" needed the people's freedom. Then the question asked students to comment that, if they were intellectuals in China in 1945, would they support the CCP? Such a question was liberally phrased – a position that naturally aroused the political sensitivity of pro-Beijing and pro-CCP critics, who must regard the question setter as politically "incorrect" and "disloyal" to the CCP. Another question in the 2017 history examination paper was to ask students whether they agreed that the question of Hong Kong's future after 1997 "increased the political consciousness of the Hong Kong people."[154] Such a question appeared to encourage students to express their views toward the identity of Hong Kong people. Unfortunately, after the anti-extradition movement in 2019, PRC's hardline and conservatively nationalistic authorities viewed the local Hong Kong identity as a menace to the CCP. If Yeung's liberal-minded approach to setting examination questions was regarded as a potential "threat" to the PRC's national security, especially after the enactment of the national security law in late June 2020, the attacks launched by pro-Beijing media on him and Keith Lo were highly political, aiming at removing the liberal-minded managers of the HKEAA.

A careful reading of the History subject's examination questions in 2017 showed that one question, apart from the two questions mentioned above, was highly political and might arouse the sensitivity of PRC authorities. The question cited the opinion surveys of the Hong Kong people in 1982, showing that 70 percent of the respondents supported the idea of Hong Kong remaining as a colony, 15 percent supportive of the idea that Hong Kong would be "a trustee city under the management of the United Nations but it would not be autonomous," and only 4 percent accepting Hong Kong's sovereignty administrative return to China.[155] While the opinion survey's answers were already politically sensitive to pro-Beijing elites and PRC authorities, the question asked in 2017 was really provocative – by using the materials in the opinion survey, do you think that the worries expressed by the respondents in the survey "still existed in 1990"? Since 1990 was the year immediately after the June 4th 1989 Tiananmen tragedy during which the People's Liberation Army (PLA) was sent to suppress the student demonstrators on the Tiananmen Square, and since many Hong Kong people in 1990 were deeply anxious about Hong Kong's political future, the examination question asked in the 2017 History subject paper was highly politically sensitive. The year 2017 had already been politically sensitive to PRC officials responsible for Hong Kong matters, because the anti-national education campaign in the summer of 2012, the Occupy Central movement in 2014, the Mongkok riots in early 2016 and the disqualification of two localist legislators-elect in late 2016 prompted Beijing to see localism in the HKSAR as a "threat" to its sovereignty over Hong Kong. Therefore, the examination questions designed for the 2017 History subject paper were politically provocative and likely unacceptable to PRC authorities, who eventually seized a golden opportunity of purging the HKEAA's liberal-minded managers less than one year after the promulgation of the national security for Hong Kong in late June 2020.

Yeung unveiled that he had to resign earlier for the purpose of maintaining his long service payment.[156] If a report on the controversial examination question was completed, he could have been dismissed immediately without the right of acquiring long service payment and with his reputation damaged.[157] As such, early resignation was his best option. Yeung referred to the entire controversy as a kind of Cultural Revolution in the HKSAR.[158] Objectively speaking, if the PRC's Cultural Revolution was characterized by personnel struggles, media attacks and factional rivalries, the saga over the history examination question in May 2020 did exhibit the features of Cultural Revolution-style struggles. In August 2021, Yeung left Hong Kong for the UK.

The mainlandization of Hong Kong's education system could be vividly seen. First, the liberal-minded managers of the HKEAA were the targets of political struggles. Purging them would pave the way for the occupation of the examination scrutiny committee of the history subject by politically "correct" and "patriotic" elites. Second, the pro-Beijing media led by Orange News, *Wen Wei Po* and *Ta Kung Pao* were very effective in attacking, labeling and removing the political "troublemakers" in the HKEAA, opening the door to a much smoother process of implementing national security education and Chinese history education. The version of modern Chinese history has to be politically "correct" and "loyal" to the CCP – a point emphasized in China's "comprehensive jurisdiction" over the HKSAR. Third, as the CCP approached its centennial anniversary in the year 2021, the attack on the HKEAA and the removal of its liberal-minded managers could be regarded as the precondition paving the way for the celebration of the CCP's achievements and contributions to China during its centennial anniversary in 2021.

Fourth, the philosophy of designing the history subject's examination questions changed significantly in May 2020, when the HKSAR government, under the PRC's pressure, instructed the HKEAA to cancel the controversial examination question. Hans Yeung revealed in May 2021 that, from 2012 to May 2020, he and his colleagues adopted the philosophy of designing examination questions for students to express their views flexibility in "an unfamiliar but a pluralistic and complex setting."[159] However, given that political "correctness" emerged as the most important ideological principle in May 2020, when PRC authorities objected to the controversial examination question, the different philosophies between Yeung and his examination team on the one hand and PRC authorities on the other could be easily seen. Specifically, while Yeung and his colleagues adopted a liberal, flexible but critical approach, PRC authorities opted for a far more politically monolithic and "correct" attitude toward Chinese history-related examination questions. Obviously, the liberal ideology adopted by Yeung and his like-minded examination officers was contrary to the authoritarian ideology held by PRC officials. The leaders of the HKSAR government, including Chief Executive Carrie Lam and Secretary for Education Kevin Yeung, became the loyal agents following the order from the central authorities in Beijing.

Fifth, a new pattern of "Cultural Revolution" could be seen in the HKSAR: the first shot was made by *Orange News*, the second one followed by *Wen Wei Po* and *Ta Kung Pao*, the third powerful trigger was made by the OCMFA and *Xinhua*, exerting tremendous pressure on the HKSAR government to follow suit and HKEAA to make concessions. Given that a company controlled by the Liaison Office, Guangdong Xin Wenhua, owned 88 percent of *Wen Wei Po* and 99.9 percent of *Ta Kung Pao* as early as 2015, that the two newspapers are filled with mainland reporters and editors sticking to the line of the CCP and that Orange News was controlled by the pro-Beijing Sino United Publishing Company, their attacks on the examination question and the HKEAA managers represented an official line of initiating the political purge.[160] If political struggle characterized Chinese politics during the Cultural Revolution, a Hong Kong-style of political struggle could be seen in the controversy over the history examination question in May 2020.

Targeting Students and Student Unions

A row erupted in July 2021 when the Hong Kong University Students' Union Council (HKUSUC) passed a resolution to "mourn" and "appreciate" a man named Leung Kin-fai who stabbed at the back of a police officer in Causeway

Bay on July 1 and who then committed suicide and died on the same day.[161] The incident aroused the criticisms of pro-government elites and the media. In response to public criticisms, the HKUSUC withdrew the resolution while 11 members of the HKUSUC and 4 members of the Student Union's executive committee resigned. On August 4, the Council of the University of Hong Kong (CHKU), which was chaired by Professor Arthur Li, held a special meeting and decided that all those students participating in the HKUSUC would be barred from entering the HKU campus and utilizing the university facilities and services until further notice.[162] Cheung Tat-ming, a law professor, resigned from his position as a member of the CHKU, saying that the decision of the Council to stop the students who attended the HKUSUC meeting on July 7 from entering the campus and using university services appeared to "exceed its power."[163] According to the terms of reference of the CHKU, it is a governing body of the university and is responsible for the management, human resources and future development. However, on August 6, seven members of the Court of the HKU, which has the power to make, repeal and amend statutes, issued an open letter to the CHKU, requesting that the decision of barring the students concerned from entering the campus and using its services and facilities should be withdrawn.[164] The seven members of the Court included the deputy convenors of the HKU Alumni Concern Group, Mak Tung-wing and Chiu Kit-yee. Their open letter said that the CHKU penalty on the students did not touch on the behavior under the HKU Ordinance, that a discipline committee should deal with the cases of students even if they were ruled by the local court for violating the law, and that the CHKU decision was made on the basis of depriving the learning opportunity of students – a decision not in conformity with the educative expectation of guiding university students to the right path.[165]

The letter from the Court members aroused a strong reaction from *Ta Kung Pao*, which editorialized on August 7 and accused the Court of mixing up black and white.[166] It said that the resolution of the HKUSUC aroused a public outcry and prompted the police's national security section to investigate. Moreover, the decision adopted by the CHKU was "affirmed" by all societal sectors.[167] Yet, seven members of the Court issued an open letter that "did not mention a single word on the act of students in beautifying a terrorist."[168] The editorial said that it was natural for the school management to punish students who commit mistakes or who were suspected of violating the law, and that there was no need to wait for the students to be arrested first and then followed by punishment.[169] The editorial criticized the logic of the open letter as "tolerating and cultivating traitors."[170] It went so far as to criticize the letter as "ridiculous" and seven Court members as "singing songs curvedly for terrorist activity."[171] *Ta Kung Pao* concluded that the letter's content reflected the "deep-seated contradictions" in Hong Kong's education, which should be rectified and where "the dirty waters" should be cleaned and eliminated.[172] The strongly worded editorial of *Ta Kung Pao* reflected the official line of PRC authorities in the HKSAR.

In response to the open letter, the HKU spokesman said that the CHKU adopted the necessary measure to deal with risk management rather than penalizing the students concerned.[173] As the highest managerial body, the CHKU had to ensure proper risk management. The decision of the CHKU, according to the spokesman, did consider the safety, reputation and legal liability incurred by the HKUSUC. The way in which the CHKU handled the student activists showed that the controversy over the "mourning" of a "terrorist" who attempted to kill a police officer became heavily politicized and polarized.

Impacts on Teachers and Students: Outward Migration

The impacts of the Hong Kong style of Cultural Revolution could be felt among many teachers and students, whose middle-class backgrounds tended to opt for outward migration. In November 2020, many middle-class families migrated from Hong Kong to other places, leading to the withdrawal of some students from their studies in prestigious schools. The Diocesan Girls' School made a rare move in admitting students to join the first semester of Form 1 to Form 4 classes from 2020 to 2021 – a move that showed not only the withdrawal of some middle-class students but also the impact of the implementation of the national security law, which frightened many middle-class parents.[174] Another famous school, the Ying Wah College, admitted that the first semester of 2020 witnessed the withdrawal of 50 students and that the second semester lost 10 more students.[175] The Heep Yunn School saw 30 students withdrawing from their studies in the first semester of 2020–2021. One of the schools that belonged to the Anglican Church group acknowledged that a withdrawal rate of two to three percent could be seen in the semesters of 2020.[176] One unnamed school envisaged the loss of 40 students at one Form alone, showing the sudden withdrawal of students and their immigration.[177] Some schools continued to admit students in the whole academic year of 2020–2021, reflecting the rapid loss of students and the quest for replacing their loss. A school principal who refused to be named said: "My school has a high rate of students being admitted to local universities. Normally very few students changed schools at the senior high level, but this year is exceptional in that there are many withdrawals."[178] Prestigious private and public schools were most affected, according to him. The tide of student withdrawal meant that schools at the second tier saw their students moving up to fill in the places at the first-tiered prestigious schools. The impact of student migration filtered downward to the primary and secondary schools, creating a vicious cycle in which schools at higher tiers had to care about their number of students and to grasp students from lower tiers.

Tang Fei, the FEW vice-chairman, admitted that international schools also advertised to admit students in September 2020, showing the outflow of students. He remarked that "parents and students use their legs to vote," and that the situation of schools in the Northern, Tsuen Wan and Kwai Tsing districts was serious because of the combined effects of relying on students who lived across the border in the mainland and students who withdrew to either migrate or move up to higher-tiered schools.[179] In the past, schools had an unwritten consensus that they did not accept students in the middle of the semester, but now there was no need for coordination after the semester began because the withdrawal of students was continuous and serious.[180] Tang Fei added that schools that were affected by student withdrawal had to admit students with weaker capability because the priority was to fill up the vacant places.[181] A school principal concluded that the second tier of schools was the most affected ones, because students with weak capability would continue to stay in schools at the third tier. Many students at Form 5 and Form 6 at the secondary level tended to move to other schools at the higher tier. Some principals worried that, in the long run, some schools would be eliminated because of their inability of getting enough students.[182] Ultimately, how to restore the confidence of parents would be a factor shaping the survival and sustainability of schools at the primary and secondary levels.

In February 2021, a survey of 98 principals conducted by the Hong Kong Secondary School Principals Association (HKSSPA) showed that the number of withdrawal of students from their studies between July and November 2020 reached 1,474 – an increase of 23 percent compared with 1,195 during the same period in 2019.[183] Forms 1, 2, 3 and 6 were the most affected in the phenomenon of student withdrawal. Half (723) of the 1,474 students left their schools because of immigration. Similarly, 235 teachers left their schools in 2020 – an increase of almost 50 percent compared with the situation of 205 teachers leaving their schools in 2019. Many teachers who left their schools were experienced ones with more than 20 years of teaching experience. Among the 235 teachers who left, 28 of them retired earlier and 4 of them decided to change professions. Moreover, 80 percent of the school principals believed that the number of students withdrawing from their studies would increase, while 75 percent of them perceived the same situation for teachers. Many school principals were worried about the problems of having difficulties retaining good students, who would move to study in other schools, and maintaining the development of schools in many aspects, such as good teaching quality, group solidarity, planning and sustainability. They urged that the EDB should allow more autonomy to schools, reduce intervention in school planning, promote the policy of small class teaching, allow students residing in the mainland to return to study in Hong Kong, and minimize the crisis of eliminating classes in schools that were affected by the decline in student enrolment.

The anxiety of school principals was reasonable, especially the question of replenishing the teachers who left the HKSAR. In August 2021, it was reported that the EDB advertised for 26 teaching assistant positions, including positions vacated at famous schools such as King's College and Queen's College.[184] The FEW vice-chairman Tang Fei regarded this phenomenon as "rare," adding that teaching positions would demand for replacement even in September, and that schools were in a passive situation in response to the tide of immigration. On the other hand, some experienced teachers at the directly subsidized schools changed their jobs to work in government schools in the capacity of being freelancers and they enjoyed good pay and a more relaxed teaching schedule.[185] Tang observed that the teaching atmosphere at some traditionally famous schools was "very bad" because the departure of students affected the mood of teachers, who also wanted to leave their positions.[186] He appealed to the government to look for solutions, such as freezing the structure of classes at various levels and allowing students who resided in the mainland to return to study in the HKSAR.

Many middle-class families lost their political confidence in the HKSAR. A family of four members immigrating to Britain in July 2020 revealed that its father abandoned his job in the HKSAR, while his daughter and son changed from studying in Hong Kong to that in Britain.[187] The father said that the Hong Kong education system collapsed, making him lose the confidence and prompting him to bring his family to Britain. He added that the national security law was intimidating and leading to social instability. The implementation of the national security law "accelerated my decision to leave as the society was too unstable and unsafe."[188] Another father with a son and a daughter told the authors that he decided to bring the whole family, including his wife and parents, to Britain, because the education system in the HKSAR under the national security law was "chaotic," especially as his wife was a secondary school teacher.[189] Some secondary school teachers were frightened to teach politically sensitive courses, like Citizenship and Social Development, under the national security law. The suggestion from some pro-government legislators that video cameras should be installed in classrooms had the unintended consequence of frightening many teachers at the primary and secondary school levels.

For some teachers teaching Liberal Studies, they had to find a way out of the political predicament as some were reluctant to teach the new Citizenship and Social Development subject. One experienced teacher who taught Liberal Studies decided to immigrate to Britain. He wrote in June 2020: "I think you understand that the forthcoming socio-political environment in Hong Kong will not be optimistic. As a Hong Kong high school teacher who teaches Liberal Studies, Chinese History and History, I feel that the socio-political environment may not permit me to stay in Hong Kong to teach students in the long run. Permanent departure from Hong Kong is not an easy decision and I hope that God will lead and bless me."[190] Indeed, those teachers who taught increasingly politically sensitive subjects, like History, Chinese History and Citizenship and Social Development, have to be careful in their teaching pedagogy, remarks and comments inside and outside classrooms under the national security law. Faced with tremendous pressure, some of them decided to leave the teaching profession. For those who stay and persist, they must adapt to the changing political circumstances.

One case highlighted in the media was Cheung Yui-fai, who was a Liberal Studies teacher and who decided in June 2020 to opt for early retirement. Teaching for 30 years and joining the teaching profession after the democracy movement in the PRC in 1989, Cheung belonged to the first generation of Liberal Studies teachers, but he admitted that the EDB had already set the red lines and that it would be "difficult to return to the professional autonomy in the past."[191] In June 1989, Cheung was a social science student at the HKU and the Tiananmen massacre in the mainland prompted him to write up a slogan on the pavement at the HKU. He was imbued with the idea of imparting the knowledge of democracy, freedom and China's development into the minds of secondary school students.[192] In 1995, Cheung began to teach Liberal Studies, choosing the two topics of Hong Kong studies and China's development. He said that Liberal Studies aimed at allowing students to "rationally discuss and care about social topics under the foundation of respecting diversity."[193] Cheung sharply observed that the guidelines under Citizenship and Social Development set out the red lines, making it difficult for not only teachers to teach but also students to think and discuss openly. He predicted that many teachers under the new subject would be under pressure because they would have to visit the mainland. Cheung encouraged the young generation of teachers to maintain their space to think critically from different angles instead of being "unreasonably intimidated by the ruling authorities."[194] According to Cheung, he no longer discussed the 1989 June 4th incident in June 2020 because he wanted to protect himself and prevent anyone from criticizing him easily.[195]

Another Liberal Studies teacher, Tin Fong-chak, admitted that many teachers resigned mainly because of the political pressure and partly because of the "deteriorating school atmosphere."[196] Fong pointed to the phenomenon of revoking the licenses of some teachers – a move that frightened many teachers who were afraid of receiving anonymous complaints. He added that, under the national security law and the new Citizenship and Social Development subject, teachers would have to express the official viewpoints without the autonomy to question the governmental perspective.[197] According to Tin, most social topics are debatable with the affirmative and negative sides, but the new pedagogy is that teachers will be unable to criticize the government and express their views different from the administration.[198] However, Tin said teachers may still have the discretion to discuss with students freely outside the classroom.

While Cheung's assessment of the teachers' lack of autonomy under the Citizenship and Development Studies subject was the same as Tin's evaluation, both differed in the discretion of teachers outside classrooms. Tin identified some degree of autonomy and discretion on the part of teachers outside the classroom setting, but Cheung implied that, even if the teachers may raise politically sensitive issues outside classrooms, they would likely be a target of easy criticisms and complaints from students, parents and pro-Beijing media and elites.

Cheung's observation did have evidence; some schools have already banned teachers from discussing politically tabooed topics. For example, the Pui Ling School of the Precious Blood and its sister schools issued guidelines to ban teachers from discussing politically tabooed topics, such as "Hong Kong independence" as early as August 2016, four years before the promulgation of the national security law.[199] Its guideline described the discussion of "Hong Kong independence" as equivalent to a discussion of suicide and bank robbery; moreover, if such sensitive topics were raised by students, the teachers should guide them properly.[200] Teachers were also forbidden to discuss "Hong Kong independence" outside classrooms – a move that could actually protect teachers and that turned out to be a proper one in light of the enactment and implementation of the national security law.

Objectively speaking, teachers who are teaching subjects like History, Chinese History and Citizenship and Social Development have to be careful and to abide by the national security law. In a sense, some degree of self-censorship is necessary for teachers to protect themselves. Under the new political circumstances in which the 1989 June 4th incident and the role of the police in the 2019 anti-extradition bill movement are increasingly sensitive topics, it is and will be normal for teachers to stay on the safe side rather than taking any political and legal risks.

A discussion with four secondary school teachers in May 2020 showed that they were politically neutral but decided not to immigrate, and that they did adapt to the changing political circumstances.[201] First, they agreed that Liberal Studies could increase the awareness of students, but whether students were interested in political participation was another matter shaped by a whole range of factors, such as peer influences, the mobilization of student participation through social media and the support from their parents. Second, their schools showed a multiplicity of methods in handling the national flag; one school required students to attend a flag-raising ceremony once a month, another school doing it on important days. Third, they all knew that the government required each school to set up a committee to deal with the national security education. Usually, the discipline master and the student counselor are appointed to such a committee, which would have to report its activities related to national security education to the EDB. Fourth, they all believed that the new subject of Citizenship and Social Development would have to be taught carefully; teachers would simply follow the required textbook word by word without the need to involve students in discussions. Nor would there be any critical thinking imparted to students. Unless their school principals require them to organize student activities, they would not do so. Fifth, they all agreed that the so-called "controversial" public examination question on whether Japan did more harm than good to China actually had "no problem" because students could disagree with the statement in the first place. One teacher argued that Japan did have contributions to China's modernization. But they all agreed that the EDB exerted pressure on the HKEAA to cancel the public examination question. Sixth, they all said that they would not discuss politics with their colleagues, whom they would not trust, for the sake of protecting themselves. They merely discussed politics among good and close friends who, to them, were reliable. Seventh, they would sign the oath of obeying the national security law, if necessary and especially those teachers in public schools, because of their need to protect their jobs. Eighth, they all noted that some school principals and teachers were very active in organizing the national security education because of the need to demonstrate to the government authorities that the schools performed well. After all, some school principals and teachers are pro-government and would like to climb up the promotion and political ladder if they are regarded as performing well in the implementation of the national security education. Ninth, they revealed that the librarians of their schools were checking whether some books might be politically sensitive and banned by the government – a kind of self-censorship on the part of librarians in accordance with the law. Tenth, they revealed that if teachers were all required by the schools to have vaccination against Covid-19, they would have no choice but to do so; nevertheless, any school survey conducted on whether they would have vaccination would be completed by them carefully to protect their own privacy. In short, those teachers who opt for staying in the HKSAR and who would continue to teach tend to adapt strategically to the rapidly changing socio-political circumstances.

At the university level, many students withdrew from their studies in the 2019–2020 academic year for various reasons, including the 2019 protests that disrupted their studies and the outbreak of Covid-19 in early 2020. The University Grants Council released the figures of student at all government-funded universities, showing that 2,121 students withdrew from their undergraduate and graduate studies, including 1,816 undergraduates – a figure that increased by 19 percent compared to the situation in the 2018–2019 academic year.[202] Among those who withdrew from their studies, HKU had 342 students, PolyU 329 and CUHK 305. Some of the students who withdrew from their studies included mainland students as they returned to the PRC. The increase in the number of students withdrawing from their studies hit the PolyU most, because only 224 students had withdrawn in the academic year from 2018 to 2019. The 2019–2020 academic year witnessed a rise of 47 percent in student withdrawal at the PolyU. Of course, the fierce battles between some students and the police at both PolyU and CUHK in late 2019 might have an immediate impact on the withdrawal decision.

Conclusion

The promulgation of the national security law in late June 2020 had immediate and profound impacts on the education sector. The most important impact was the beginning of the Hong Kong-style of "Cultural Revolution." This Cultural Revolution in the HKSAR has been evolving since June 30, 2020. It comprises four major components of transformation: (1) teachers; (2) the PTU; (3) the struggle over a politically "incorrect" public examination question and the "yellow" officers of the HKEAA and (4) students and student unions. However, a hallmark of the Cultural Revolution in Hong Kong was that it was led by highly nationalistic and patriotic Chinese and triggered by the determination to transform the political culture of targeted citizens and institutions, including the HKEAA. The impact of conducting the Hong Kong style of Cultural Revolution could be felt, namely the migration of teachers and students from Hong Kong to other places. Many teachers and students who cannot afford to migrate, and whose political values are more pragmatic and less idealistic, prefer to stay in the HKSAR and adapt to the changing circumstances.

Notes

1. The high tide of the PRC's Cultural Revolution took place from 1966 to 1969. For details, see Maurice Meisner, *Mao's China and After: A History of the People's Republic* (New York: The Free Press, 1999), pp. 312–351.
2. "Defiant teacher Ng Mei-lan," *Next Magazine*, no. 1174 (September 6, 2012), in 叛逆教師　吳美蘭 @ 明星八掛大分享★☆ :: 痞客邦 :: (pixnet.net), access date: August 6, 2021.
3. *Ibid*.
4. *Ibid*.
5. *Ibid*.
6. See a brief message of the Social Democratic Front, July 15, 2012, in 社會民主連線 – 敢於表達政見的「良心教師」吳美蘭, 新學年將會離開任教了10個年頭的庇利羅士女子中學, 轉往教授少數族裔... | Facebook, access date: August 6, 2021.
7. *Headline News*, October 7, 2020.
8. *Epoch Times*, July 5, 2021.
9. "Two Police Unions reprimanded Lam See-wai," July 28, 2013, in 兩警察協會譴責林慧思 – 新傳網 (symedialab.com), access date: August 6, 2021.
10. *Apple Daily*, August 5, 2013.
11. "The dispute over Lam See-wai's foul language, EDB four years later rules that the complaint was established," July 16, 2017, in 林慧思粗口風波　事隔4年教局突發信裁定違操守 | 香港01 | 社會新聞 (hk01.com), access date: August 6, 2021.
12. *Oriental Daily*, January 27, 2018, in 拒唱國歌 辱罵國家 爆粗教師林慧思辭職 – 東方日報 (on.cc), access date: August 6, 2021.
13. *Ibid*.
14. Nicola Chan, "Hong Kong extradition bill: Liberal Studies teacher resigns from HKEAA post over anti-police Facebook post," July 8, 2019, in Hong Kong extradition bill: Liberal Studies teacher resigns from HKEAA post over anti-police Facebook post – YP | South China Morning Post (scmp.com), access date: August 8, 2021. Lai was named as one of the "yellow teachers" in a "pro-blue" or pro-government website, 賴得鐘-亂港黃師-亂港檔案-香港解密 (hkleaks.pk), access date: August 8, 2021.
15. "Sacred Heart Cannossian College is suspected to try cleaning the record of Lai Tak-chung," *Wen Wei Po*, September 3, 2019, in 嘉諾撒聖心校疑圖為賴得鐘「洗底」(tap2world.com), access date: August 8, 2021.
16. *Wen Wei Po*, August 22, 2021, p. A9.
17. "A secondary school teacher has a working sheet that depicts police having conspiracy with triads, teacher admitting mistake and apologizes," September 25, 2019, in【逃犯條例】有中學工作紙以警黑勾結為題　老師承認過失並致歉 | 香港01 | 社會新聞 (hk01.com), access date: August 6, 2021.
18. *Ibid*.
19. "Kevin Yeung: 'Glory to Hong Kong' belongs to political propaganda, a teacher at Heung To Middle School does not have her contract renewed as she had allowed students to sign it in the campus," *Sky Post*, June 12, 2020, in 楊潤雄:《榮光》屬政治宣傳 校園禁唱 允學生演奏 香島中學教師不獲續約 – 晴報 – 港聞 – 要聞 – D200612 (ulifestyle.com.hk), access date: August 8, 2021.
20. *Ibid*.
21. *Ibid*.
22. *Ibid*.
23. *Ibid*.
24. "Heung To Teacher allowing students to sing "Glory to Hong Kong" has the contract discontinued, over 100 students form human chain to support her," June 12, 2020, in 香島中學教師疑因允奏《榮光》被拒續約 過百學生築人鏈聲援 | 獨媒報導 | 獨立媒體 (inmediahk.net), access date: August 8, 2021.
25. *Ibid*.
26. *Ibid*.

27 *Ibid.*
28 "Kowloon Tong Alliance Primary School teacher has his license revoked, EDB says he has a plan to spread the idea of 'Hong Kong independence,'" October 5, 2020, in 九龍塘宣道小學教師遭取消教師資格　教育局: 有計劃散播港獨信息 | 香港01 | 社會新聞 (hk01.com), access date: August 7, 2021.
29 *Ibid.*
30 *Ibid.*
31 *Ibid.*
32 *Ibid.*
33 However, the Amnesty International criticized the punishment for sending a warning to educators in classrooms and having the impact of "eroding the freedom of speech." See Amnesty International's statement, October 6, 2020, in 教育局以「有計劃散播史獨信息」為由取消教師資格　— 國際特赦組織香港分會 Amnesty International Hong Kong, access date: August 7, 2021.
34 "Ho Lap teacher whose license was revoked apologizes and he loses his job, feels directionless and remembers his students," November 16, 2020, in 遭釘牌可立教師認歷史知識貧乏致歉　失夢想職業感迷惘　不捨學生 | 香港01 | 社會新聞 (hk01.com), access date: August 7, 2021.
35 *Ibid.*
36 *Ibid.*
37 *Oriental Daily*, November 12, 2020.
38 *Oriental Daily*, May 3, 2021.
39 *Ibid.*
40 *Ibid.*
41 "Kevin Yeung says the government revises the law to suspend the license of teachers and to deduct their salaries temporarily," November 9, 2020, in 楊潤雄稱正研究修例容許取消教師資格一段時間或扣糧等 | Now 新聞, access date: August 7, 2021.
42 "Government school teacher's license is revoked, while a visual arts teacher whose comics criticized the police was regarded as lacking professional conduct," May 1, 2021, in 首有官校教師因反修例被「釘牌」　課餘漫畫批警方亦被指專業失德 (rfi.fr), access date: August 7, 2021.
43 "Visual art teacher Vawongsir published political comics and he was a target of complaints, he was ruled as lacking professional ethics," April 29, 2021, in 【清算教師】視藝教師「vawongsir」被裁專業失德　或成釘牌第三人　教局指諷警暴漫畫為「無理指控」 | 立場報道 | 立場新聞 (thestandnews.com), access date: August 7, 2021. See also *Oriental Daily*, April 29, 2021.
44 "Tin Shui Wai teacher distributed *Apple Daily* to teachers and was stopped teaching temporarily, and the PTU criticizes the school's action," June 18, 2021, in 天水圍有小學教師派《蘋果》予同事遭暫停課堂　教協斥上綱上線 | 香港 01 | 社會新聞 (hk01.com), access date: August 8, 2021.
45 *Ibid.*
46 *Ibid.*
47 *Ibid.*
48 *Ibid.*
49 "Teacher bought *Apple Daily* and distributed it to teachers, Kevin Yeung says there should be no political propaganda and school itself handles the case," June 23, 2021, in 教師買《蘋果》回校派同事　楊潤雄: 不得政治宣傳　信學校能處理 | 香港 01 | 政情 (hk01.com), access date: August 8, 2021.
50 "Cheung Yu-yan advocates installing video cameras to supervise teachers' remarks and teaching situation," Radio Television Hong Kong, January 22, 2021, in 張宇人倡教室安裝閉路電視集中攝錄教師監察教學情況 – RTHK, access date: August 8, 2021.
51 "Teacher bought *Apple Daily* and distributed it to teachers, Kevin Yeung says there should be no political propaganda and school itself handles the case," June 23, 2021, in 教師買《蘋果》回校派同事　楊潤雄: 不得政治宣傳　信學校能處理 | 香港 01 | 政情 (hk01.com), access date: August 8, 2021.

52 New China News Agency, "Hong Kong Education needs to be rectified and cleared of its root, and it is necessary to dig out the 'poisonous fester' of the Professional Teachers Union," July 31, 2021, in 新华社: 香港教育要正本清源必须铲除"教协"这颗毒瘤 (locpg.gov.cn), access date: August 1, 2021.
53 The Alliance's five operational goals," in About Hong Kong Alliance | 香港支聯會 Hong Kong Alliance in Support of Patriotic Democratic Movements of China (wordpress.com), access date: August 1, 2021.
54 Ibid.
55 Ibid.
56 Ibid.
57 Ibid.
58 Ibid.
59 Ibid.
60 Ibid.
61 "EDB announces the termination of its full-scale working relations with the Professional Teachers Union," July 31, 2021, in 教育局宣布全面終止與教協工作關係 – RTHK, access date: August 1, 2021.
62 Ibid.
63 Ibid.
64 *Wen Wei Po*, August 1, 2021, p. A1.
65 Ibid.
66 Ibid.
67 Ibid.
68 Ibid.
69 *Ta Kung Pao*, August 1, 2021.
70 Ibid.
71 Ibid.
72 Ibid.
73 *Oriental Daily*, October 10, 2021.
74 Ibid.
75 "Alliance School teacher had his license revoked, and PTU survey showed 70 percent of principals found the ruling unreasonable," November 10, http://www.hk01.com, access date: August 1, 2021.
76 *Ta Kung Pao*, August 1, 2021, p. A1.
77 Ibid.
78 Ibid.
79 Ibid.
80 Ibid.
81 Tommy Cheung, "'Father' of Hong Kong nationalism? A critical review of Wan Chin's city-state theory," *Asian Education and Development Studies*, vol. 4, no. 4 (October 2015), pp. 460–470.
82 *Ta Kung Pao*, August 1, 2021, p. A1.
83 See the website of the Education Commission, in Education Commission - Membership (e-c.edu.hk), access date: August 1, 2021.
84 *Ta Kung Pao*, August 1, 2021, p. A2.
85 Ibid.
86 "PTU responds to the EDB's termination of working relations," PTU press release, July 31, 2021, in 新聞稿／立場書 | 香港教育專業人員協會 (hkptu.org), access date: August 2, 2021.
87 Ibid.
88 "PTU responds to the commentary of *Xinhua* and *People's Daily*," PTU press release, July 31, 2021, in 教協回應新華社及人民日報的評論 | 香港教育專業人員協會 (hkptu.org), access date: August 2, 2021.
89 *Wen Wei Po*, August 1, 2021, p. A1.

90 *Ibid.*
91 *Ibid.*
92 *Ibid.*
93 Editorial, "Realizing the PTU's damage and harm, deeply analyze and correct the situation," *Wen Wei Po*, August 2, 2021, p. A4.
94 *Ming Pao*, August 2, 2021.
95 Sonny Shiu-hing Lo, "Ideologies and factionalism in Beijing-Hong Kong relations," *Asian Survey*, vol. 58, no. 3 (June 2018), pp. 392–415.
96 Lau Yung-fei, "Registry of Trade Unions should 'revoke' PTU license according to the law," *Ta Kung Pao*, August 3, 2021.
97 *Ibid.*
98 *Ta Kung Pao*, August 3, 2021, p. A10.
99 *Ibid.*
100 *Ibid.*
101 *Ming Pao*, August 3, 2021, p. A8.
102 *Ibid.*
103 *Ibid.*
104 *Ibid.*
105 Fong Ching-chi, "Education governance needs a thunderbolt means, softline approach will be considered only after the river, water and seas are calmed down," *Ta Kung Pao*, August 6, 2021, p. A12.
106 *Ibid.*
107 *Ibid.*
108 Editorial, "PTU makes a new move, but this cannot eliminate its 'cruel action' of damaging Hong Kong," *Wen Wei Po*, August 6, 2021, p. A7.
109 "PTU press conference: announcing its dissolution, chair Fung Wai-wah says many solutions cannot tackle the crisis," August 10, 2021, in 教協記者會｜宣布解散 會長馮偉華: 多個方案都難解當前危機｜香港01｜社會新聞 (hk01.com), access date: August 10, 2021.
110 "The disbandment of PTU is self-inflicted and Hong Kong education embraces the historical chance of returning to the correct path," *Xinhua*, August 11, 2021, in "教協"解散咎由自取 香港教育迎来重回正轨历史契机－港澳－人民网 (people.com.cn), access date: August 12, 2021.
111 *Ta Kung Pao*, August 12, 2021, p. A1.
112 *Wen Wei Po*, August 12, 2021, p. A2.
113 *Ming Pao*, August 11, 2021, p. A2; *Wen Wei Po*, August 12, 2021, p. A3; and *Ta Kung Pao*, August 10, 2021, p. A5.
114 Mok Pui-fan, "Leaders of the PTU must be brought to justice," *Wen Wei Po*, August 11, 2021, p. A13. Also see Lee Kai-ting, "PTU crimes remain despite its disbandment, its leaders who violate the law must be pursued," *Ta Kung Pao*, August 11, 2021, p. A12.
115 *Wen Wei Po*, August 11, 2021, p. A3.
116 *Ibid.*
117 *Ibid.*
118 *Ibid.*
119 Fung Yiu-cheuk, "From an Examination Paper to look at History Subject: A Chronology of the DSE History Subject Examination Controversies," in www.mpweekly.com, June 30, 2020, access date: July 22, 2021.
120 *Ibid.*
121 *Ibid.*
122 *Ibid.*
123 *Ibid.*
124 Chalmers A. Johnson, *Peasant Nationalism and Communist Power: The Emergence of Revolutionary China, 1937–1945* (Stanford: Stanford University Press, 1962).

125 Tang Wing-lam, "So Kwok-sang responds to non-renewal: personal reasons without being pressured," HK01, September 1, 2020, in DSE 2021 | 考評局秘書長蘇國生回應不續任：個人考慮、不涉施壓 | 香港01 | 社會新聞 (hk01.com), access date: July 25, 2021.

126 "So's contract not renewed, Ip Kin-yuen speculates it is related to the examination question controversy," *Epoch Times*, August 18, 2020, in 考評局秘書長蘇國生不續任 葉建源推測涉歷史科試題爭議 | 大紀元時報 香港 | 獨立敢言的良心媒體 (epochtimes.com), access date: August 6, 2021.

127 "Formerly a member of the Shenzhen CPPCC, background was questioned: Wei says he does not how to define patriots," *Sky Post*, March 25, 2021, in 歷史科爭議 | 曾任深圳政協 背景受質疑 考評局魏向東：不知怎定義愛國者 – 晴報 – 時事 – 要聞 – D210325 (ulifestyle.com.hk), access date: July 25, 2021.

128 "Wei says government's move of appointing people to go into examination scrutiny committee does not influence the independence of the Examination Authority," March 25, 2021, in 【DSE】魏向東指教育局人員加入審題委員會　不影響考評局獨立性 – 香港經濟日報 – TOPick – 新聞 – 社會 – D210325 (hket.com), access date: July 25, 2021.

129 Po Lanping, "Hong Kong's Education System needs to be scratched in its bones and remedied for its poison," *People's Daily*, May 16, 2020, in 香港教育需要"刮骨療毒" (peopleapp.com), access date: July 24, 2021.

130 Fung Yiu-cheuk, "From an examination paper to look at history subject: A chronology of the DSE history subject examination controversies," in www.mpweekly.com, June 30, 2020, access date: July 22, 2021.

131 *Ibid*.

132 Fung Cheuk-yiu, "Judicial review from DSE students fails, expectations of thousands of students become empty," July 3, 2020, in DSE 考生司法覆核敗訴 數以千計學生願望落空 -教育- 明周文化 (mpweekly.com), access date: July 24, 2021.

133 *Ibid*.

134 "Ip Kin-yuen worries that 2 of the 7 members who were officials had to 'report' to the authorities and leak out the question," March 9, 2021, in 歷史科審題委員會名單曝光　7 成員最少 2 人任職教育局　葉建源憂被要求「向上級交代」洩密 | 立場報道 | 立場新聞 (thestandnews.com), access date: July 24, 2021.

135 *Ibid*.

136 *Ibid*.

137 Tang Wing-lam, "DSE controversy: Three days before the resignation of two examination managers are making people shivering," HK01, May 16, 2020, in DSE　歷史科 | 一文看清考評風波　兩經理辭職前三日間如何驚心動魄 | 香港01 | 社會新聞 (hk01.com), access date: July 24, 2021.

138 *Sing Tao Daily*, May 14, 2020.

139 *Wen Wei Po*, May 17, 2020.

140 *Ibid*.

141 *Ibid*.

142 *Oriental Daily*, May 16, 2020.

143 "High level of examination authority: Black hands covering the sky," *Ta Kung Pao*, May 14, 2020.

144 Wu Ka-yan, "Facebook saying Carrie Lam should go, two Examination Authority managers resign," HK01, May 16, 2020, in 【01 獨家】FB 發「林鄭滾蛋」　考評局評核發展部通識科兩經理辭職 | 香港01 | 社會新聞 (hk01.com), access date: July 24, 2021.

145 "Rumors that government officials join the examination committee, but the Examination Authority said it was confidential," March 10, 2021, in 傳多名教局人員加入歷史科委員會 考評局重申屬高度機密 | 頭條日報 (stheadline.com), access date: July 24, 2021.

146 Ip Kin-yuen, "History subject's examination controversy showed white terror in the resignation of two officers," *Ming Pao*, August 5, 2020.
147 *Hong Kong Free Press*, December 1, 2020.
148 "Professional autonomy is a history of the past. Hans Yeung says that his mistake was being open-minded," The Standnews, December 27, 2020, in 【專訪】當專業自主成為歷史　前考評局經理楊穎宇: 我錯在 Open-minded | 立場人語 | 立場新聞 (thestandnews.com), access date: July 24, 2021.
149 *Ibid.*
150 *Ibid.* Also see "Dr. Hans Yeung talks about the beginning and the end of the controversial history examination question: an indicator of Hong Kong's 'degradation,'" December 23, 2020, in 眾新聞 – 【首度開腔】離職考評局經理楊穎宇博士　親述歷史科試題內情始末　「香港隋落嘅指標性事件」 (hkcnews.com), access date: July 25, 2021.
151 "Professional autonomy is a history of the past. Hans Yeung says that his mistake was being open-minded," *The Standnews*, December 27, 2020.
152 *Ming Pao*, May 16, 2020.
153 "Dr. Hans Yeung talks about the beginning and the end of the controversial history examination question: An indicator of Hong Kong's 'degradation,'" December 23, 2020, in hkcnews.com.
154 "DSE History subject examination questions: Citing 1982 public opinion poll to show 70 percent of Hong Kong people wanted Hong Kong to remain a colony and asking question to analyze the people's worries," April 20, 2017, in 【多話題】DSE歷史科試卷　引82年民調七成人盼港維持殖民地　要考生分析港人憂慮 | 立場報道 | 立場新聞 (thestandnews.com), access date: August 6, 2021.
155 *Ibid.*
156 "Dr. Hans Yeung talks about the beginning and the end of the controversial history examination question: An indicator of Hong Kong's 'degradation,'" December 23, 2020, in hkcnews.com.
157 *Ibid.*
158 *Ibid.*
159 Hans Yeung, "A critique of the History Subject paper in 2021," May 8, 2021, in 眾新聞 – 盤點2021年歷史科試卷 (hkcnews.com), access date: August 6, 2021.
160 Yuen Chan, "Test balloon, warning shot, attack dog: Is Hong Kong witnessing a rebirth of the 'mainland mouthpiece'?" *Hong Kong Free Press*, May 15, 2020, in hongkongfp.com, access date: August 5, 2021. A former student told one of the authors that she had observed only two to three Hong Kong-born reporters in a 20-member political reporting team led by two mainland editors, that the reports had to be written in a more "leftwing" way critical of the Hong Kong democrats, and that the adherence to political "correctness" was prominent. Personal discussion with the former student who worked in one pro-Beijing newspaper in 2019 on May 3, 2021.
161 *Wen Wei Po*, August 5, 2021.
162 *Ming Pao*, August 4, 2021.
163 *Ming Pao*, August 5, 2021.
164 *Now TV News*, August 6, 2021.
165 *Ibid.*
166 "HKU even has such court members!" *Ta Kung Pao*, August 7, 2021, p. A4.
167 *Ibid.*
168 *Ibid.*
169 *Ibid.*
170 *Ibid.*
171 *Ibid.*
172 *Ibid.*

150 Cultural Revolution in the Education Sector

173 *Ming Pao*, August 6, 2021, p. A8.
174 *Ming Pao*, November 3, 2020.
175 *Ibid*.
176 "Political troubles see the withdrawal of students in Hong Kong's primary and secondary schools," November 7, 2020, in 政治困擾 香港中小學現退學潮 (rfi.fr), access date: August 8, 2021.
177 *Ibid*.
178 *Headline News*, October 8, 2020.
179 *Ibid*.
180 *Ibid*.
181 *Ibid*.
182 *Ibid*.
183 "Secondary Schools Principal Association: Student departure increases by 52 percent and teachers leaving their position increase by 15 percent, including early retirement," February 23, 2021, in 中學校長會: 學生離港退學按年增52% 教師離職增15%部份提早退休 | 香港01 | 社會新聞 (hk01.com), access date: August 8, 2021.
184 *Oriental Daily*, August 8, 2021, p. A7.
185 *Ibid*.
186 *Ibid*.
187 "Hok Yau Club: The tide of withdrawal is the most serious one in ten years, a father says the national security law prompts him to leave," November 4, 2020, in 【香港要聞】港多間名校爆「退學潮」 學友社: 十年來最嚴重 港爸:「國安法」真是加速了我要走 – GNEWS, access date: August 8, 2020.
188 *Ibid*.
189 Discussion with this gentleman, who was an academic and whose wife was a secondary school teacher, on July 25, 2021.
190 Email communication with the teacher, June 4, 2020.
191 "Joining the teaching profession because of the 1989 democracy movement, Cheung Yui-fai as a first generation Liberal Studies teacher decides to retire early, saying that the red lines are established," June 10, 2021, in 因八九民運投身教育界 首代通識老師張銳輝提早退休: 教學設紅線 | 香港01 | 社會新聞 (hk01.com), access date: August 8, 2021.
192 *Ibid*.
193 *Ibid*.
194 *Ibid*.
195 "Liberal Studies teacher Cheung Yui-fai retires earlier, he teaches for 30 years and says the red lines are making teachers losing their professional autonomy," June 10, 2021, in 資深通識教師張銳輝提早退休 任教近30年 指「紅線」下教師失專業自主 | 立場報道 | 立場新聞 (thestandnews.com), access date: August 8, 2021.
196 *Ibid*.
197 *Ibid*.
198 *Ibid*.
199 "The Precious Blood schools ban teachers to talk about 'Hong Kong independence' even in private capacity outside classrooms." August 23, 2016, in 寶血會培靈學校 被指明言禁老師在校談港獨 個人身份在校外討論也不適合 | 立場報道 | 立場新聞 (thestandnews.com), access date: November 23, 2021.
200 *Ibid*.
201 Informal and relaxed chats with four secondary school teachers, who were the former students of one of the authors, May 8, 2020.
202 "Eight universities have 1,816 students withdrawing from their studies, a figure highest in eleven years with the University of Hong Kong at the top," March 2, 2021, in 八大 上學年共1816 學士生退學 創至少11年新高 港大佔最多 | 香港01 | 社會新聞 (hk01.com), access date: August 8, 2021.

5 Adaptation to the Mainlandization, Decolonization, Legalization and Migration

This chapter discusses how the education sector of Hong Kong has been adapting to the rapid processes of mainlandization, decolonization, legalization and migration. Mainlandization refers to the process of making Hong Kong's education system more like the mainland counterpart than ever before, especially considering the PRC's education reforms under the Xin Jinping era. One of the essential ingredients of mainlandization is the strengthening of patriotic education, which can also be seen as a phenomenon of decolonizing Hong Kong's education. The legalization of Hong Kong's education can be seen in the imposition of the national security law and more legal restrictions on the schools. Some students and teachers were punished legally, leading to the fear of some parents and young students. As a result, the migration of many Hong Kong students began in early 2021, leading to a brain drain and an upward mobility of teaching assistants to the position of teachers. Still, many stakeholders in Hong Kong's education system have to adapt to the rapid political and environmental changes.

China's Education Reform and Implications for Hong Kong

In 2021, the centennial anniversary of the CCP was marked by a series of education reform in the PRC. In August 2021, the Ministry of Education announced that a guide on Chinese-style socialism during the Xi Jinping era would have to be integrated into the curriculum reform.[1] Moreover, national security education would have to be incorporated into the new curriculum at the primary school level, including the 16 dimensions of national security, the emphasis on the threat of "Taiwan independence," Tibet independence," "Xinjiang independence" and "Hong Kong independence."[2] All these emphases would be built into the suitable curricula at the primary, secondary and university levels. If ideological indoctrination was naturally integrated into China's education reform, the emphasis on the implementation of the national security education in the HKSAR was understandable and reflective of the mainland's transformation.

In the PRC, the thought of Xi Jinping has been integrated into the curricula of mainland schools at various levels, illustrating the importance of "political

DOI: 10.4324/9781003147268-5

Table 5.1 Education Reforms in the PRC

Teaching materials and topic	University	Secondary	Primary
Chinese-Style Socialism Thought In New Era under Xin Jinping	Implement with examination	Implement	Implement
Chinese Excellence in Tradition, Culture and Education; and Propaganda Education in the Revolutionary Tradition		Implement with examination	Implement
Labor Education	Implement with practice	Implement with practice	Implement with practice
National Security Education	Implement with examination	Implement with examination	Implement with examination
Lecture on General Secretary Xi Jinping's Important Remarks	Implement	Implement	Implement
Party Leadership and Its Content	Implement	Implement	Implement
Study and Construction Work of Marxism in the New Era	Implement	–	–
National Defense Education	–	Implement	Implement
Life Safety and Health Education	–	Implement	Implement

Source: Adapted from *Ming Pao*, August 25, 2021, p. A17.

renaissance" in the primary schools and the consolidation of the Chinese national identity among the psyche of the mainland youths.[3] Table 5.1 shows the scope of education reforms in the PRC, including the teaching of national security education at the primary, secondary and university levels. The construction of a batch of teachers knowledgeable in national security is necessary, according to a leading guideline on national security education.[4] While the education of Xi Jinping thought focuses on university students, party leadership and its content have to be taught at all levels of the schools in China.

Comparatively speaking, education reforms in the PRC are more comprehensive and political than those in the HKSAR. In Hong Kong, students are taught under the national security education to respect the CCP – a kind of soft indoctrination compared with the direct indoctrination in the mainland. In September 2021, CCP General Secretary Xi Jinping appealed to the students in the Central Party School that they should have faith in their political beliefs in their lifetime, and that their loyalty to the CCP is a must for the sake of shouldering more responsibilities to be the pillars of the society in the future.[5] He added that students in the Party School who "do not want to struggle are unrealistic," meaning that they should have faith to fight for their beliefs and protect China's national sovereignty, security and development interest.[6] Students in the Party School have to study Marxism, Chinese history, the reform policy, the history of socialism and other disciplines such as politics, economics, law, culture, society, ecology, management and international relations. Clearly, while ideological indoctrination is a must for the students at all levels, party members have to shoulder the responsibility of carrying out the CCP's mission and vision for the PRC.

Decolonization and Patriotic Education in Hong Kong

The consolidation of patriotic education can be seen as part and parcel of the process of decolonizing Hong Kong's education system. For the supporters of the PRC, decolonization and patriotic education go hand in hand and should be warmly embraced. From July 3 to 9, 2021, a seven-day exhibition of the centennial achievements of the CCP at the Hong Kong Wanchai Convention and Exhibition Center immediately after the celebration of the CCP's centennial anniversary in Beijing on July 1, marked the beginning of patriotic education in the HKSAR.[7] The exhibition was co-organized by the Bauhinia Cultural Consortium and the National Museum of China with the collaboration from the Hong Kong Constitutional and Mainland Affairs Bureau, the Bauhinia Magazine and the Hong Kong Wen Wei Ta Kung Media Group.

The content of the exhibition was divided into two main parts: the first one covering the history of China and the rise of the CCP as well as its recent achievements; and the second one focusing on the scientific progress and achievements of the PRC. Many schools organized students to visit the exhibition on China's scientific progress and achievements, while many individual citizens and groups went into the exhibition hall that depicted China's turbulent history and the rise of the CCP, including the heroic Dongjiang guerillas that fought against the Japanese invaders in South China during the Second World War.

Several characteristics of the exhibition could be observed. First, the history of China and its recent scientific and economic achievements were depicted in the format of descriptive bulletin boards and in the form of virtual reality. Models of airplanes, tanks and aircraft carriers were shown to attract the young audience. Second, patriotic groups were mobilized to visit the exhibition, leading to the report of the organizers that the seven-day exhibition attracted 62,500 citizens. Third, the content of the exhibition could be turned into textbook and references easily, as advocated by some patriotic elites, so that the schoolchildren would be able to understand the history of China, the CCP's rise and the PRC's achievements in a more in-depth and comprehensive manner. Fourth, at least 80 Hong Kong scouts and the Hong Kong Army Cadets aged between eight and twenty were mobilized every day to act as tour guides and demonstrators, explaining to the visitors the content of the various bulletin boards. As such, the exhibition served the purpose of educating the young people of Hong Kong on the history of China, the CCP and the PRC. Fifth, an important highlight of the exhibition was a detailed historical account of foreign invasion into China during the Qing dynasty and all the related indemnities involved – a detailed account that attracted a lot of visitors to take photographs. Sixth, the rise of the CCP was depicted comprehensively, including the repeated television coverage of Chairman Mao Zedong's remarks on the Tiananmen rostrum that the Chinese people stood up on October 1, 1949.

The exhibition was accompanied by other activities to foster patriotic education in Hong Kong. First, patriotic groups led by the Solidarity Force of Loving China and Protecting Hong Kong, together with some alumni of the CUHK, organized a series of national education activities from July 9 until the end of November 2021. The activities included the mobilization of schoolchildren to sing the PRC national anthem, and to participate in the creative artwork and quizzes. It was expected that 600,000 schoolchildren would be mobilized to participate in these national education activities. The honorary chairman of the organizer, Yuan Mo, said that the education sector, the business, youth groups and patriotic organizations actively supported and participated in the "engineering" activities, which aimed at "promoting positivism, calling upon the young generation and recollecting Hong Kong's momentum.[8]

Second, curriculum reform was accompanying the national education activities so that patriotism could be instilled into the psyche of more young people. In early July, the Education Bureau issued two teaching briefs on "Hong Kong under 'one country, two systems.'" The teaching materials covered two important aspects: the HKSAR's political system and the spirit of the rule of law. In the curriculum concerning Hong Kong's political system, six main points are emphasized. First, students must understand that the decision power of the HKSAR political system stems from the central government.[9] Second, the Chief Executive of the HKSAR must be accountable to the central people's government and the HKSAR in accordance with the Basic Law. Third, the HKSAR political system is characterized by its executive-led nature, the mutual checks and coordination between the executive and legislative branches and judicial independence. Fourth, students must understand the duties and operation of the following leaders and institutions: the Chief Justice, the Chief Secretary for Administration, the Financial Secretary and their related government departments; the composition and the duties of the legislature; and the composition and duties of the judiciary. Fifth, students need to understand the principle and realization of "patriots governing Hong Kong," the oath-taking of the Chief Executive and civil servants and the National Security Law's stipulation on "patriots governing Hong Kong." Sixth, students should build up the value of loving and cherishing Hong Kong, respecting and protecting the HKSAR political system under "one country, two systems," and recognizing their national identity. Clearly, the emphasized features in the curriculum on Hong Kong's political system, patriotic education and national identity are injected into the teaching pedagogy so that teachers and students will understand their proper role in the society of Hong Kong.

Regarding the curriculum on the spirit of the rule of law, five points were emphasized.[10] First, students should understand the content of the rule of law and its spirit, including the respect of the authority of the law; the precondition of obeying the law; the support of judicial independence; and the upholding of the principles of equality before the law, fair trial, procedural due process, and the transparency and stability of law. Second, students should understand the important meaning of protecting the rule of law spirit, including the protection of human rights as an important element. Nevertheless, students have to understand that human rights are not without limits; one cannot affect the human rights of another person and one cannot affect social

Adaptation to Mainlandization and Decolonization 155

order and national security. If there are contradictions, individual freedom must be constrained by the law. Third, students need to realize that the protection of the rule of law is Hong Kong's common value, thereby facilitating the establishment of good order, social stability and the foundation of Hong Kong's society and China's national development. Fourth, students should, through the court verdicts of the Court of Final Appeal, "correctly understand that whatever demands they request, any violent and illegal act must violate the spirit of the rule of law."[11] Fifth, students should understand that the judicial branches do not face any interference in its process of adjudication and that "the HKSAR enjoys independent judicial power and the power of final adjudication." Clearly, the revamped curriculum guide sought to rectify the previously "distorted" societal interpretations over the meaning of the rule of law and judicial independence in Hong Kong.

On July 10, 2021, Chief Executive Carrie Lam attended a high-level forum on patriotic education. She remarked that patriotic education was "stigmatized" in the past, and that "all societal sectors must implement patriotism education, promote the spirit of patriotism, and correct the values of the young people."[12] She added that loving the country is natural and necessary, while rebelling against the country is by no means acceptable. Lam pointed to the lack of systematic patriotic education in the HKSAR in the past, and she deplored the media distortion of the need for patriotic education. The Chief Executive also revealed that the Chinese history subject would become a compulsory subject in schools – a correct path away from the distorted development in the past when Chinese history was regarded only as an elective for senior secondary schoolchildren.

In the summer of 2021, patriotic education was accelerated and deepened in the HKSAR. The Radio Television Hong Kong (RTHK) cooperated with the China Central Television (CCTV) to promote the programs on patriotic education; it showed the mainland television programs and documentaries on the PLA, CCP's history and China during the Second World War.[13] On the other hand, the EDB organized and held talks for teachers at primary, secondary and special school levels to understand how to teach national security education in classes.[14] In August 2021, the workshops held by the EDB on national security education attracted the registration of teachers from 90 percent of the local schools – an indication that all the schools and their teachers took the national security education seriously.[15] The EDB required all schools to organize a national flag-raising ceremony; 37 out of 511 primary schools started to do so in September 2021.[16] It revised the handbook for school administration and incorporated the principles of requiring all teaching staff to retain the professional conduct, to do anything to prevent and stop student activities that violate the national security law, and to enhance the law-abiding consciousness of students.[17] Some school principals admitted that while national education in the past was politically stereotyped and opposed by the society, the situation changed completely after the promulgation of the national security law in June 2020.[18] In September 2021, one month after the government gazette on the need to respect the national flag and anthem was published, each kindergarten was provided with HK$3,000 subsidy to buy the national flag and its flag-raising pole; the elements of the national flag and emblem were injected into the curriculum of kindergartens; and plans were made to groom some kindergarten children to be the model persons raising the national flag in official ceremonies.[19] Patriotic education is increasingly entrenched into schools after the promulgation of the national security law in late June 2020.

The pro-government and pro-Beijing FEW pushed the HKSAR government to set up a teaching center to provide professional training for teachers to promote national security education.[20] The chairman of the Education Convergence, Ho Hon-kuen, called for the HKSAR government to set up a special committee to reform the education system and its related consultation with stakeholders with the aim of making Hong Kong's education become a hub for education in the Greater Bay Area.[21] The Education Professional Alliance (EPA), a pro-Beijing organization composed of ten groups with the participation of school principals from primary and secondary schools and kindergartens, advocated a "full-scale" promotion of national education and suggested the formation of a special committee on national education.[22] The EDB, in mid-August 2021, submitted a proposal of opening three senior positions, including two principal assistant secretaries, to formulate the policy on national security and national security education and to implement them in schools.[23] One of the three officials would oversee the formulation and implementation of the policy and the supervision of schools, while another would provide logistical support and materials for the schools, scrutinize the quality of textbooks and references and monitor the primary and secondary students' visits and exchanges to the mainland.[24] In response to the request for additional personnel from the EDB, legislators supported it, but the pro-Beijing lawmakers questioned how the government would "depoliticize" the teaching materials and how it would ensure that national security education would not become a "formality" wasting resources.[25] In short, while the government accelerated the speed of entrenching patriotic education at the school level, pro-Beijing groups and elites have been not only collaborating with but also checking against the HKSAR administration to sustain the momentum of national education.

Patriotic education has been strengthened through various extra-curricular activities in the HKSAR. In late September, the Junior Police Call's Buddy Scheme arranged a group of primary students to visit the headquarters of the Ta Kung and Wen Wei Group, where an exhibition on national education was shown to them.[26] On September 3, 2021, 300 teachers and students were provided with the opportunity to ask questions in a live broadcast interview at the Wanchai Exhibition and Convention Center with three mainland Chinese astronauts in the space.[27] The event was covered extensively in the pro-Beijing media and it was organized by the Liaison Office, whose deputy director Tan Tieniu attended together with Chief Executive Carrie Lam. Two days later, the Liaison Office's technology division deputy director Xu Kai severely criticized the Hong Kong education system as "chaotic," and he added that only patriotic education and patriotic people ruling Hong Kong would be able to stop the chaos.[28]

Apart from the deepening of patriotic education, higher education institutes began to deal with the "excessive" activities left from the 2019 anti-extradition movement. After the criticisms from pro-Beijing media, campuses at various universities, including the HKU and the HKUST, cleaned up the posters, stickers and placards in support of the 2019 anti-extradition bill movement.[29] In the name of resuming the classes for September 2021, the HKUST sent the cleaning staff to remove all the words, slogans and banners resisting the extradition bill.[30] The Student Union at the CUHK strategically removed the head of a statue that showed a protestor opposing the extradition bill. The Polytechnic University ordered a student newspaper to be removed on the grounds that its content was "factually inaccurate," but it was rumored that the university authorities found the student newspaper's interview with an organization that assisted and supported the democrats who were imprisoned for their illegal protest activities in 2019 as inappropriate.[31] Clearly, while the management of local universities cooperated with the HKSAR government to remove the legacies of the 2019 anti-extradition movement, some university students were aware of the necessity of having a strategic withdrawal amid the widespread crackdown of political interest groups and individual democrats involved in the 2019 anti-extradition movement.

Moral education has also been strengthened at the school level to ensure that students are trained to be more law-abiding and behaviorally more responsible than the turbulent riots in the latter half of 2019. In August 2021, 85 classic works, including Chinese literature and poems, were added to the curriculum development of primary and secondary schools.[32] To restore socio-political order in the HKSAR and to reshape the political culture of Hong Kong students, four pillars of education have been established after the promulgation of the national security law: national security education, national education, Chinese history and culture and moral education. These four pillars have been integrated into all the subjects and the extra-curricular activities of students at the kindergarten, primary and secondary levels, diluting their local Hong Kong identity and consolidating the mainland Chinese politico-cultural identity. Indeed, it remains to be seen whether the politico-cultural identity of Hong Kong students will change, because in the past, they tended to separate their cultural identity of being Chinese from their political identification with the CCP.[33]

Legalization of Education: Political Participation Costs of Students and Teachers

The new emphasis on patriotic education and the swift imposition of the national security law onto the HKSAR in June 2020 led to the arrest, prosecution and imprisonment of many lawbreakers during the 2019 anti-extradition bill movement, which was led by students and intellectuals. Former Chief Executive C. Y.

158   *Adaptation to Mainlandization and Decolonization*

Leung set up an 803 Fund to seek judicial review in asking the EDB to release the data on those teachers who were adjudicated as having misconduct.[34] Leung remarked that parents had the right to know more about these teachers, and that the EDB should strike a balance between the protection of the privacy of the teachers concerned and the interest of the public.[35] The Secretary for Education, Kevin Yeung, said that the EDB handled those teachers who had misconduct with proper procedures.[36] Regardless of the court's verdict on the appeal, some teachers are now increasingly under more psychological pressure than ever before.

Frightened by the prospect of their children being penalized by the HKSAR government, many middle-class parents preferred to migrate out of Hong Kong to other countries, including the UK, Canada, Australia and the United States, especially as the UK government in 2021 opened a new visa program to allow the holders of the British National Overseas (BNO) passports to migrate to the UK and apply for British citizenship later.[37]

Table 5.2 shows that many student leaders were arrested and prosecuted for their involvement in the 2019 anti-extradition movement. The founders and leaders of the Scholarism and later Demosisto, such as Joshua Wong, Agnes Chow, Tiffany Yuen and Ivan Lam were all eventually arrested, prosecuted and imprisoned. Except for Issac Cheng, who finally left the HKSAR for Taiwan, the fate of the leaders of the Demosisto revealed the huge costs of political participation of some young Hong Kong people. Similarly, for the former leaders and activists of the Hong Kong Federation of Students (HKFS), Lester Shum's experiences again unveiled the cost of youth participation in politics. Other leaders such as Willis Ho, Alex Chow and Nathan Law showed that the earlier the activists left the political arena, the more freedom they tended to enjoy, especially Chow and Law, who decided to pursue their overseas graduate studies. Witnessing the political experiences of all these young political leaders and activists, many members of the younger generation have pondered whether they are willing to sacrifice their time and energy in political participation. For many parents whose children participated in social and political movement from 2012 to 2019, they also developed their anxiety over whether their sons and daughters should participate in politics at the expense of their safety and future development.

There are many other examples of young people who have to encounter huge political costs due to their participation in politics. Edward Leung Tin-kei, one of the founders of the localist group named Hong Kong Indigenous, was imprisoned for six years in June 2018 for his participation in the Mongkok riot in early 2016. Born in the mainland and knowing that his grandfather had been a KMT member persecuted by the CCP, Leung migrated to Hong Kong when he was a child.[38] Leung studied philosophy and politics at the University of Hong Kong, developing his political perspectives on both the mainland and the HKSAR. The HKSAR government, to Leung, failed to respond to public opinion for democratization. He began to participate actively in politics by joining the Occupy Central movement in November 2014 and forming the Hong Kong

Table 5.2 Student Activists and the Costs of Their Political Participation

Student leaders	Their participation in politics and its political cost
Joshua Wong, General Secretary of the Demosisto, 2016–2020	Wong was a convener and founder of the student activist group named Scholarism in May 2011 when he was 15 years old. Wong became politically active in the anti-national education movement in 2012 and in the 2014 Occupy Central movement. His crucial role in the Occupy movement resulted in his nomination by *Time Magazine* as one of the most influential teens, and by *Fortune* magazine as one of the world's greatest leaders in 2015. Wong was also nominated for the Nobel Peace Prize in 2017. However, in August 2017, Wong and two other democracy activists were convicted and jailed for their roles in the occupation of Civic Square at the incipient stage of the 2014 Occupy Central protests; in January 2018, Wong was convicted and jailed again for failing to comply with a court order for clearance of the Mongkok protest site during the Hong Kong protests in 2014. He played a major role in lobbying and persuading US politicians to pass the Hong Kong Human Rights and Democracy Act during the 2019–2020 Hong Kong protests. Wong was disqualified by the HKSAR government from running in the 2019 District Council elections. In December 2020, Wong was convicted and imprisoned for the third time over an unauthorized protest outside police headquarters in June 2019. In January 2021, Wong was among 53 members of the pro-democratic camp arrested under the national security law, for being involved in a primary election held in the summer of 2020 before the originally scheduled LegCo election. In April 2021, Wong was sentenced to 4 months in jail, followed by another imprisonment for 10 more months in May for his participation in an assembly marking the Tiananmen incident in June 2020.
Agnes Chow Ting, Deputy Secretary of Demosisto, 2016–2020	A former spokesperson of Scholarism. In 2014, Chow studied at the Hong Kong Baptist University for her specialization in government and international relations. In January 2018, she tried to participate in the 2018 LegCo by-election but was disqualified by the Electoral Affairs Commission for failing to comply with the relevant electoral law. Agnes Chow is very fluent in Japanese, and she got a lot of interviews and coverage in the Japanese media. Her YouTube channel once attracted 300,000 subscribers in 2020. The Japanese media described Chow as the "Goddess of Democracy" for her active promotion of democracy in the HKSAR. In June 2020, the political party she founded with Joshua Wong and Ivan Lam, namely Demosisto, was disbanded. In December 2020, she was sentenced to 10 months' imprisonment. Chow was released from prison in June 2021 after serving six months sentence. Her Facebook profile was then deleted.

(Continued)

Table 5.2 Student Activists and the Costs of Their Political Participation *(Continued)*

Student leaders	Their participation in politics and its political cost
Issac Cheng Ka-long, vice-chairman of Demosisto, 2019–2020	Cheng was a volunteer of the Federation of Trade Union when he was a primary school student. In 2012, he participated actively in the anti-national education movement. Later he became the student union council's chairman at the Shu Yan University. In 2019, he protested in the LegCo hearing on the national anthem law and later was prosecuted for not respecting the LegCo's order. He was fined HK$1,000. In July 2000, the pro-Beijing media reported that Cheng escaped to the UK or Taiwan. In March 2021, it was reported that he left the HKSAR for Taiwan.
Tiffany Yuen Ka-wai, vice-chairwoman, Demosisto, 2017–2018	She studied Chinese at the Chinese University of Hong Kong and was directly elected as a District Council member in the Southern district. In the primary election held by the democrats before the September 2020 LegCo elections, Yuen was also selected by voters. In January 2021, Yuen was arrested together with other democrats for violating the national security law by organizing and participating in the primary election. In May 2021, she was imprisoned for four months for her participation in all illegal assembly for the Tiananmen candlelight vigil on June 4, 2020. In September 2021, Yuen was named by the media as one of the "troublemakers" who tried to organize a prison "gang" resisting the officers of the Correctional Services Department.
Ivan Lam Long-yin, member of the Executive Committee of the Demosisto, 2016–2018 and chairman from 2018 to 2020	Both Ivan Lam and Joshua Wong were classmates in the United Christian College and they were the founders of Demosisto. Lam and Wong were also the student leaders of the 2014 Occupy Central movement. In June 2014, Lam participated in a protest opposing the LegCo's discussion of the northeast development and plunged into the legislature illegally. In August 2017, Lam was sentenced to 13 months' imprisonment. In December 2020, he was sentenced to seven months' imprisonment for his illegal participation in an assembly that surrounded the police headquarters on June 21, 2019.
Willis Ho Kit Wang, Deputy Secretary of the Hong Kong Federation of Students (HKFS), 2013–2014	She was a former reporter of HK01. In June 2014, she participated in a protest against the LegCo's deliberation and financial approval of the development in northeast development. Ho was arrested. In February 2016, she was sentenced to 120 hours of social service for her participation in an illegal protest. In August 2017, after the government appeal, the court ruled that Ho should be imprisoned for 13 months. In 2019, she was a filmmaker of a documentary on the anti-extradition bill movement.
Alex Chow Yong-kang, Secretary of the HKFS, 2014–2015	Chow was the vice-president (external) of the Hong Kong University Students' Union, and he was one of the student organizers of the 2014 Occupy Central movement. In February 2015, he spoke at the Geneva Summit for Human Rights and Democracy together with Lester Shum in front of an international audience of human rights activists. Chow and two other student leaders, Nathan Law and Joshua Wong, were convicted in July 2016 of participation and organization of an unlawful assembly at the Civic Square in the Central Government Complex. Later in 2016, Chow began his master's studies at the London School of Economics, followed by his doctoral studies at the University of California, Berkeley.

(Continued)

Adaptation to Mainlandization and Decolonization 161

Table 5.2 Student Activists and the Costs of Their Political Participation *(Continued)*

Student leaders	Their participation in politics and its political cost
Lester Shum, Deputy Secretary of the HKFS, 2014–2015	Shum studied for his undergraduate degree in government and public administration at the CUHK. He was elected as the vice president of the CUHK Student Union from 2013 to 2014. Chow was also one of the main organizers of the 2014 Occupy Central movement and continued with his political activism. After the 2016 LegCo election, Shum was hired by localist legislator Eddie Chu as an assistant. In September 2019, Shum joined Eddie Chu and Joshua Wong to participate in a forum at Taipei, where they talked about the anti-extradition bill movement at the headquarters of the Democratic Progressive Party. In November 2019, Shum was elected as a district council member in the Hoi Bun constituency in the Tsuen Wan district. In June 2020, he declared his intention to run for the September 2020 LegCo election. Nevertheless, in January 2021, he was arrested together with other 53 democrats who organized the primary election in the summer of 2020. In May 2021, Shum was sentenced to six months' imprisonment for his participation in an unlawful assembly in June 2019.
Nathan Law Kwun-chung, Secretary General (2015–2016)	He received his secondary education at FEW Wong Cho Bau Secondary School and later specialized in cultural studies at Lingnan University, where he was the chair of the Representative Council and the acting president of the Student Union. In September 2016, Law was directly elected as a legislator, making him the youngest lawmaker in the history of the LegCo. However, following the disqualification of two legislators-elect Baggio Leung and Yau Wai-ching, in November 2016, Law was also disqualified from bringing a legislator in July 2017. Together with Alex Chow and Joshua Wong, Law was imprisoned in 2018 for his organization and participation in the activities that stormed into the Civic Square during the 2014 Occupy Central movement. In 2019, Law accepted an offer with a full scholarship from the Council on East Asian Studies at Yale University and he began to pursue his studies for a master's degree in East Asian Studies in August. After the enactment of the national security law in late June 2020, Law announced that he had already moved to London, where he was granted political asylum in April 2021. The Hong Kong police ordered the arrest of Nathan Law for his alleged activities of "inciting secession and collusion" with foreign forces. In March 2021, Law was named a Pritzker Fellow at the University of Chicago's Institute of Politics.

Sources: Compiled from open sources and news reports, including the following websites: Democracy Activists on Trial – Hong Kong Watch and https://hkdc.us/nathan-law/, access date: September 12, 2021; "Student activist Isaac Cheng reported to have left HK for Taiwan," *The Standard*, March 9, 2021, in https://www.thestandard.com.hk/breaking-news/section/4/167014/Student-activist-Isaac-Cheng-reported-to-have-left-HK-for-Taiwan, access date: September 12, 2021.

Indigenous in 2015. In February 2016, Leung was defeated in a by-election held for the LegCo, but he impressively got 66,500 votes. Most importantly, his fiery political speeches revealed his profound sense of Hongkongism and his belief in the need for both Hong Kong and China to be democratized. Although Leung was imprisoned, his slogan advocating the need to "recover Hong Kong during revolutionary times" stimulated and inspired many young participants in the 2019 anti-extradition movement.

Other localists who were imbued with a strong sense of Hong Kong identity became the targets of arrests, prosecutions and imprisonment. One of them was Sunny Cheung, a localist who studied at HKBU, who represented the student sector to lobby the United States for the passage of the Hong Kong Human Rights and Democracy Act, and who eventually left Hong Kong for the UK in August 2020, two months after the promulgation of the national security law. In August 2021, Cheung announced that he would pursue his graduate studies at John Hopkins University.[39] Unlike Sunny Cheung, who can be regarded as a lucky localist, other localists like Ventus Lau Wing-hong, Tony Chung Hon-lam and Wong Yat-chin. Ventus Lau studied Chinese language and literature at the CUHK and was elected as a District Council member in 2015. In June 2019, Lau and his like-minded supporters appealed to the netizens to petition the consulates of 19 countries in the HKSAR to oppose the extradition bill.[40] In January 2021, Lau was arrested for his participation in the primary election held for the pro-democracy candidates in July 2020. As of September 2021, Lau was remanded in custody. Tony Chung Hon-lam was a founder of Studentlocalism in April 2016, and it was disbanded immediately after the promulgation of the national security law in late June 2020. In October 2020, Chung was arrested by the police together with two other members of Studentlocalism for using an Internet platform to "spread information that instigated others to engage in secession."[41] From 2017 to 2019, Chung's activities were followed by the reporters of *Wen Wei Po* and *Ta Kung Pao*, including his January 2019 visit to Taiwan, where he and his friends were accused of meeting the special envoys from President Tsai Ing-wen. Eventually, the reporters of *Wen Wei Po* and *Ta Kung Pao* were barred from entering Taiwan for three years for their "fake news" produced.[42] In December 2020, Chung was sentenced to four months' imprisonment for his disrespect to the PRC national flag and participation in an illegal assembly. Wong Yat-chin is not only a youngster active in Student Politicism, which was set up in May 2020, but also a student with a strong sense of Hongkongism.[43] In October 2020, Student Politicism organized an anti-extradition movement photograph exhibition in different districts. In November, four members of Student Politicism, including Wong, were arrested for illegal assembly. In December 2020, the group helped the prisoners to collect logistical materials and acquired 40 bags just within an hour, showing its popularity and public support. In June 2021, Wong attended the DSE public examination and his English subject's result was unsatisfactory; he admitted that he had spent a lot of time in organizing Politicism and that his dream would be a student enrolling in government and public administration at the CUHK. Wong hoped that he would study politics in Taiwan, but he was afraid that he might not be allowed to leave the HKSAR.[44] When asked whether he regretted his political participation, Wong said having real political experiences is different from what he read from books. Wong's experience showed that a minority of localist students are persisting in political participation even though its cost is potentially tremendous. In September 2021, Wong was arrested with three leaders of Student Politicism for allegedly violating the national security law.

Because of the political transformation of the HKSAR from a partially pluralistic system to an authoritarian system where politically active students were legally punished, the fate of teachers at the high education level is the same. Joseph Cheng Yu-shek, a professor in political science formerly at CUHK and later at CityU, became a target of political attacks and persecution by the authorities. Cheng became increasingly participatory in politics, being the convener of the Power for Democracy, a political group responsible for coordinating the candidates of the pan-democratic camp in LegCo and district elections from 2002 to 2019. He was also a former secretary of the Civic Party in 2003 and a convener of the Alliance for True Democracy from 2013 to 2015. After the promulgation of the national security law in late June 2020, it was rumored that Cheng was on the list of targets prepared by the national security apparatus, because he had been accused of having "close foreign connections" during the 2014 Occupy Central movement.[45] Cheng had a practice of hiring research assistants for his research projects, but one of them took photographs of his alleged contacts with foreign organizations, such as the National Democracy Institute, and published a book critical of him.[46] As a citizen of Australia, Cheng decided to return to his home country. His experiences showed that, as an overseas Chinese scholar, it might be much better to maintain political neutrality in the HKSAR; any political participation in support of the local democracy movement could bring about personal costs, including the accusations that he had "foreign connections" and was one of the "black hands" behind the 2014 Occupy Central movement.

Other examples of local scholars whose political participation brought about personal costs are numerous. They include law professor Benny Yiu-ting Tai, an organizer of the 2014 Occupy Central movement and one of the planners of the primary election held for the democrats in July 2020; Chan Kin-man, another organizer of the Occupy Central movement and a former sociologist at the CUHK; Ip Iam-chong, an assistant professor in cultural studies at Lingnan University and whose contract was not renewed for his possible active participation in social and political movement; and Benson Wong Wai-kwok, a former assistant professor at HKBU whose contract was also not renewed for his possible participation in union politics and social movement. In July 2020, Benny Tai was fired by the University of Hong Kong for his misconduct after the court sentenced him to 16 months' imprisonment for his leadership and participation in the 2014 Occupy Central movement.[47] His dismissal was criticized as an "infringement" of "academic freedom."[48] As with Benny Tai, Chan

Kin-man was sentenced in 2019 to 16 months' imprisonment for his leadership and organization of the 2014 Occupy Central movement, but he quickly retired from the CUHK in 2019 without facing the fate of being dismissed by his university. Unlike Tai and Chan, who apparently got substantiation from their universities, Ip and Wong were on contractual terms. As such, Ip and Wong's situation was far more academically and politically vulnerable than Tai and Chan's. Both Ip and Wong can be seen as politically active academics whose contracts were not renewed apparently on political grounds, regardless of whether their academic merit and publications were strong enough. While Ip was active in social and political participation in defense of Hong Kong's sustainable development and environmental protection, Wong was the former chair of the academic staff union at Baptist University and was often critical of the university authorities. Under the pretext of not commenting on individual cases, local universities found it relatively easy to deal with the fate of Ip and Wong. If Benny Tai, who had substantiation, was also vulnerable to being dismissed due to his political participation and criminal conviction, the fate of other academics who were and are on contractual terms must be more politically vulnerable even though their academic merit and publications were defensible.

The question of academic freedom is problematic in the HKSAR. As Hong Kong's publicly funded universities are all eager to be ranked high by international agencies that rank all universities in the world, they tend to focus on cutting-edge research, funded research projects and academic journal publications with high impact factor. Under this environment of academic capitalism, academics who are interested in advocating their political theory and philosophy, like Benny Tai and Horace Chin Wan of Lingnan University, tended to be high profile in public but raised the eyebrows of university authorities who attached importance to quiet research outputs.[49] Moreover, academics whose academic merit and publications were strong but who participated in politics, like Joseph Cheng and Johannes Chan Man-mun, could be politically targeted and perhaps deliberately blocked in their career advancement.[50]

After the promulgation of the national security law, academic freedom has been arguably most affected in the area of political science and history, especially those who teach and research in Hong Kong. An academic at the HKUST, Lee Ching-kwan from the University of California, was openly criticized by the pro-Beijing media for making remarks at a forum organized by the US-based Hong Kong Democracy Council that the HKSAR was "not" part of China.[51] Two other professors of journalism at the HKU were a target of complaint by a mainland student, who complained to the national security commission in the HKSAR.[52] One local university canceled a course on Hong Kong politics, partly because the instructor who taught the course left and partly because of self-censorship.[53] A few academics who taught Hong Kong history changed a course outline by deleting sensitive topics, such as the Tiananmen incident in the PRC and the local democracy movement, and by adding politically correct topics, such as Japan's invasion of Hong Kong and the mainland's ancient and historical relations with Hong Kong.[54] Creeping self-censorship can be hiddenly seen in the disciplines of history and political science, while academic freedom appears to thrive in other disciplines – a phenomenon that reflects the limited but targeted impacts of the national security law on academia in the HKSAR.

On the other hand, some academics continue to teach politically sensitive subjects, like Hong Kong politics and Chinese politics. Topics like Xinjiang, Tibet and the anti-extradition movement in the HKSAR in 2019 remain highly sensitive. However, if the teachers concerned describe the facts and allow students to do so without adopting an advocacy and a normative approach, the prospects of academic freedom may not be so bleak as outsiders may have portrayed.[55] For inexperienced teachers, their self-censorship is understandable. The challenges are for teachers and students to adapt to the political transformations and yet to cherish the existing freedom of thought, speech and publications. One of the authors is an external examiner of political science courses at two local universities. Students continue to write their answers freely and critically. From this perspective, the quality assurance mechanisms at local universities, including the use of external examiners, to ensure the quality of the delivery of courses in politics appear to work well. Of course, the academic freedom of teachers and students depends on the tolerance of not only external examiners but also university authorities. Arguably, all university teachers and authorities should strive for the protection of the existing academic space to defend their cherished academic freedom, bearing in mind the limitations imposed on them by the national security law. Students, on the other hand, should not be afraid of speaking out within the parameters of the national security law. Indeed, it is easier said than done and the developments of academic freedom remain to be observed carefully.

Migration of Students and Teachers Out of Hong Kong

A total of 89,200 citizens left the HKSAR from mid-2020 to mid-2021.[56] It was unclear how many students and teachers were among these 89,200 immigrants. Figure 5.1 shows the student enrolment in day schools by level from 2002 to 2020. It shows that student enrolment declined over time, especially after 2019. It must be noted that primary school students tended to increase in the period from 2005 to 2012, when the Donald Tsang administration was characterized by social stability and economic prosperity. Although students enrolling in kindergartens increased from 2019 to 2020, students enrolling in primary and secondary schools dropped by 12,636 (1,707 at the secondary level and 12,636 at the primary level). The figures showed a significant decline in student population, perhaps pointing to the likelihood that many parents decided to send their children out of the HKSAR because many arrested, prosecuted and imprisoned democrats were young students.

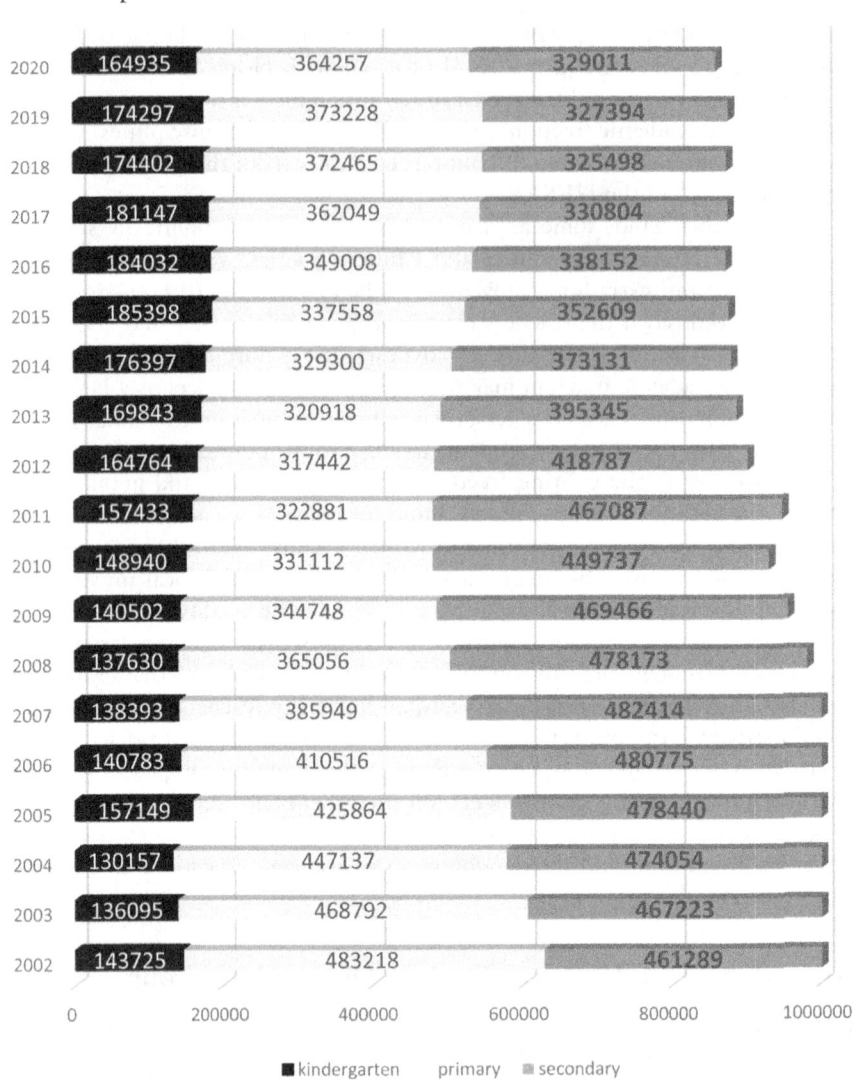

166 *Adaptation to Mainlandization and Decolonization*

Year	Kindergarten	Primary	Secondary
2020	164935	364257	329011
2019	174297	373228	327394
2018	174402	372465	325498
2017	181147	362049	330804
2016	184032	349008	338152
2015	185398	337558	352609
2014	176397	329300	373131
2013	169843	320918	395345
2012	164764	317442	418787
2011	157433	322881	467087
2010	148940	331112	449737
2009	140502	344748	469466
2008	137630	365056	478173
2007	138393	385949	482414
2006	140783	410516	480775
2005	157149	425864	478440
2004	130157	447137	474054
2003	136095	468792	467223
2002	143725	483218	461289

Figure 5.1 Student Enrolment in Day Schools by Level, 2002 to 2020

Note: Starting from 2009, the education system was changed from 3-2-2-3 (2-year higher forms and 2-year pre-university) to 3-3-4 (3-year higher forms) such that the two systems coexisted from 2009 to 2012.

Sources: Students Enrolments Statistics, Education Bureau, 2012/2013 and 2020/2021, in websites: https://www.edb.gov.hk/attachment/en/about-edb/publications-stat/figures/Enrol_2012.pdf and https://www.edb.gov.hk/attachment/en/about-edb/publications-stat/figures/Enrol_2020.pdf, access date: August 3, 2021.

Table 5.3 Operating Classes, Accommodation and Student Enrolment in Primary and Secondary Schools by Religious Background of School, 2019 and 2020 (Numbers in Primary Schools/Secondary Schools)

Religious background of school	Classes 2019/2020	Accommodation 2019/2020	Enrolment 2019/2020
All	13,725/12,130	383,845/381,664	373,228/327,394
	13,713/12,219	383,379/383,405	364,257/329,011
No religion	5,867/5,241	160,438/164,686	155,185/140,308
	5,860/5,300	160,148/165,347	150,864/141,692
Christianity/Protestantism	4,511/3,977	129,504/124,067	126,657/108,557
	4,517/4,005	129,650/124,876	124,299/108,807
Catholicism	2,598/2,154	74,082/69,386	72,075/58,902
	2,590/2,155	73,806/69,418	70,503/58,567
Buddhism	363/448	9,960/12,740	9,849/11,354
	365/452	9,972/14,014	9,562/11,568
Taoism	220/143	5,799/4,621	5,726/3,947
	218/143	5,775/4,621	5,481/3,992
Confucianism, Buddhism and Taoism	99/114	2,475/3,582	2,381/3,090
	99/113	2,475/3,582	2,238/3,115
Other religions	67/53	1,587/1,562	1,355/1,236
	64/51	1,553/1,547	1,310/1,273

Source: Student Enrolment Statistics, 2019 and 2020, Education Bureau, in websites: https://www.edb.gov.hk/attachment/en/about-edb/publications-stat/figures/Enrol_2019.pdf and https://www.edb.gov.hk/attachment/en/about-edb/publications-stat/figures/Enrol_2020.pdf, access date: August 3, 2021.

Table 5.3 highlights the student enrolment in 2019 and 2020. The drop in the number of primary and secondary school students was prominent in schools without religious affiliation and schools that were Christian/Protestant and Catholic. Buddhist and Confucian schools tended to witness a slight increase in student numbers. The prominent decline in student numbers could be found in Christian/Protestant and Catholic schools, where students tended to be taught with the values of liberalism. Because many student activists in the 2019 anti-extradition bill movement were legally punished, the potentially intimidating impact on the students enrolling in Christian/Protestant and Catholic schools could not be underestimated.

Figure 5.2 shows the demographic characteristics of the one-way permit holders from the mainland with implications for Hong Kong's education from 1998 to 2019. The age group of those four or under four years old jumped from 2,272 in 1998 to 9,122 in 1999, but the number tended to decline from 2002 onward to 2,915 in 2019. Due to the outbreak and persistence of Covid-19, the number dropped to 743 in 2020. On the other hand, the age group from 5 to 14 years old dropped from a high level of 27,899 in 1998 to 14,566 in 1999, and then the number steadily declined from 2001 onward to 4,787 in 2019. Again, Covid-19 dragged down the number of one-way permit holders coming to Hong Kong in 2020 when only 1,417 of them in the age group of 5 to 14 years old came to the HKSAR. The age group of 15 to 24 years old, however, increased

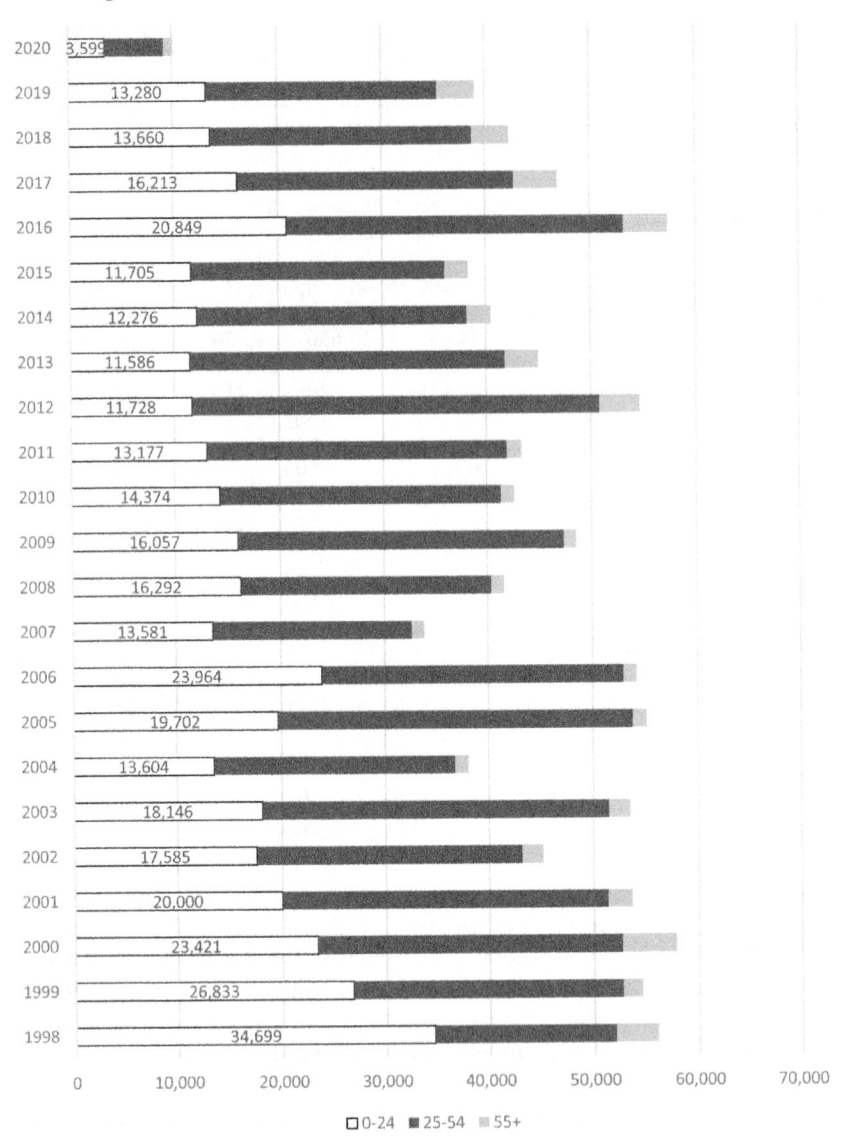

168 *Adaptation to Mainlandization and Decolonization*

Year	0-24
2020	3,599
2019	13,280
2018	13,660
2017	16,213
2016	20,849
2015	11,705
2014	12,276
2013	11,586
2012	11,728
2011	13,177
2010	14,374
2009	16,057
2008	16,292
2007	13,581
2006	23,964
2005	19,702
2004	13,604
2003	18,146
2002	17,585
2001	20,000
2000	23,421
1999	26,833
1998	34,699

□ 0-24   ■ 25-54   ■ 55+

Figure 5.2 Demographic Characteristics of One-Way Permit Holders: Implications for Education, 1998–2019

Sources: See government statistics, in websites: https://www.had.gov.hk/file_manager/tc/documents/public_services/services_for_new_arrivals_from_the_mainland/2020%20Q4%20Report.pdf, https://www.had.gov.hk/file_manager/tc/documents/public_services/services_for_new_arrivals_from_the_mainland/report-2019q4.pdf, https://www.had.gov.hk/file_manager/tc/documents/public_services/services_for_new_arrivals_from_the_mainland/report_2017q4.pdf, https://www.had.gov.hk/file_manager/tc/documents/public_services/services_for_new_arrivals_from_the_mainland/report_2012q4.pdf, https://www.had.gov.hk/file_manager/tc/documents/public_services/services_for_new_arrivals_from_the_mainland/report_2007q4.pdf, https://www.had.gov.hk/file_manager/tc/documents/public_services/services_for_new_arrivals_from_the_mainland/report_2002q4.pdf, access date: March 3, 2021.

slightly over time; the number rose from 4,528 in 1998 to 6,117 in 2008, and then it declined to 5,578 in 2019. It must be noted that the occurrence of the anti-extradition bill movement in the latter half of 2019 tended to frighten many mainlanders, who hesitated to come to Hong Kong even if they held one-way permits. It can be anticipated that the number of one-way permit holders would gradually increase as Covid-19 would gradually weaken in the coming years.

The implications for Hong Kong's education are twofold: (1) the number of some 3,000 one-way permit holders at four years old and below would have to increase further if the HKSAR wishes to compensate for the seemingly large number of primary schoolchildren who left Hong Kong after the imposition of the national security law in June 2020 and (2) similarly, the annual entry of about 5,000 one-way permit holders at the age of 5 to 14 would not be sufficient to compensate for the migration of many secondary schoolchildren who also left the HKSAR after June 2020. As such, the EDB will have to study how to increase the number of schoolchildren who are one-way permit holders for the sake of maintaining the student population at a level that would not necessitate a cut in the number of primary and secondary schools.

Table 5.4 shows the student enrolment in government-funded university programs in the HKSAR from the 1996–1997 academic year to the 2019–2020 one. It demonstrates that, with the passage of time, the number and total percentage of the local students declined while that of the mainland students increased significantly. In 1996, 97.9 percent of the students enrolling in local universities were local and only 1.26 percent were from the mainland. By 2006, 90 percent of the students studying in local universities were local and 9 percent were from the mainland. In 2020, however, only 79.7 percent of the students studying in local universities were local and 14.1 percent were from the mainland. A considerable degree of mainlandization in the student population at local universities could be seen. In late August 2021, the pro-Beijing media reported that more mainland students came to study for their master degree at Hong Kong universities, and that the educational agencies helping mainland students to pursue studies out of China revealed that the percentage of mainland students making inquiries on their studies in the HKSAR increased by 126 percent from January to July 2021 – a reflection that the Covid-19 continuation and Washington's restrictions on the entry of mainland students to study in the United States might produce a combined effect of driving more mainlanders to consider studying in neighboring Hong Kong.[57]

In fact, a similar trend of mainlandization of the profile of academics could be witnessed, especially as many local Hong Kong students have not been keen to pursue graduate and doctoral studies, while local universities striving for research excellence have been recruiting many top researchers from overseas. These new recruits have been composed of many mainland-born academics who acquired their doctorates in top foreign universities in North America and Europe. The irreversible trend of the mainlandization of students and teachers at Hong Kong's universities means that their political culture of having a much stronger mainland Chinese identity and a stronger sense of Chinese nationalism is different from the Hong Kong-born academics and students. The continuous

Table 5.4 Student Enrolment (Headcount) in University Grants Council-Funded Programs at Hong Kong Universities from 1996–1997 to 2019–2020

Mode of programs	Total	Local	Mainland	Asia	Other	Sub-total (mainland + Asia + others)	% Total
Ug	48,525	48,438	5	24	58	87	0.18%
TPg	10,539	10,398	16	45	80	141	1.34%
RPg	3,620	3,514	769	101	136	1,006	27.79%
Y1996	62,684	61,391	791	170	278	1,293	2.06%
% Total	100%	97.9%	1.26%	0.27%	0.44%	2.06%	–
Ug	48,345	48,270	7	15	53	75	0.16%
TPg	11,056	10,891	39	43	83	165	1.49%
RPg	3,823	2,712	899	97	116	1,111	29.06%
Y1997	63,224	61,889	946	155	255	1,355	2.14%
% Total	100%	97.86%	1.50%	0.25%	0.40%	2.14%	–
Ug	47,644	47,541	36	21	40	97	0.20%
TPg	11,103	10,937	43	47	76	166	1.50%
RPg	3,875	2,764	919	87	105	1,111	28.67%
Y1998	62,622	61,245	1,000	155	222	1,377	2.20%
% Total	100%	97.80%	1.60%	0.25%	0.35%	2.20%	–
Ug	47,467	47,243	177	26	21	224	0.47%
TPg	11,350	11,163	62	59	66	187	1.65%
RPg	4,021	2,825	1,022	81	93	1,196	29.74%
Y1999	62,838	61,227	1,263	167	181	1,611	2.56%
% Total	100%	97.44%	2.01%	0.27%	0.29%	2.56%	–
Ug	47,606	47,244	333	12	17	362	0.76%
TPg	11,255	11,063	69	68	55	192	1.71%
RPg	3,962	2,744	1,059	88	70	1,218	30.7%
Y2000	62,823	61,042	1,462	170	148	1,781	2.83%
% Total	100%	97.17%	2.32%	0.27%	0.24%	2.83%	–
Ug	48,054	47,518	506	10	20	536	1.12%
TPg	10,959	10,718	101	71	69	241	2.20%
RPg	4,284	2,815	1,301	101	67	1,469	34.29%
Y2001	63,297	61,044	1,912	183	158	2,253	3.56%
% Total	100%	96.4%	3.02%	0.29%	0.25%	3.56%	–
Ug	49,170	48,494	633	21	22	676	1.37%
TPg	10,947	10,667	121	74	85	280	2.56%
RPg	4,445	2,799	1,475	109	62	1,646	37.03%
Y2002	64,562	61,958	2,230	204	170	2,604	4.03%
% Total	100%	95.97%	3.45%	0.32%	0.26%	4.03%	–
Ug	50,129	48,751	842	37	29	908	1.81%
TPg	10,674	10,653	137	39	45	221	2.07%
RPg	5,225	3,163	1,868	116	78	2,062	39.46%
Y2003	66,028	62,824	2,849	197	158	3,204	4.85%
% Total	100%	95.15%	4.31%	0.30%	0.24%	4.85%	–
Ug	50,898	49,520	1,284	60	34	1,378	2.71%
TPg	80,89	7,949	71	29	40	140	1.73%
RPg	5,233	3,031	2,003	121	78	2,202	42.08%
Y2004	64,220	60,492	3,362	210	156	3,728	5.81%
% Total	100%	94.19%	5.24%	0.33%	0.24%	5.81%	–

(Continued)

Table 5.4 Student Enrolment (Headcount) in University Grants Council-Funded Programs at Hong Kong Universities from 1996–1997 to 2019–2020 *(Continued)*

Mode of programs	Total	Local	Mainland	Asia	Other	Sub-total (mainland + Asia + others)	% Total
Ug	51,625	49,481	2,007	99	38	2,144	4.15%
TPg	5,628	5,519	56	25	28	109	1.94%
RPg	5,474	2,954	2,307	120	94	2,520	46.04%
Y2005	62,728	62,255	4,370	244	160	4,773	7.61%
% Total	100%	92.39%	6.97%	0.39%	0.26%	7.61%	–
Ug	52,513	49,314	2,973	161	65	3,199	6.09%
TPg	4,668	4,571	59	19	19	97	2.07%
RPg	5,716	2,554	2,722	111	87	2,920	51.08%
Y2006	62,897	56,511	5,754	292	171	6,217	9.88%
% Total	100%	90.12%	9.15%	0.46%	0.27%	9.88%	–
Ug	53,359	49,380	3,658	218	103	3,979	7.5%
TPg	4,506	4,418	56	19	13	88	2.0%
RPg	5,871	2,646	3,036	110	79	3,225	54.9%
Y2007	63,736	56,443	6,751	347	195	7,293	11.4%
% Total	100%	88.6%	10.3%	0.8%	0.3%	11.4%	–
Ug	55,050	50,260	4,348	286	156	4,790	8.7%
TPg	3,951	3,893	39	13	6	58	1.5%
RPg	5,959	2,420	3,324	118	98	3,539	59.4%
Y2008	64,960	56,586	7,713	418	262	8,392	12.9%
% Total	100%	87.1%	11.9%	0.6%	0.4%	12.9%	–
Ug	56,610	51,419	4,562	436	193	5,191	9.2%
TPg	3,611	3,558	35	12	6	53	1.5%
RPg	6,322	2,239	3,830	146	107	4,083	64.6%
Y2009	66,543	57,210	8,429	596	308	9,333	14.0%
% Total	100%	86.0%	12.7%	0.9%	0.5%	14.0%	–
Ug	57,565	51,967	4,638	721	239	5,598	9.7%
TPg	3,578	3,513	43	12	10	65	1.8%
RPg	6,462	6,056	4,041	216	149	4,406	668.2%
Y2010	67,605	57,531	8,724	950	400	10,074	14.9%
% Total	100%	85.1%	12.9%	1.4%	0.6%	14.9%	–
Ug	58,412	52,498	4,583	1,057	274	5,914	10.1%
TPg	3,686	3,599	55	17	15	87	2.4%
RPg	6,572	1,805	4,299	280	188	4,767	72.5%
Y2011	68,625	57,855	8,937	1,355	478	10,770	15.7%
% Total	100%	84.3%	13.0%	2.0%	0.7%	15.7%	–
Ug	76,351	67,951	6,315	1,750	334	8,399	11.0%
TPg	3,721	3,627	62	19	13	94	2.5%
RPg	6,819	1,653	4,586	335	246	5,166	75.8%
Y2012	86,891	73,232	10,963	2,105	593	13,659	15.7%
% Total	100%	84.3%	12.6%	2.4%	0.7%	15.7%	–
Ug	78,219	69,277	6,510	2,096	325	8,942	11.4%
TPg	3,427	3,316	86	14	11	111	3.2%
RPg	7,014	1,557	4,767	385	305	5,457	77.8%
Y2013	91,585	87,075	11,374	2,495	641	14,510	15.8%
% Total	100%	84.2%	12.4%	2.7%	0.7%	15.8%	–

(Continued)

Table 5.4 Student Enrolment (Headcount) in University Grants Council-Funded Programs at Hong Kong Universities from 1996–1997 to 2019–2020 *(Continued)*

Mode of programs	Total	Local	Mainland	Asia	Other	Sub-total (mainland + Asia + others)	% Total
Ug	80,914	71,540	6,630	2,416	328	9,374	11.6%
TPg	3,475	3,380	69	15	11	95	2.7%
RPg	7,118	1,438	4,909	400	371	5,680	79.8%
Y2014	91,507	76,356	11,610	2,831	710	15,151	16.6%
% Total	100%	83.4%	12.7%	3.1%	0.8%	16.6%	–
Ug	82,603	72,984	6,712	2,692	9,709	9,709	11.8%
TPg	3,421	3,346	52	14	9	75	2.2%
RPg	7,370	1,442	5,112	424	392	5,928	80.4%
Y2015	93,394	77,681	11,877	3,130	706	15,713	16.8%
% Total	100%	83.2%	12.7%	3.4%	0.8%	16.8%	–
Ug	83,920	73,564	6,847	3,192	317	10,356	12.3%
TPg	3,212	3,149	54	8	1	63	2.0%
RPg	7,567	1,518	5,131	503	415	6,049	79.9%
Y2106	94,699	78,230	12,032	3,707	733	16,469	17.4%
% Total	100%	82.6%	12.7%	3.9%	0.8%	17.4%	–
Ug	85,119	74,278	6,911	3,599	331	10,841	12.7%
TPg	3,000	2,917	70	10	2	83	2.8%
RPg	7,603	1,387	5,117	575	433	6,216	81.8%
Y2017	85,722	68,672	12,099	4,184	766	17,050	19.9%
% Total	100%	80.1%	14.1%	4.9%	0.9%	19.9%	–
Ug	86,037	74,436	6,933	4,300	368	11,601	13.5%
TPg	2,932	2,830	90	9	3	102	3.5%
RPg	7,911	1,553	5,299	618	441	6,358	80.4%
Y2018	96,800	78,739	12,322	4,927	812	18,061	18.7%
% Total	100%	81.3%	12.7%	5.1%	0.8%	18.7%	–
Ug	86,867	74,618	7,096	4,760	393	12,249	14.1%
TPg	2,873	2,773	81	10	6	100	3.5%
RPg	8,378	1,514	5,735	663	466	6,864	81.9%
Y2019	98,118	78,905	12,914	5,446	865	19,213	19.6%
% Total	100%	80.4%	13.2%	5.6%	0.9%	19.6%	–
Ug	85,551	73,074	7,645	4,441	391	12,477	14.6%
TPg	2,054	1,953	81	11	9	101	4.9%
RPg	8,427	1,517	5,879	605	426	6,910	82.0%
Y2020	96,032	76,544	13,580	5,081	824	19,488	20.3%
% Total	100%	79.7%	14.1%	5.3%	0.9%	20.3%	–

Source: Statistical Data on the University Grants Committee, University Grants Committee, in website: https://cdcf.ugc.edu.hk/cdcf/searchStatSiteReport.action, access date: September 12, 2021.

Notes: Level of study: SD – Sub-degree, Ug – Undergraduate, TPg – Taught Postgraduate and RPg – Research Postgraduate.

Sub-total – the number of students coming from the areas outside Hong Kong.

Y – the total number of students in that particular year.

% Total – the number of students divided by the total number of students.

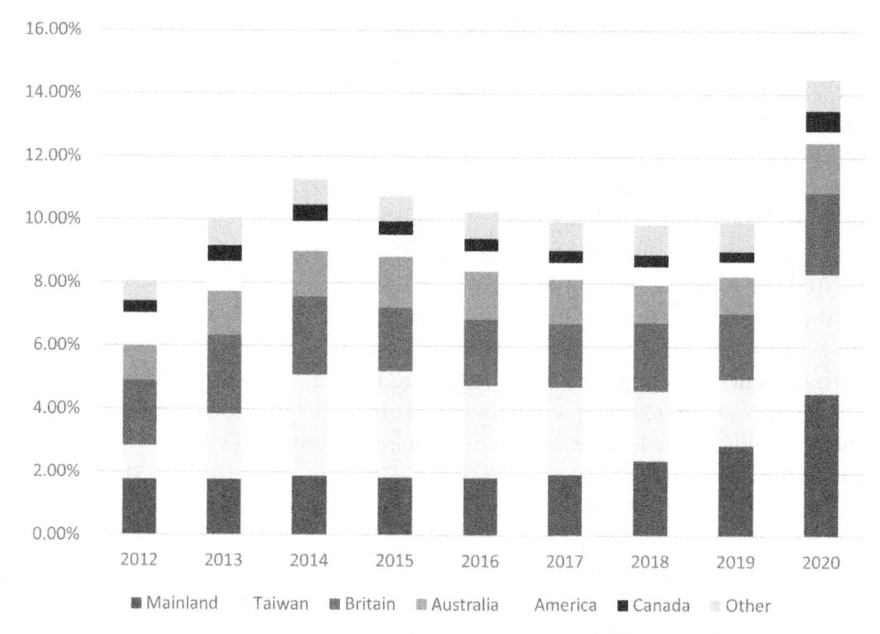

Figure 5.3 Percentage of Students Studying Outside Hong Kong after S6 Graduations, 2012–2020

Source: School Education Statistics Section, Report on Secondary 6 Students' Pathway Survey, 2012–2020, Education Bureau, website: https://www.edb.gov.hk/en/about-edb/publications-stat/figures/index_2.html, access date: September 12, 2021.

migration of mainland-born students and academics to the HKSAR will likely bring about a more "patriotic" and nationalistic education sector in the long run, even though some of them may be politically assimilated into the core values of Hong Kong, such as civil liberties and the rule of law.[58]

As mainland universities have been increasing their international ranking and status, more Hong Kong graduates from the DSE examination have gone to the PRC for further studies than ever before. Figure 5.3 shows that the percentage of Hong Kong students who attended the DSE examination and who went to the mainland increased from 21.9 percent of the total DSE students in 2012 to 31.24 percent in 2020. Other popular destinations of students' outward study include Taiwan, the UK, Australia, Canada and the United States.

Individual Adaptation to Politico-Educational Change

The education sector in the HKSAR has been rapidly adapting to political changes since the imposition of the national security law in late June 2020 and the increasing emphasis on the need for Hong Kong to integrate into the Greater Bay Area (GBA) both economically and socially. While individual stakeholders in the education sector have been adapting to such transformations in various ways, Hong Kong's universities have established their campuses in the GBA to forge greater cooperation with mainland universities and institutes.

Many young teachers, especially the qualified teachers who graduated from local universities, are encountering tremendous pressure to adapt to the political, educational and curriculum changes in the HKSAR. One young qualified teacher who graduated from the Education University revealed that, in the process of job interviews, political questions were asked by the school panels, such as whether a teacher should set a question like "the Nazi party had more good than harm to Jews" and whether she would report to the office if a student showed misconduct in the process of raising the national flag.[59] To protect herself, she deleted her remarks and comments on her social media.[60] Another young qualified teacher revealed that, during his job interview, the school panel asked him on how to enhance the Chinese national identity of students and how to deal with students who might raise a foreign flag in the flag-raising ceremony.[61] He admitted that his teaching content would have to be very careful, especially the wordings in his lecture. A school principal unveiled that a complaint from parents, who were civil servants and pro-government, about a video shown by a teacher on the June 4th incident in China in 1989.[62] Under the circumstances in which stakeholders like parents and students can complain about the teachers' pedagogy and teaching content, the school management and teachers find it not easy to adapt to the new and politically sensitive circumstances.

Professionally and objectively speaking, young teachers who teach history must get the facts accurate. There were cases in which a few teachers who had their licenses revoked by the EDB did show lapses in their teaching pedagogy and content. For instance, the young teacher at the Alliance Primary School was severely criticized for making three errors in his teaching content: (1) claiming that the triads were not tackled by the Hong Kong government, which in fact did and does crack down on their illegal activities; (2) asserting that Andy Chan of the banned Hong Kong National Party just mentioning "independence" once and yet touching on the CCP's bottom line (actually Chan had been criticized for distributing leaflets supportive of "independence" more than once); and (3) interest groups could be easily regarded as "triads" under the Societies Ordinance.[63] Teachers must check the facts of their teaching materials during the preparatory process. As such, the case of revoking the license of the young teacher at the Alliance Primary School did have important implications for teaching: all teachers, young or old, must be professional and factual in their description of historical and current events. Otherwise, their students could be taught wrongly, and parents could complain against inaccurate information conveyed to their children. The adaptation of teachers to the need for not only accuracies in their teaching materials but also professionalism in their preparation is a must.

Indeed, individual teachers encounter tremendous pressure from the environment. Any individual teacher who is deemed to be "politically yellow" or liberal in outlook could run the risk of being criticized and labeled by the pro-Beijing mass media, just like a case in which a "poisonous" and "yellow" teacher, who said in his social media that the police "crazily suppressed" protestors, was regarded by *Wen Wei Po* as "anti-China and making Hong Kong chaotic."[64] Pro-government and pro-Beijing parents urged that the EDB should follow up with this case.[65]

Hence, teachers are under pressure to be very cautious in their public remarks and comments on social media. Any view supportive of the 2019 protests could be construed as holding "yellow" or "unpatriotic" political orientation.

The case of revoking the license of the teacher at the Alliance Primary School did have chilling effects on other teachers. A survey conducted by the PTU, before it was disbanded, showed that 39.2 percent of the 125 respondents strongly disagreed with the view that this teacher had "a plan to spread Hong Kong independence," that 22.4 percent disagreed with the perception, that 18.4 percent had no opinion, that 11.2 percent agreed and 8.8 percent strongly agreed.[66] Most importantly, 50.4 percent of the respondents believed that the materials provided by the EDB were very inadequate, that 22.4 percent thought they were inadequate, that 5.6 percent had no opinion, that 9.6 percent believed that they were adequate and that 12 percent perceived them as very adequate.[67] Although it could be argued that opinion survey of such a small sample might not be representative of all the teachers and principals, the revocation of the license of the teacher at the Alliance Primary School did have both deterrence and chilling impacts on teachers, whose teaching materials would have to be far more professional, accurate and cautious than ever before.

Individual and school adaptation to the new curriculum of Citizenship and Social Studies remains a challenge. The Hong Kong Youth Association conducted a survey of 395 teachers at the senior high level. It found that, on average, teachers gave 6 marks out of a total of 10 marks to express their feeling that the new curriculum change was "clear."[68] When asked about their preparedness of the Chinese subject and new Citizenship and Social Development subject, teachers gave an average of only 4–8 marks and 2.49 marks, respectively – an indication that they did not feel comfortable in dealing with the new subject of Citizenship and Social Development.[69] The crux of the problem was that 67.7 percent of the teachers surveyed said that the new subject had "inadequate content." Most significantly, 72.9 percent of them believed that it would be the most difficult task to teach "Hong Kong under 'one country, two systems.'"[70] The Association suggested that the HKSAR government should publicize and explain the new subject, and that more reference materials should be provided to the teachers, including the organization of talks, seminars and lessons plans. In fact, the ED provided 12 sets of pedagogical materials for teachers to teach the new subject of Citizenship and Social Development in September 2021.[71] Still, many teachers found that the time was too tight and that the materials were inadequate for them to teach the new subject. Moreover, some teachers expressed the view that, if the national security law was still evolving in September 2021, it was not the ripe time for teachers to be required to teach the law concerned.[72] On the other hand, some students found the content of national security law difficult, "complex" and boring.[73] They believed that less efforts should be spent on the subject of Citizenship and Social Development, for students would be assessed on the basis of pass or failure.[74] If so, while the new subject of Citizenship and Social Development is expected to inculcate the content of national security into the psyche of students, their interest in the subject would be no match with their need and determination to perform better in the three core subjects of Chinese,

English and Mathematics. If so, it would be doubtful whether the new subject of Citizenship and Social Development would be able to stimulate the patriotic sentiment among the Hong Kong students.

Perhaps the pro-Beijing elites have understood the limitation of the new subject of Citizenship and Social Development and some of them advocated the need to enhance the content of the battle of Hong Kong during World War Two as a means of increasing the nationalistic sentiment of local students. Chan Hak-kan, a member of the pro-Beijing political party DAB, called for the need to strengthen the patriotism of Hong Kong youth through education.[75] In fact, the EDB in September 2021 made use of the Japanese invasion of China on September 18, 1931 as a pedagogical event to teach students and teachers to be aware of Chinese history and to stimulate their nationalistic sentiment.[76] Various subjects at the primary and secondary school level have integrated the element of the Chinese resistance to the Japanese invasion during the Second World War, including General Studies (primary), Chinese History (junior high and senior high) and History (junior high and senior high).[77] Under these circumstances, teachers and students are destined to adapt to the more nationalistic content of various subjects in the HKSAR.

Institutional Adaptation to Economic Integration with Greater Bay Area

In response to the central government's push for socio-economic integration between the HKSAR and the GBA, many local Hong Kong universities have established their branches and campuses in the mainland. The HKBU set up its United International College (UIC) in Zhuhai in 2005, one year after the CUHK established its campus in Shenzhen. The UIC was jointly founded by HKBU and the Beijing Normal University.[78] Its charter was approved by the PRC Ministry of Education. The CUHK in Shenzhen was established in accordance with the PRC Regulations on Chinese-foreign Cooperation in Running Schools.[79] In July 2012, the Shenzhen Hospital of the HKU went into operation, and it was built by the Shenzhen municipal government with the adoption of a management model under HKU.[80] In April 2020, HKU planned to set up a new medical school in Shenzhen.[81] In 2020, the HKUST planned to set up its new campus in Guangzhou and to admit students in 2022.[82] In March 2020, the CityU planned to set up its new campus with a graduate school in Dongguan and to operate in the year 2023 with a recruitment of 6,000 students.[83] In March 2020, the PolyU planned to establish its research school and campus in the city of Foshan.[84] At the same time, the Open University of Hong Kong (now renamed as Metropolitan University) planned to build up a campus in the city of Zhaoqing and to admit 4,000 students within four years of its operation.[85] In May 2021, the HKU planned for a campus in Shenzhen's Nanshan district where students would travel freely between Hong Kong and the mainland.[86] In July 2021, Lingnan University deepened its cooperation with the Shenzhen Open University, strengthening research and talent training.[87] Clearly, Hong Kong's universities have been utilizing the physical space in the GBA, opening new campuses there and participating in the process of forging closer collaboration in research and teaching with mainland institutes. The central government's GBA blueprint published in February 2019 did stimulate Hong Kong's universities to move further to the mainland to set up campuses, recruit mainland students, conduct cross-border research and fully utilize the funding and research resources in the GBA.[88] On the other hand, mainland universities in the GBA can tap the research talents and expertise from the HKSAR, conducting cutting-edge research while forging cooperation in various disciplines, ranging from medicine to science, and from engineering to artificial intelligence.[89] Innovation in technological advancement can be made through cross-border cooperation among universities, leading to the maintenance and an increase in the economic competitiveness of the HKSAR and the cities in the GBA.[90] As such, a win-win situation can be developed between the mainland universities in the GBA and their Hong Kong counterparts, especially as many of the Hong Kong universities have relatively high international ranking and solid reputation in research.

The Politics of Migration of Students and Teachers

The last chapter touched on the migration of students and teachers after the imposition of the national security law in the HKSAR; this section utilizes the calculation of newspaper advertisements as an indicator of calculating the extent to which teachers migrated out of Hong Kong. In early September 2021, a directly subsidized school in Shatin lost 40 teachers, including some who changed jobs and some who immigrated to other countries.[91] Another school in the Eastern district lost 140 students in the new semester year of 2021–2022.[92] Immigration affected some primary schools; in early September 2021, 54 out of a total of 534 primary schools reduced their number of classes.[93] In Kowloon City district, four schools cut eight classes, while eight classes were eliminated by three schools in Kwun Tong district.[94] Some primary school principals expressed their hope that classes would be allowed to be maintained in small size so as to avoid their schools from being "slaughtered."[95]

The decision of some teachers to leave their teaching profession for other jobs or immigration was due to several factors.[96] First, the national security law and education deterred them from teaching the politically sensitive Citizenship and Social Development subject and History. Second, many teachers had to handle the cases of students who were arrested and prosecuted because of the latter's participation in the 2019 anti-extradition protests. Some teachers believed that students who were arrested and prosecuted were the victims of political struggle between the HKSAR government and radical protestors. Some teachers also felt that the government "suppressed" students and decided to leave the teaching profession, which they did not see as having prospects.[97] As with some students, a minority of teachers felt depressed and upset with the government's determined efforts at penalizing the students who participated in the 2019 anti-extradition movement. Third, some teachers believed that their autonomy and freedom of speech were going to be seriously affected by the national security law, and that outsiders especially the pro-Beijing camp, pointed the accusing fingers at them unfairly without understanding the difficulties they encountered. Fourth, after the promulgation of the national security law, the complaints channels opened by the national security authorities made some teachers feel pressured and depressed. They felt that they were pressured to "indoctrinate" students on the national security law and education – a government policy that some of them resisted and opposed.[98] Fifth, for the teachers who decided to quit the teaching position, they had a strong sense of Hong Kong identity and disagreed with the mainland Chinese political identity imposed on their Hong Kong students. They disagreed with the arguments made by Kevin Yeung, the Secretary for Education, who openly said in early September 2021 that the objectives of national security education "are to develop in students a sense of belonging to the country, an affection for the Chinese people, a sense of national identity, as well as an awareness of and a sense of responsibility for safeguarding national security, and to develop students into law-abiding citizens."[99] In the minds of teachers who quit their profession, the autonomy of teachers and students is far more important than the imposition of Chinese national identity into their psyche. Hence, for those teachers who left their profession, their relatively strong local identity played a crucial role in shaping their decision.

Table 5.5 compares the number of schools and student enrolment in day schools in 2019 with that in 2020. No matter whether students enrolled in primary or secondary schools, most of them studied in aided schools. In 2020, a total of 270,930 primary school students enrolled in aided schools out of an overall of 364,257 students – 74.4 percent of all primary school students. In the same year, a total of 235,991 students enrolled in aided schools out of an overall

Table 5.5 The Number of Schools and Student Enrolment in Day Schools by Type in 2019 and 2020

Type	Number of schools 2019/2020	Student enrolment 2019/2020
Primary School		
Government	34/34	23,043/22,393
Aided	421/421	278,030/270,930
Direct Subsidiary Scheme	21/21	15,935/15,918
International	44/45	23,156/22,783
Other Private	67/68	33,064/32,233
Subtotal	587/589	373,228/364,257
Secondary School		
Government	31/31	20,551/20,467
Aided	359/359	234,319/235,991
Caput[a]	2/2	1,256/1,215
Direct Subsidiary Scheme	59/59	46,049/45,586
International	33/33	17,977/18,232
Other Private	20/22	7,242/7,520
Subtotal	504/506	327,394/329,011

Source: Student Enrolment Statistics 2019–2021, Education Bureau, in websites: https://www.edb.gov.hk/attachment/en/about-edb/publications-stat/figures/Enrol_2019.pdf and https://www.edb.gov.hk/attachment/en/about-edb/publications-stat/figures/Enrol_2020.pdf, access date: September 18, 2021.

Note: [a]Caput schools refer to those schools subsidized by the government in accordance with their student numbers. For details, see EDB – Aided Schools and Caput Schools, access date: September 18, 2021.

of 329,011 students – 71.7 percent of all secondary school students. Hence, most teachers were also hired by aided schools. In government schools, the teachers who were hired were civil servants; their establishment was like that of the aided schools, but less than 10 percent of the total number of students enrolled in these government schools. Private schools are managed in a way parallel to the schools under the direct subsidy scheme with a high degree of flexibility in dealing with the establishment. The number of private primary schools was larger than that of the directly subsidized schools. Yet, this situation is reversed in secondary schools where directly subsidized schools outnumbered private ones.

It can be estimated that 80 percent of all the teachers in Hong Kong are working in aided schools and government schools. They have a standardized salary pay structure and scale; after a teacher is hired, he or she has one point salary increase in accordance with the scale until he or she reaches the maximum point of the rank concerned. The starting and maximum salaries of teachers in Hong Kong's primary schools and secondary school, respectively are shown in Table 5.6.

In the 1980s, when Hong Kong's financial and monetary center developed quickly with prosperous salaries enjoyed by private-sector employees, the pay scale in the teaching profession was unattractive to many people. At that time, those university graduates who wanted to join the teaching profession found it relatively easy to get hired by primary and secondary schools. After an increase in the enrolment of students at the university level in the early 1990s, more university graduates were found in the market. At this juncture, the teaching profession was seen by many university graduates as a career that promised stable salary and good prospects, leading to more university graduates competing for teaching positions. Under these circumstances, primary and secondary schools found it relatively easy to recruit teachers and to choose the most qualified candidates. Nowadays, a teacher's entry salary is already over HK$30,000 and his or her salary can reach over HK$60,000 (for primary school) or HK$70,000 (for secondary school) after working for 15 years.[100] In addition to the mandatory provident fund in which

Table 5.6 The Pay Scale of School Teachers in Hong Kong

Primary school	Secondary school	Salary point	Master pay scale HK$ (monthly)	Currency in USD (monthly)
–	Principal I	49	135,470	17,422
–	Principal II	44	110,170	14,168
HMI	PGM	41	97,745	12,570
HMII	SGM	39	89,845	11,554
SPSM	–	35	75,265	9,679
PSM	GM	33	73,775	9,488
APSM	–	29	61,415	7,898
Starting	Starting	15	31,750	4,083

Notes: APSM: Assistant Primary School Master/Mistress; PSM: Primary School Master/Mistress; SPSM: Senior Primary School Master/Mistress (Vice School Headmaster/Mistress); HM: School Headmaster/Mistress (for Primary School); GM: Graduate Master/Mistress; SGM: Senior Graduate Master/Mistress; PGM: Principal Graduate Master/Mistress (Secondary School Vice Principal); Principal: Secondary School Principal. The currency in USD is counted as HK$100 to USD12.86 as of mid-September 2021.

the government contributes 15 percent of the salary of an individual teacher, the prospects of the teaching profession remain quite attractive.

Moreover, a teacher can secure a regular position after he or she works for two years if there is no misconduct on his or her part. Indeed, after the implementation of education reforms, teachers are often assessed in accordance with their performance in carrying out these reforms and they have encountered more work pressure than before. Still, teachers, in general, have good prospects and enjoy a certain degree of career protection and security. Unless an individual teacher has misconduct, he or she cannot be easily dismissed. Of course, some teachers who were involved in the power struggle in schools could be vulnerable to be dismissed or discontinued in their contractual relations with the schools. Overall, teachers who teach in government schools and aided schools tend to have a certain degree of career security.

Yet, teachers who teach in private schools and directly subsidized schools do not have such protection as mentioned above. The contractual relations between the teachers and the private/direct subsidized schools can be terminated by the schools concerned. Normally, the contracts of teachers in these private and directly subsidized schools are on one-year duration with the possibility of renewal. Although these schools can pay the teachers by taking reference to the pay scale of the government and aided schools, such pay scale is not necessarily followed by private and directly subsidized schools. Usually, private and directly subsidized schools pay less to the teachers, especially the private schools where teachers lack sufficient career protection.

Since the implementation of various education reforms in the 2000s, schools have been allowed to hire teaching assistants, associate teachers and assistant teachers to maintain the manpower and resources so that the workload of the regular teachers could be reduced. These new positions, including teaching assistants, lacked career protection as they were and are of temporary nature. Schools can hire a few more assistants if the government provides more subsidies. Also, those university graduates who were hired as teaching assistants hoped to move up the career ladder if any regular teacher may leave or retire. Teaching assistants could also secure the support of schools for them to study for the teaching certificates to gain professional recognition and acquire further promotion opportunities. However, some teaching assistants might wait for eight to ten years without being promoted, a situation depending on the financial situation of the schools and their fortune.

To estimate the extent of those teachers who left the teaching position after the imposition of the national security law in June 2020, we calculated the advertisement on the teaching vacancies from June to early September 2021. Normally, any teacher who resigns needs to give three months' notice to the school authorities. Because the national security law was imposed in late June 2020, those teachers who were worrying about its impacts might not have the time to resign until the summer of the next academic year. Hence, calculating the teaching vacancies from June to the beginning of the school year in early September 2021 can give us a better picture of the attrition of teachers from schools. Table 5.7 collects the advertisement on teaching vacancies from

Table 5.7 Teaching Vacancies Advertisement from June to Early September 2021

Date: 18 June, 4.35 pages, 170 posts, 18 non-teaching posts and 18 SKT					
Number of posts	1	2	3	4+	Total posts
Aided Primary T	19	5	2	7	>56
Aided Primary TA	12	6	1	0	25
Aided Secondary T	33	11	4	0	67
Aided Secondary TA	16	6	3	4	>53
DSS T	8	4	4	5	>48
DSS TA	8	1	1	1	>17

Date: 29 June, 3.4 pages, 130 posts, 10 non-teaching posts and 11 SKT					
Number of posts	1	2	3	4+	Total posts
Aided Primary T	10	10	4	7	>70
Aided Primary TA	12	12	0	2	>44
Aided Secondary T	23	10	2	4	>65
Aided Secondary TA	14	5	3	3	>45
DSS T	6	2	2	3	>28
DSS TA	3	3	1	0	12

Date: 8 July, 5 pages, 184 posts, 22 non-teaching posts and 8 SKT					
Number of posts	1	2	3	4+	Total posts
Aided Primary T	32	4	0	5	>60
Aided Primary TA	15	8	3	4	>56
Aided Secondary T	25	11	1	3	>62
Aided Secondary TA	20	19	5	9	>109
DSS T	12	5	0	4	>36
DSS TA	6	1	1	1	>15

Date: 17 July, 4.3 pages, 163 posts, 19 non-teaching posts and 3 SKT					
Number of posts	1	2	3	4+	Total posts
Aided Primary T	29	7	2	7	>77
Aided Primary TA	24	11	5	0	61
Aided Secondary T	22	4	1	1	>37
Aided Secondary TA	15	11	7	5	>68
DSS T	3	5	3	0	22
DSS TA	6	1	0	0	8

Date: 2 August, 3 pages, 116 posts, 13 non-teaching posts, 3 SKT					
Number of posts	1	2	3	4+	Total posts
Aided Primary T	11	4	0	0	19
Aided Primary TA	11	7	0	0	25
Aided Secondary T	12	3	1	0	21
Aided Secondary TA	27	13	3	3	>74
DSS T	8	6	1	0	23
DSS TA	2	2	0	1	>10

(Continued)

Table 5.7 Teaching Vacancies Advertisement from June to Early September 2021 *(Continued)*

Date: 17 August, 3.3 pages 126 posts, 18 non-teaching posts and 5 SKT						
Number of posts	1	2	3	4+	Total posts
Aided Primary T	7	1	0	2	>17
Aided Primary TA	17	2	1	2	>32
Aided Secondary T	20	3	0	0	26
Aided Secondary TA	20	9	6	4	>72
DSS T	3	2	1	0	10
DSS TA	4	4	1	2	>23

Date: 2 September, 3 pages, 111 posts, 33 non-teaching posts and 3 SKT						
Number of posts	1	2	3	4+	Total posts
Aided Primary T	1	0	0	0	1
Aided Primary TA	11	2	0	2	>23
Aided Secondary T	10	2	0	0	14
Aided Secondary TA	20	12	1	4	>63
DSS T	3	0	0	0	3
DSS TA	3	1	0	0	5

Date: 8 September, 3.3 pages, 121 posts, 33 non-teaching posts and 20 SKT						
Number of posts	1	2	3	4+	Total posts
Aided Primary T	8	6	0	0	20
Aided Primary TA	14	4	1	0	25
Aided Secondary T	4	3	0	0	10
Aided Secondary TA	13	2	3	3	>38
DSS T	3	1	0	0	5
DSS TA	1	1	0	0	3

Date: 17 September, 3.8 pages, 128 posts, 28 non-teaching posts and 28 SKT						
Number of posts	1	2	3	4+	Total posts
Aided Primary T	9	0	0	0	9
Aided Primary TA	14	5	0	1	>28
Aided Secondary T	13	2	0	0	17
Aided Secondary TA	16	6	4	4	>56
DSS T	2	0	0	0	2
DSS TA	2	0	0	0	2

Note: The non-teaching posts refer to those advertisements made by schools, but they employ non-teaching positions; SKT – the number of posts advertised by special schools, kindergarten and private tutoring; T – teachers may include various teaching positions and supply (or substitute) teachers; TA – teaching assistants may include teachers' assistants, associate teachers, assistant teachers or teaching assistants; Aided – aided schools; DSS – Direct Subsidy schools, international schools or private schools; > denotes bigger than; 4+ means more than four.

June to September 2021 by focusing on *Ming Pao*, which is the key newspaper advertising the teaching vacancies. Our statistics count the number of pages of teaching vacancies advertisement and the number of advertisement posts. Some posts were provided by schools with non-teaching posts, and some were the advertisements from kindergartens, special schools and private tutor schools. Indeed, the limitation of our methodology in Table 5.7 is that the advertisements might not reflect the true attrition of teachers, not to mention their migration and decision to change profession. In the past, teaching vacancies could be advertised on the PTU website and newspaper; nevertheless, the PTU was disbanded in the summer of 2021. Hence, focusing on the teaching advertisement in *Ming Pao* might provide us with a better picture of the attrition of teachers. In May 2021, the PTU estimated that the attrition rate of teachers in primary and secondary schools would be about 10 percent of the total number of teachers – an estimation that appeared to be true from our calculation of teaching vacancies that were later advertised. Moreover, the PTU estimated that an individual teacher, who worked in aided school and who reached the age of 50, should be able to save HK$5 million, including his or her mandatory provident fund.[101] As such, some of the teachers who reached their 50s and who were dissatisfied with the education reforms could afford to immigrate, especially as they had personal investment apart from the deposit from their earned salaries. The PTU estimated that an individual teacher who opted for migration to other countries might have at least HK$10 million so that he or she would be able to secure himself or herself in the new destination of migration.

As mentioned before, a teacher who resigns needs three-month prior notice, meaning that he or she must resign on June 1 for the sake of leaving the school that starts its semester on September 1. From June to September 2021, *Ming Pao* had three to five pages of advertisements on teaching vacancies every day – an unprecedented phenomenon indicative of the attrition of teachers. From Table 5.7, we can observe that the vacant positions of teachers and teaching assistants were numerous from June to July. On one single day, *Ming Pao* advertised more than 200 teaching positions, with many positions from directly subsidized schools. On July 8 alone, *Ming Pao* advertised 338 teaching positions. In August, almost 200 positions were advertised on *Ming Pao* every day. On September 17, there were 28 teaching vacancies for regular teaching positions and 86 posts for teaching assistants. Clearly, a lot of teachers left their profession.

Usually, a school only has several teaching assistants. But under the circumstances of the attrition of teachers, many schools promote the existing teaching assistants to be regular teachers. The vacancies of teaching assistants could be easily seen in the advertisements from June to early September. Although the priority of filling the vacancies was to recruit university graduates, the inadequacy of manpower supply due to the sudden increase in teachers' attrition meant that many schools preferred to fill up the vacancies through the promotion of teaching assistants. At the same time, teaching assistants found more opportunities of moving to work in other schools as regular teachers. Due to the combined results of the promotion of teaching assistants in their original schools and their mobility to move to other schools, the inadequate supply of teaching assistants as shown in the advertisements was understandable.

Conclusion

This chapter traces the development of the PRC's education reforms which had an immediate impact on Hong Kong, where patriotic and national education has begun extensively. The HKSAR government, as required by the national security law, has to deepen and broaden the national security education, patriotic education and national education. The year 2021 witnessed all the reforms undertaken in all these areas, including various extra-curricular activities for students, training sessions for teachers, governmental subsidies for schools, EDB's personnel changes to propel the reforms further, the efforts made by pro-Beijing groups and elites to push for faster transformations, the utilization of the GBA as a platform to conduct patriotic education and united front work, the active participation of Hong Kong's universities in their campus expansion in the GBA, the migration of many teachers and students to overseas countries and the inevitable adaptation of all the stakeholders (principals, teachers, students and parents) to the environmental changes and the curriculum reforms at the school level. Specifically, the brain drain in the education sector, especially the migration of experienced teachers out of Hong Kong, has provided an impetus for the schools to replenish and refill the vacancies by moving the available teaching assistants upward, thereby witnessing a certain degree of upward mobility of teachers. Yet, many schools have envisaged the reduction in their class size, which may or may not be a positive phenomenon. Negatively, this phenomenon can be a precursor to the closure of some schools. Positively, the HKSAR government may tolerate and allow the phenomenon of persistent small classes so that the existing number of schools would be kept. Whatever the policy adopted by the HKSAR government in the short run, education reforms in Hong Kong have been heavily shaped by the political factors, namely the imposition of the national security law and its concomitant result of triggering reforms in patriotic education, national education and national security education.

Notes

1 *Ta Kung Pao*, August 25, 2021, p. A20.
2 *Ibid*. Also see *Ming Pao*, September 2, 2021, p. A13.
3 *Ming Pao*, August 25, 2021, p. A17.
4 *Wen Wei Po*, August 25, 2021, p. A10.
5 *Wen Wei Po*, September 2, 2021, p. A16.
6 *Ming Pao*, September 2, 2021, p. A13.
7 The authors visited the exhibition on July 7, 2021, and we made the observations in this section.
8 *Ta Kung Pao*, July 10, 2021, p. A8.
9 *Wen Wei Po*, July 9, 2021, p. A7.
10 *Ibid*.

11 *Ibid.*
12 Her remarks were reported in www.hk01.com, July 10, 2021.
13 *Ta Kung Pao*, August 10, 2021, p. A3.
14 *Ta Kung Pao*, August 11, 2021, p. A5.
15 *Ta Kung Pao*, September 2, 2021, p. A6.
16 *Ming Pao*, September 3, 2021, p. A14.
17 *Ming Pao*, September 2, 2021, p. A4.
18 *Ibid.*
19 *Ming Pao*, September 15, 2021, p. A9. For the government gazette on the national flag and anthem, see *Ta Kung Pao*, August 12, 2021, p. A5. It is a criminal offense to denigrate the national flag and national anthem, according to the national flag and national anthem ordinance's article 7. Moreover, any person using the Internet to denigrate the national flag and anthem will also commit a criminal offense and be liable for three years' imprisonment. *Wen Wei Po*, August 12, 2021, p. A5.
20 *Oriental Daily*, August 25, 2021, p. A11.
21 *Wen Wei Po*, August 31, 2021, p. A4.
22 *Ta Kung Pao*, August 30, 2021, p. A4.
23 *Wen Wei Po*, August 19, 2021, p. A5.
24 *Ibid.*
25 *Ibid.*
26 *Wen Wei Po*, August 26, 2021, p. A13.
27 *Wen Wei Po*, September 4, 2021, p. A1.
28 *Ming Pao*, September 6, 2021, p. A11.
29 *Wen Wei Po*, September 14, 2020, p. 1.
30 *Oriental Daily*, September 5, 2021, p. A15.
31 This organization tried to provide logistical support to the pro-democracy prisoners, but after the police and pro-Beijing media criticized it, its core organizers toned down their activities and refrained from using Facebook to show off their activities.
32 *Wen Wei Po*, August 13, 2021, p. A12.
33 Many young Hong Kong people tended to see themselves as culturally Chinese, but they did not identify themselves with the CCP in the mainland. See Sonny Shiu-Hing Lo, *The Dynamics of Beijing-Hong Kong Relations: A Model for Taiwan?* (Hong Kong: Hong Kong University Press, 2008).
34 *Ta Kung Pao*, October 14, 2020, p. A10.
35 *Ta Kung Pao*, October 4, 2020, p. A7.
36 *Ibid.*
37 There were 34,300 applications in the first two months after the applications began in late January 2021. See Maisy Mok, "Brits fear BNO route open windows for China spies," *The Standard*, August 10, 2021, access date: September 7, 2021.
38 For Leung's family background, see *Ta Kung Pao*, August 16, 2019, in 梁天琦何來「反共家仇」 出生屋出售套現百萬 (archive.org), access date: September 12, 2021.
39 "Sunny Cheung applies for political asylum in the US and gets admitted to a master program," August 16, 2021, in 【流亡海外】張崑陽正向美國申請政治庇護　獲大學取錄碩士課程 – 香港經濟日報 – TOPick – 新聞 – 政治 – D210816 (hket.com), access date: September 12, 2021.
40 *Headline News*, June 26, 2019.
41 "Studentlocalism was disbanded four years after it was founded, Tony Chung once advocated Hong Kong could have military conscription to have its own army," October 27, 2021, in 國安法 | 學生動源成立4年即解散　鍾翰林曾倡港應徵兵建立軍隊 | 香港01 | 政情 (hk01.com), access date: September 12, 2021.
42 *Oriental Daily*, January 17, 2019.
43 See Wong's Facebook, 王逸戰 Wong Yat Chin – Home | Facebook, access date: September 12, 2021.

186 *Adaptation to Mainlandization and Decolonization*

44 See his interview, July 22, 2021, in 身負 7 罪的重考生 #賢學思政 王逸戰: 終將入獄的人 考得再好也徒勞 – YouTube, access date: September 12, 2021.
45 "Occupy adviser Cheng Yu-shek escapes to Australia and claims to struggle through distance," no date, in 「佔中軍師」鄭宇碩著草澳洲 揚言會「遙距抗爭」– 港聞 – 橙新聞 (orangenews.hk), access date: September 12, 2021.
46 Cheung Tat-ming, *What is Evidence? The Black Hand behind the Occupy Central* (in Chinese) (Macau: San Si Publisher, 2018).
47 "Benny Tai: Hong Kong university fires professor who led protests," July 28, 2020, in BBC News, access date: September 12, 2021.
48 Rachel Wong, "'End of academic freedom': University of Hong Kong to fire pro-democracy activist and law professor Benny Tai," July 28, 2020, in Hong Kong Free Press HKFP (hongkongfp.com), access date: September 12, 2021.
49 Horace Chin was an assistant professor in Chinese at Lingnan University from 2009 to 2016 and was a prolific writer. His famous book on Hong Kong as a city-state aroused great academic and popular interest. In 2016, Lingnan University did not renew his contract, but it was possible that Chin's outspoken remarks might have alarmed and alienated the university authorities there. After Chin was defeated in the September 2016 LegCo election, he decided to withdraw from the social movement.
50 Johannes Chan is a legal scholar. In 2015, he was recommended as a candidate for the position of pro-vice-chancellor at the University of Hong Kong. But some conservative members of the University Council blocked him because, according to news reports, Chan was a liberal and an outspoken academic. He also participated in the Hong Kong 2020, which was a group led by the former Chief Secretary Anson Chan. The group studied how to achieve universal suffrage in the HKSAR. Apparently, Chan's political inclination and activities might have alarmed and alienated the university's high authorities. See "Meeting point: Behind the original sin. Who made the dirty river affecting the sky?," in 【匯點: 原罪背後 4】是誰令濁流滔天 | 立場報道 | 立場新聞 (thestandnews.com), access date: September 12, 2021. According to the news report above, there were rumors saying that the former Chief Executive C. Y. Leung exerted pressure on the members of the University Council to stop the appointment of Johannes Chan as the pro-vice-chancellor.
51 *Ta Kung Pao*, November 16, 2020; *Wen Wei Po*, November 17, 2021, p. A4.
52 One showed the video of Andy Chan Ho-tin, the former leader and founder of the banned Hong Kong National Party, while another professor talked about "the five demands" of the protestors in mid-2019. Information from a professor at HKU, May 2021.
53 Personal discussion with a scholar, August 2021.
54 Personal observation of a tertiary institution's courses, August 2021.
55 Personal discussion with an academic who taught on sensitive topics like Xinjiang, September 2021.
56 "Almost 90,000 citizens leave Hong Kong in mid-2021," *The Standard*, August 12, 2021, access date: September 5, 2021.
57 *Ta Kung Pao*, August 30, 2021, p. A9; and *Wen Wei Po*, August 30, 2021, p. A14.
58 With the imposition of the national security law, however, the core values of Hong Kong have been arguably diluted to a limited extent, for political cases involving the 2019 anti-extradition movement have been dealt with by national security court judges selected by the top security authorities of the HKSAR. Some of the judgments appeared to be quite politically conservative and legally hardline.
59 *Apple Daily*, August 13, 2020, p. A19.
60 *Ibid*.
61 *Ibid*.
62 *Ibid*.
63 *Ta Kung Pao*, November 11, 2020, p. A7.

64 *Wen Wei Po*, August 7, 2020, p. A 12.
65 *Ibid.*
66 *Ming Pao*, November 11, 2020, p. A11.
67 *Ibid.*
68 *Oriental Daily*, August 30, 2021, p. A12.
69 *Ibid.*
70 *Ibid.*
71 *Ta Kung Pao*, August 12, 2021, p. A4.
72 *Ming Pao*, September 4, 2021, p. A4.
73 *Ibid.*
74 *Ibid.*
75 *Wen Wei Po*, September 8, 2021, p. A14.
76 *Wen Wei Po*, September 9, 2021, p. A7.
77 *Ibid.*
78 See website: https://uic.edu.hk/en/about-us/introduction/about-uic, access date: September 14, 2021.
79 See website: https://www.cuhk.edu.cn/en/about/overview, access date: September 14, 2021.
80 See website: 医院介绍 (hku-szh.org), access date: September 14, 2021.
81 *South China Morning Post*, February 25, 2019.
82 *Hong Kong Commercial Daily*, March 3, 2020.
83 *Wen Wei Po*, March 6, 2020. Also see *Wen Wei Po*, April 23, 2021.
84 *Headline News*, March 12, 2020.
85 *Sing Tao Daily*, March 19, 2020.
86 *Wen Wei Po*, May 20, 2021.
87 Press release of Lingnan University, July 15, 2021.
88 For the details of the GBA plan, see Guangdong-Hong Kong-Macao Greater Bay Area – Outline Development Plan, access date: September 14, 2021.
89 Cheung Yuet, "Hong Kong higher education institutions come," *Economic Observer News* (Chinese), September 6, 2021, p. 2.
90 Ailei Xie, Gerard A. Postiglione and Qian Huang, "The Greater Bay Area development strategy and its relevance to higher education," *ECNU Review of Education*, vol. 4, no. 1 (2021), pp. 210–221.
91 *Oriental Daily*, September 2, 2021, p. A4.
92 *Ibid.*
93 *Oriental Daily*, September 3, 2021, p. A7.
94 *Ibid.*
95 *Ibid.*
96 Personal discussions with an executive committee member of the PTU, July 2021.
97 *Ibid.*
98 *Ibid.*
99 "Implementation of national security education in schools," September 1, 2021, in LCQ20: Implementation of national security education in schools (info.gov.hk), access date: September 18, 2021.
100 Personal discussions with several former students and principals, August 2021.
101 "PTU says 40 percent of teachers would leave their profession as the increase in political pressure is the main reason," May 9, 2021, in 【教師流失】教協調查指4成教師有意離開教育界　政治壓力日增成主因 – 香港經濟日報 – TOPick – 新聞 – 社會 – D210509 (hket.com), access date: September 18, 2021.

Conclusion

This book shows that the China factor has tremendous political impacts on Hong Kong's education reform, especially after the imposition of the national security law onto the HKSAR in late June 2020. The mainlandization of Hong Kong's education reforms is characterized by the dilution of the liberal elements in the Liberal Studies subject and its replacement by the Citizenship and Social Development curriculum; the strengthening of Chinese history and culture in the school curricula; the emphasis on national security in different subjects and at varying levels of schools (kindergarten, primary, secondary, tertiary); the inculcation of Chinese culture and national education in the kindergartens, primary and secondary schools; the organization of extra-curricular activities, ranging from exhibition to exchanges and visits, to consolidate Chinese patriotism and nationalism in the psyche of students; and the retraining of teachers and students on the need to respect the PRC's national security interest and sovereignty and to understand the Chinese history and culture in a much deeper way than ever before. In the PRC's practices, these moves constitute an indispensable part of political socialization and indoctrination. Undoubtedly, the Hong Kong education system has already witnessed the mainlandization in a prominent manner. The implication is that "one country, two systems" has to be readjusted in such a way that the interests of the "one country" dominate those of the "two systems." From the PRC's perspective, the autonomy of the "two systems" originates from "one country." As such, the freedom of speech, of thought and of publication enjoyed in the HKSAR is all the rights conferred upon the people of Hong Kong by the central government in Beijing – a top-down and an authoritarian perspective to which Hongkongers must adapt.

During the British colonial era, education reform in Hong Kong was deliberately depoliticized to avoid the local Chinese imbued with a strong sense of Chinese patriotism and nationalism. After July 1, 1997, the HKSAR government began to politicize the content of education reform by introducing the national education policy, which however was opposed and resisted in the summer of 2012 by some liberal-minded students, intellectuals and parents. As the local identity of Hong Kong people gained further momentum from 2012 to the Occupy Central movement in September-December 2014, from the Mongkok riots in early 2016 to the disqualification of two legislators-elect in November 2016,

DOI: 10.4324/9781003147268-6

and from the public opposition to the extradition bill between June and December 2019, the PRC authorities were infuriated and determined to introduce the national security law to change the entire political landscape of Hong Kong. Unlike London, which decentralized education reform to the British colonial administration, Beijing centralized education reform in the HKSAR where the local government was seen by PRC authorities as relatively weak from 2012 to 2019.

The national security law was undoubtedly a watershed in Hong Kong's education development and reforms. To reverse the trend of public success in opposing the national education policy in the summer 2012 and the extradition bill in 2019, the national security law empowered the HKSAR government to legalize the education system, to penalize the political and pro-democracy activists, to impose national security education and to accelerate and deepen the process of implementing national education and national culture in Hong Kong. While the PRC's education system under President Xi Jinping has envisaged a consolidation of national security education, the same phenomenon can be found in Hong Kong, where the power struggle between the mainland Chinese nationalistic policymakers and the Hong Kong localists was eventually tipped in favor of the former. The HKSAR government as the local agent of the central administration must carry out the directives of Beijing, pushing forward all aspects of education reform, including national security education, national education, patriotic education, moral education and Chinese culture education. Local Hong Kong identity has to be suppressed while national Chinese identity has to be elevated to a much higher level than ever before.

The politics of education reforms in China's Hong Kong is marked by several features. First, pro-Beijing groups and elites are playing a crucial role in assisting the process of implementing education reforms; and they also exert pressure on the HKSAR government to accelerate and deepen the process of reforms. The pro-Beijing groups and elites are making use of the new electoral system designed by the National People's Congress in March 2021, participating actively in the election held for the 1,500-member Election Committee that would select 40 out of the 90-member LegCo and that would elect the Chief Executive in March 2022. In short, the pro-Beijing interest groups and elites are like the transmission belt in an increasingly mainlandized political system of Hong Kong, playing the functions of being the supporters, facilitators, promoters, precursors and participants in revamping the education system in the HKSAR. The pro-Beijing elites and media are also the fighters and vanguard of mainland Chinese nationalism in the push for education reform in Hong Kong, as the controversy over the public examination question set by the HKEAA in 2020 showed. They have been playing a crucial role as the fighter of the Hong Kong style of Cultural Revolution in the education sector.

In brief, the China factor is the most prominent shaper influencing the political context and content of education reforms in the HKSAR. Beijing's political clients include the HKSAR government and the pro-Beijing politicians, elites, groups and organizations. The pro-Beijing elites and groups are important vehicles through which the central government in Beijing can easily exert pressure on the HKSAR government to implement education reforms, which include the national security education, the enhancement of the Chinese culture in Hong Kong's curriculum reform, and the acceleration of national security education in local schools. All these pressures achieve the objectives of enhancing the degree of Chinese nationalism and patriotism in the psyche of the Hong Kong people, especially the young people who are undergoing education at the primary, secondary and university levels. Indeed, it remains to be seen whether the mainlandization of Hong Kong's education system can and will really make the Hong Kong students more patriotic, more nationalistic and having stronger Chinese politico-cultural identity than ever before. Traditionally, the people of Hong Kong have separated their Chinese cultural identity from their political identification with the regime in the mainland. The anti-extradition movement in the latter half of 2019 proved that many young Hong Kong people were anti-CCP and did not want to witness the mainlandization of Hong Kong. Nevertheless, the message of education reform in the HKSAR since the imposition of the national security law in late June 2020 has been clear: the young generation should ideally combine their cultural identity of being Chinese with their political identification with the CCP rule in both the mainland and Hong Kong. Whether this objective will be successful remains to be observed and assessed. However, given that the young people of Hong Kong still have relatively free access to information, sensitive political topics like the June 4th 1989 tragedy and the 2019 anti-extradition movement will still be accessible through the Internet. As such, there would likely be difficulties in the promotion of a mixed politico-cultural Chinese identity among many Hongkongers.

Education reforms are composed of three main elements: (1) school-based reforms focusing on administrative change, the operation of school boards, the participation of parents in running the schools; (2) teachers' professionalism, which is expected to facilitate the implementation of school reforms and national security education introduced by the government and (3) curriculum reforms in conformity with the national security law, national security education and the enhancement of Chinese culture and history knowledge in the psyche of Hong Kong students. School-based reforms were emphasized in the pre-national security law period of the HKSAR government. But since late June 2020, teachers' professionalism has been emphasized along the line of national security law and education, while students' values and attitudes toward their motherland are expected to be far more patriotic and nationalistic than ever before.

Under the circumstances in which education reforms have been politicized since June 2020, the migration of some teachers out of Hong Kong provided an impetus for the schools to refill the vacancies by moving the available teaching assistants upward, thereby witnessing a certain degree of upward mobility of teachers. However, many schools have envisaged the reduction in their class size, which may or may not be a positive development. Negatively, this development can be a prelude to the closure of some schools. Positively, the HKSAR government may tolerate the persistence of small classes so that the number of schools would be largely maintained. Whatever the policy adopted by the HKSAR government in the coming years, education reforms in Hong Kong have been heavily shaped by the political factors, namely the imposition of the national security law and its concomitant of triggering reforms in patriotic education, national education, moral education, Chinese history and culture education and national security education. The chain effects of the national security law have to be understood and continuously monitored by scholars studying Hong Kong's education reforms.

In the final analysis, the depoliticization of Hong Kong's education system during the British colonial rule is a thing of the past. Since July 1, 1997, a gradual process of politicization could be seen, but the national education policy was opposed by an assertive civil society in the summer of 2012. Yet, authoritarian China does not allow the persistence of such a strong civil society in the HKSAR, where social groups sprung up again to oppose the extradition bill in 2019. The civil society in the HKSAR has to be tamed and suppressed by PRC authorities together with the security apparatus of Hong Kong. The imposition of the national security law can be interpreted as the legalization and mainlandization of Hong Kong's education system. Re-politicization of the Hong Kong education is a must, accompanied by political socialization and indoctrination parallel to but not exactly the same as the mainland. Political indoctrination in the HKSAR appears to be relatively softer than that of the mainland; nevertheless, the soft power imposed by the PRC's overlord onto the young students of Hong Kong may have far-reaching repercussions, including the gradual transformations of their politico-cultural identity and political culture.

Hence, national security law, national education, Chinese culture education and patriotic education have already been emphasized in the school and curriculum reforms in the HKSAR. Although local universities in Hong Kong do not have the formal installation of the party-secretaries like their mainland counterparts, they have been toeing the line of the official PRC policies, including the need to expand their campuses and cooperation into the GBA, their necessity of forging research collaboration with mainland institutes and scholars, and their importance of maintaining and elevating the competitiveness of all the cities in the GBA in a win-win situation. While these efforts at maximizing the research potential in Hong Kong are natural and much cherished, it remains to be seen whether the local university authorities in the HKSAR continue to respect academic freedom and allow local academics to exercise their freedom of thought, speech and publications within the parameters of the Basic Law and the national security law. If some university authorities are only power-hungry and yearn for political influence, their academic integrity can run the risk of being easily compromised without the determination to strike a balance between political loyalty towards their motherland and the respect for academic freedom in the HKSAR.

Although self-censorship is by no means explicit in the HKSAR after the imposition of the national security law in late June 2020, it does persist in a few disciplines, notably political science and history. Still, it is arguably more a matter of individual scholar's personal disposition and psychological struggle with the rapidly changing political environment than an outright structural intervention from their higher university authorities. The national security law and its impacts on academics remain to be observed further, but preliminary observations point to the necessity of individual adaptation to the tremendous political and psychological pressure exerted from the China factor. For many secondary school teachers, the national security law was a threat to their personal autonomy and liberties. As such, some opted for emigration. For others who could not afford to emigrate or leave their profession, they continue to adapt strategically to the political transformations. It can be said that, for those teachers who choose to stay in Hong Kong and who continue to teach politically sensitive subjects, they would likely play a crucial role in maintaining the existing space for their freedom of thought, speech and publication.

If politics, as Harold Laswell defined, refers to who gets what, when and how, the politics of education reform in China's Hong Kong was obviously triggered by the China factor in response to the strong local identity of many Hongkongers from 2012 to 2019. The consequences of the national security law on the teaching profession remain to be researched. However, unlike the British who depoliticized the education system and who decentralized education reform to avoid political challenges to the colonial rule, the PRC overlord has re-politicized the education system and centralized the education reform of Hong Kong to consolidate its political legitimacy and authority in the eyes of the Hong Kong people. It remains to be seen whether this political project of the PRC will be successful in the long run.

Bibliography

"Alliance School teacher had his license revoked, and PTU survey showed 70 percent of principals found the ruling unreasonable," November 10, 2020, http://www.hk01.com, access date: August 1, 2021.

"Benny Tai: Hong Kong university fires professor who led protests," July 28, 2020, in Benny Tai: Hong Kong university fires professor who led protests – BBC News, Benny Tai: Hong Kong university fires professor who led protests - BBC News, access date: September 12, 2021.

"Board chairman Lo Man-shui confirms Christine Choi resigns from her position of principal: She is not very leftwing," August 1, 2017, in 【副局政助任命】校董盧文端證蔡若蓮辭任校長：她也不是很左 | 香港01 | 社會新聞 (hk01.com), access date: August 21, 2021.

"Cheung Yu-yan advocates installing video cameras to supervise teachers' remarks and teaching situation," *Radio Television Hong Kong*, January 22, 2021, in 張宇人倡教室安裝閉路電視集中攝錄教師監察教學情況 – RTHK, access date: August 8, 2021.

"Chief Executive's speech during the 30th anniversary banquet of the SUPL," September 19, 2016, in 行政長官出席聯合出版集團成立三十周年酒會致辭全文（只有中文）（附圖／短片）(info.gov.hk), access date: August 22, 2021.

"Citizenship and Social Development: Curriculum and Assessment Guide (Secondary 4–6)," EDB, 2021, in CS_CAG_S4-6_Eng_2021 (edb.gov.hk), access date: September 6, 2021.

"Curriculum Framework of Chinese History's National Security Education," May 2021, in nse_subject_framework_chinese_history (edb.gov.hk), access date: September 5, 2021.

"Curriculum Framework of Economics Subject's (Form 4 to Form 6) National Security Education," May 2021, in nse_subject_framework_economics (edb.gov.hk), access date: September 5, 2021.

"Curriculum Framework of Life and Society's (Form 1 to Form 3) National Security Education," May 2021, in nse_subject_framework_life_and_society (edb.gov.hk), access date: September 5, 2021.

"Defiant Teacher Ng Mei-lan," *Next Magazine*, no. 1174, September 6, 2012, in 叛逆教師　吳美蘭＠明星八掛大分享★☆:: 痞客邦:: (pixnet.net), access date: August 6, 2021.

"Dr. Hans Yeung talks about the beginning and the end of the controversial history examination question: An indicator of Hong Kong's 'degradation,'" December 23, 2021, in 眾新聞 –【首度開腔】離職考評局經理楊穎宇博士　親述歷史科試題內情始末　「香港墮落嘅指標性事件」(hkcnews.com), access date: July 25, 2021.

"DSE History subject examination questions: citing 1982 public opinion poll to show 70 percent of Hong Kong people wanted Hong Kong to remain a colony and asking question to analyze the people's worries," April 20, 2017, in 【多話題】DSE歷史科試卷　引82年民調七成人盼港維持殖民地　要考生分析港人憂慮 | 立場報道 | 立場新聞 (thestandnews.com), access date: August 6, 2021.

194 *Bibliography*

"EDB announces the termination of its full-scale working relations with the Professional Teachers Union," July 31, 2021, in 教育局宣布全面終止與教協工作關係 – RTHK, access date: August 1, 2021.

"Eight universities have 1,816 students withdrawing from their studies, a figure highest in eleven years with the University of Hong Kong at the top," March 2, 2021, in 八大上學年共1816學士生退學　創至少11年新高　港大佔最多 | 香港01 | 社會新聞 (hk01.com), access date: August 8, 2021.

"Formerly a member of the Shenzhen CPPCC, Background was questioned: Wei says he does not know how to define patriots," *Sky Post*, March 25, 2021, in 歷史科爭議 | 曾任深圳政協 背景受質疑 考評局魏向東：不知怎定義愛國者 - 晴報 - 時事 - 要聞 – D210325 (ulifestyle.com.hk), access date: July 25, 2021.

"Full Text of Resolution on CCP Central Committee Report," October 24, 2017, in Full text of resolution on CPC Central Committee report (www.gov.cn), access date: August 21, 2021.

"Government school teacher's license is revoked, while a visual arts teacher whose comics criticized the police was regarded as lacking professional conduct," May 1, 2021, in 首位官校教師因反修例被「釘牌」　課餘漫畫批警方亦被指專業失德　(rfi.fr), access date: August 7, 2021.

"Handbook on Education Policy in Hong Kong, 1965–1998," Hong Kong Institute of Education, September 1992, in General Introduction to Targets and Target-related Assessment (eduhk.hk), access date: August 29, 2021.

"Heung To Teacher allowing students to sing "Glory to Hong Kong" has the contract discontinued, over 100 students form human chain to support her," June 12, 2020, in 香島中學教師疑因允奏《榮光》被拒續約 過百學生築人鏈聲援 | 獨媒報導 | 獨立媒體 (inmediahk.net), access date: August 8, 2021.

"High Level of Examination Authority: Black Hands Covering the Sky," *Ta Kung Pao*, May 14, 2020.

"Ho Hon-kuen forms a group to compete in the education sector and Wong Kam-leung from the Education Workers Federation says it breaks the PTU monopoly," August 9, 2021, in 選委會 | 何漢權等13人組隊戰教育界　教聯會黃錦良：打破教協壟斷 | 香港01 | 政情 (hk01.com), access date: September 4, 2021.

"Ho Lap teacher whose license was revoked apologizes and he loses his job, feels directionless and remembers his students," November 16, 2020, in 遭釘牌可立教師認歷史知識貧乏致歉　失夢想職業感迷惘　不捨學生 | 香港 01 | 社會新聞 (hk01.com), access date: August 7, 2021.

"Hok Yau Club: The tide of withdrawal is the most serious one in ten years, a father says the national security law prompts him to leave," November 4, 2020, in 【香港要聞】港多間名校爆「退學潮」 學友社：十年來最嚴重 港爸：「國安法」真是加速了我要走 – GNEWS, access date: August 8, 2020.

"Information Paper: Curriculum Development Institute, October 17, 1997," in Panels on Education – Papers 17 Oct 1997 (legco.gov.hk), access date: August 29, 2021.

"Ip Kin-yuen worries that 2 of the 7 members who were officials had to 'report' to the authorities and leak out the question," March 9, 2021, in 歷史科審題委員會名單曝光　7 成員最少 2 人任職教育局　葉建源憂被要求「向上級交代」洩密 | 立場報道 | 立場新聞 (thestandnews.com), access date: July 24, 2021.

"Joining the teaching profession because of the 1989 democracy movement, Cheung Yui-fai as a first generation Liberal Studies teacher decides to retire early, saying that the red lines are established," June 10, 2021, in 因八九民運投身教育界　首代通識老師張銳輝提早退休：教學設紅線 | 香港01 | 社會新聞 (hk01.com), access date: August 8, 2021.

Bibliography   195

"Kevin Yeung says the government revises the law to suspend the license of teachers and to deduct their salaries temporarily," November 9, 2020, in 楊潤雄稱正研究修例容許取消教師資格一段時間或扣糧等 | Now 新聞, access date: August 7, 2021.

"Kevin Yeung: 'Glory to Hong Kong' belongs to political propaganda, a teacher at Heung To Middle School does not have her contract renewed as she had allowed students to sign it in the campus," *Sky Post*, June 12, 2020, in 楊潤雄：《榮光》屬政治宣傳 校園禁唱 允學生演奏 香島中學教師不獲續約 - 晴報 - 港聞 - 要聞 – D200612 (ulifestyle.com.hk), access date: August 8, 2021.

"Kowloon Tong Alliance Primary School teacher has his license revoked, EDB says he has a plan to spread the idea of 'Hong Kong independence,'" October 5, 2020, in 九龍塘宣道小學教師遭取消教師資格　教育局：有計劃散播港獨信息 | 香港01 | 社會新聞 (hk01.com), access date: August 7, 2021.

"Liberal Studies: Curriculum and Assessment Guide (Secondary 4–6)," EDB, 2007 (updated in January 2014), in Liberal Studies (hkedcity.net), access date: September 6, 2021.

"Liberal Studies teacher Cheung Yui-fai retires earlier, he teaches for 30 years and says the red lines are making teachers losing their professional autonomy," June 10, 2021, in 資深通識教師張銳輝提早退休　任教近 30 年　指「紅線」下教師失專業自主 | 立場報道 | 立場新聞 (thestandnews.com), access date: August 8, 2021.

"Lui Ping-kuen interprets and dissects the blueprint of the central government on Hong Kong's governance," June 2, 2020, in https://www.businesstimes.com.hk/articles/127288/呂秉權--一國兩制-習近平-浸會大學-新聞系, access date: August 15, 2021.

"Matthew Cheung: Hong Kong has the responsibility of propelling national education and doing well in national anthem and national security education," October 18, 2020, in 指習近平重要講話對港有特殊意義　張建宗：港校推國教應有之責，望做好國歌及國安教育 | 立場報道 | 立場新聞 (thestandnews.com), access date: August 22, 2021.

"Meeting Point: Behind the original sin. Who made the dirty river affecting the sky?," in 【匯點：原罪背後 4】是誰令濁流滔天 | 立場報道 | 立場新聞 (thestandnews.com), access date: September 12, 2021.

"National Security Education," August 2021, in *National Security Law Education (NSLE0001) – NSLE0001 – Co-curricular Learning – Office of Student Affairs*, Hong Kong Baptist University (hkbu.edu.hk), access date: September 5, 2021.

"National Security Extended to Hong Kong," April 19, 2021, in 國安教育延伸至香港 分析:強迫全民參與的文革升級版 (voacantonese.com), access date: August 22, 2021.

"Next Magazine: Liaison Office violates the constitution by monopolizing the publishing industry," April 9, 2015, in 壹週刊：滅聲行動升級 中聯辦違憲壟斷出版市場.書展期間, 該重讀這篇 | by Kaykku | Jul, 2021 | Medium, access date: August 22, 2021.

"Occupy adviser Cheng Yu-shek escapes to Australia and claims to struggle through distance," no date, in 「佔中軍師」鄭宇碩著草澳洲 揚言會「遙距抗爭」 - 港聞 - 橙新聞 (orangenews.hk), access date: September 12, 2021.

"Our Hong Kong Foundation Launches Liberal Studies Research Report: Cultivating Interdisciplinary Learning, Thinking Skills, and Appreciation of Diversity," Our Hong Kong Foundation, September 7, 2020, in https://www.ourhkfoundation.org.hk/en/media/1264/education-and-youth/our-hong-kong-foundation-launches-liberal-studies-research-report, access date: August 1, 2021.

"Panel on Education: Discussion on Liberal Studies under the New Senior Secondary Curriculum," July 11, 2009, LC Paper No. CB(2)2122/08-09(01), in ed0711cb2-2122-1-e.pdf (legco.gov.hk), access date: August 31, 2021.

"Political troubles see the withdrawal of students in Hong Kong's primary and secondary schools," November 7, 2020, in 政治困擾 香港中小學現退學潮 (rfi.fr), access date: August 8, 2021.

"Polytechnic University vice-chancellor: Understand the social mood but violence is not the solution," July 3, 2019, in 【佔領立法會】無謂責示威者　理大校長：明白社會情緒但暴力非解決方法 | 立場報道 | 立場新聞 (thestandnews.com), access date: August 31, 2021.

"Professional autonomy is a history of the past. Hans Yeung says that his mistake was being open-minded," The Standnews, December 27, 2020, in 【專訪】當專業自主成為歷史　前考評局經理楊穎宇：我錯在 Open-minded | 立場人語 | 立場新聞 (thestandnews.com), access date: July 24, 2021.

"PTU press conference: Announcing its dissolution, chair Fung Wai-wah says many solutions cannot tackle the crisis," August 10, 2021, in 教協記者會 | 宣布解散　會長馮偉華：多個方案都難解當前危機 | 香港01 | 社會新聞 (hk01.com), access date: August 10, 2021.

"PTU responds to the commentary of Xinhua and People's Daily," PTU press release, July 31, 2021, in 教協回應新華社及人民日報的評論 | 香港教育專業人員協會 (hkptu.org), access date: August 2, 2021.

"PTU responds to the EDB's termination of working relations," PTU press release, July 31, 2021, in 新聞稿／立場書 | 香港教育專業人員協會 (hkptu.org), access date: August 2, 2021.

"Rumors that government officials join the examination committee, but the Examination Authority said it was confidential," March 10, 2021, in 傳多名教局人員加入歷史科委員會 考評局重申屬高度機密 | 頭條日報 (stheadline.com), access date: July 24, 2021.

"Sacred Heart Cannossian College is suspected to try cleaning the record of Lai Tak-chung," *Wen Wei Po*, September 3, 2019, in 嘉諾撒聖心校疑圖為賴得鐘「洗底」 (tap-2world.com), access date: August 8, 2021.

"Secondary Schools Principal Association: Student departure increases by 52 percent and teachers leaving their position increase by 15 percent, including early retirement," February 23, 2021, in 中學校長會：學生離港退學按年增52%　教師離職增15%部份提早退休 | 香港01 | 社會新聞 (hk01.com), access date: August 8, 2021.

"So's contract not renewed, Ip Kin-yuen speculates it is related to the examination question controversy," Epoch Times, August 18, 2020, in 考評局秘書長蘇國生不續任　葉建源推測涉歷史科試題爭議 | 大紀元時報　香港 | 獨立敢言的良心媒體 (epochtimes.com), access date: August 6, 2021.

"Studentlocalism was disbanded four years after it was founded, Tony Chung once advocated Hong Kong could have military conscription to have its own army," October 27, 2021, in 國安法 | 學生動源成立4年即解散　鍾翰林曾倡港應徵兵建立軍隊 | 香港01 | 政情 (hk01.com), access date: September 12, 2021.

"Sunny Cheung applies for political asylum in the US and gets admitted to a master program," August 16, 2021, in 【流亡海外】張崑陽正向美國申請政治庇護　獲大學取錄碩士課程 - 香港經濟日報 - TOPick - 新聞 - 政治 - D210816 (hket.com), access date: September 12, 2021.

"Teacher bought Apple Daily and distributed it to teachers, Kevin Yeung says there should be no political propaganda and school itself handles the case," June 23, 2021, in 教師買《蘋果》回校派同事　楊潤雄：不得政治宣傳　信學校能處理 | 香港01 | 政情 (hk01.com), access date: August 8, 2021.

"The disbandment of PTU is self-inflicted and Hong Kong education embraces the historical chance of returning to the correct path," Xinhua, August 11, 2021, in "教协"解散咎由自取 香港教育迎来重回正轨历史契机 - 港澳 - 人民网 (people.com.cn), access date: August 12, 2021.

"The dispute over Lam See-wai's foul language, EDB four years later rules that the complaint was established," July 16, 2017, in 林慧思粗口風波　事隔4年教局突發信裁定違操守 | 香港01 | 社會新聞 (hk01.com), access date: August 6, 2021.

"The Law of the People's Republic of China on Safeguarding National Security in the Hong Kong Special Administrative Region," June 30, 2020, in The Law of the People's Republic of China on Safeguarding National Security in the Hong Kong Special Administrative Region (elegislation.gov.hk), access date: August 21, 2021.

"The Practice of 'One Country, Two Systems' in the Hong Kong Special Administrative Region," June 10, 2014, in 《"一国两制"在香港特别行政区的实践》白皮书(英文) (scio.gov.cn), access date: August 21, 2021.

"Tin Shui Wai teacher distributed Apple Daily to teachers and was stopped teaching temporarily, and the PTU criticizes the school's action," June 18, 2021, in 天水圍有小學教師派《蘋果》予同事遭暫停課堂　教協斥上綱上線 | 香港 01 | 社會新聞 (hk01.com), access date: August 8, 2021.

"Two Police Unions reprimanded Lam See-wai," July 28, 2013, in 兩警察協會譴責林慧思 - 新傳網 (symedialab.com), access date: August 6, 2021.

"Visual art teacher Vawongsir published political comics and he was a target of complaints, he was ruled as lacking professional ethics," April 29, 2021, in 【清算教師】視藝教師「vawongsir」被裁專業失德　或成釘牌第三人　教局指諷警暴漫畫為「無理指控」 | 立場報道 | 立場新聞 (thestandnews.com), access date: August 7, 2021. See also Oriental Daily, April 29, 2021.

"Wei says government's move of appointing people to go into examination scrutiny committee does not influence the independence of the Examination Authority," March 25, 2021, in 【DSE】魏向東指教育局人員加入審題委員會　不影響考評局獨立性 - 香港經濟日報 - TOPick – 新聞 – 社會 – D210325 (hket.com), access date: July 25, 2021.

"Xi Jinping delivers important speech during the national education conference," September 10, 2018, in 习近平出席全國教育大會併發表重要講話_滾動新聞_中國政府網 (www.gov.cn), access date: August 15, 2021.

"Xi Jinping first talks about the comprehensive national security perspective," April 16, 2014, in 圖解：習近平首提"總體國家安全觀"–獨家稿件-人民網 (people.com.cn), access date: August 22, 2021.

"Xi Jinping says Chinese education can produce great experts," May 29, 2021, in 習近平稱中國教育能夠培養出大師 (rfi.fr), access date: August 22, 2021.

"Xi Jinping uses Macau to say something to Hong Kong: Article 23, Patriotic Education and the Maintenance of the Center's Power," December 20, 2019, in 习近平借澳门向香港喊话：23条、爱国教育、维护中央权力 – BBC News 中文, access date: August 15, 2021.

"Xi Jinping warns Hong Kong that students need patriotic education," July 2, 2017, in 习近平警告香港：学生需要爱国教育 (voachinese.com), access date: August 14, 2021.

"Xi Jinping's speech in the celebration meeting of the 40th anniversary of the Shenzhen special economic zone," Xinhua, October 14, 2020, in （受权发布）习近平：在深圳经济特区建立40周年庆祝大会上的讲话-新华网 (xinhuanet.com), access date: August 22, 2021.

"Zhang Xiang, Shyy Wei and Way Kuo are not eligible to be ex-officio members and change is made to the chairpersons of the Board of Directors," August 26, 2021, in 眾新聞 - 張翔史維郭位不符資格　改由校董會主席任當然選委 (hkcnews.com), access date: September 4, 2021.

Amnesty International's statement, October 6, 2020, in 教育局以「有計劃散播港獨信息」為由取消教師資格 – 國際特赦組織香港分會 Amnesty International Hong Kong, access date: August 7, 2021.

Apple Daily (Hong Kong Chinese newspaper).

Bray, Mark, "Education and Colonial Transition: The Hong Kong Experience in Comparative Perspective," in Bray, Mark and Lee, Wing-on, eds., *Education and Political Transition: Implications and Hong Kong's Change of Sovereignty* (Hong Kong: Comparative Education Research Centre, The University of Hong Kong, 1997), pp. 11–24.

Burney, Edmund, *Report on Education in Hong Kong* (London: Crown Agents for the Colonies, 1935).

Chan, Chitat, Wang, Danping, Wong, Kathy, "The Representations of Youth in Liberal Studies Student Works in Hong Kong," *The International Journal of the Humanities*, vol. 9, no. 1 (January 2011), pp. 245–256.

Chee, Wai-Chi, "Negotiating Teacher Professionalism: Governmentality and Education Reform in Hong Kong," *Ethnography and Education*, vol. 7, no. 3 (2012), pp. 327–344.

Cheng, Yin-cheong, "Education Reforms in Hong Kong: Challenges, Strategies, & International Implications," *The International Forum on Education Reform: Experiences in Selected Countries, The Office of the National Education Commission*, 30 July–2 August 2001, Bangkok, Thailand.

Cheung, Tat-ming, *What Is Evidence? The Black Hand behind the Occupy Central (in Chinese)* (Macau: San Si Publisher, 2018).

Cheung, Tommy, "'Father' of Hong Kong Nationalism? A Critical Review of Wan Chin's City-State Theory," *Asian Education and Development Studies*, vol. 4, no. 4 (October 2015), pp. 460–470.

Cheung, Tommy, "A Small Story Behind SUPL," June 2, 2018, in 聯合出版集團背後小故事. 最近大家都講三中商，其實《壹周刊》都一早已經踢爆左，三中商背後既聯合出版集團，就… | by 張秀賢 Tommy Cheung | Medium, access date: August 22, 2021.

Cho, Kai-lok, "Election Committee Election in the Education Sector Is Full of Changing Possibilities," *Hong Kong Economic Journal* (April 28, 2021).

Chong, Eric K. M., "How Does Globalization Shape the Interdisciplinary Curriculum Development in Hong Kong's Education Reform," *Curriculum and Teaching*, vol. 35, no. 1 (2020), pp. 23–51.

Curriculum Development Council and Hong Kong Examinations and Assessment Authority, *Liberal Studies Curriculum and Assessment Guide* (Hong Kong: Education Bureau, 2007).

Durkheim, Emile and Mauss, Marcel, *Primitive Classification*, translated by Rodney Needham (Chicago: University of Chicago Press, 1969).

Education and Manpower Bureau, *Review of the Academic Structure of Senior Secondary Education* (Hong Kong: Education and Manpower Bureau, May 2003).

Education and Manpower Bureau, *The New Academic Structure for Senior Secondary Education and Higher Education – Action Plan for Investing in the Future of Hong Kong* (Hong Kong: Education and Manpower Bureau, May 2005).

Education Bureau Circular, No. 6/2021, "*National Security Education in School Curriculum – Additional Curriculum Documents and Learning and Teaching Resources*," May 26, 2021, in EDBC21006E, access date: September 5, 2021.

Education Commission, *Education Commission Report Number 1* (Hong Kong: Government Printer, October 1984).

Education Department, *Annual Report of the Education Department for the year 1st May 1946 to 31st March 1947* (Hong Kong: Hong Kong Government, 1947).

Endacott, G. B., *A History of Hong Kong* (New York: Oxford University Press, 1973).

Epoch Times (pro-Falun Gong Hong Kong newspaper).

Fairbrother, Gregory P., "Rethinking Hegemony and Resistance to Political Education in Mainland China and Hong Kong," *Comparative Education Review*, vol. 52, no. 3 (2008), pp. 381–412.

Fairbrother, Gregory P., *Toward Critical Patriotism: Student Resistance to Political Education in Hong Kong and China* (Hong Kong: Hong Kong University Press, 2003), pp. 185–186.

Fairbrother, Gregory P. and Kennedy, Kerry J., "Civic Education Curriculum Reform in Hong Kong: What Should Be the Direction under Chinese Sovereignty?" *Cambridge Journal of Education*, vol. 41, no. 4 (2011), pp. 425–443.

Forestier, Katherine, Adamson, Bob, Han, Christine, and Morris, Paul, "Referencing and Borrowing from Other Systems: The Hong Kong Education Reforms," *Educational Research*, vol. 58, no. 2 (2016), pp. 149–165.

Fu, Gail Schaeffer, "Bilingual Education in Hong Kong: A Historical Perspective," a working paper in *Language and Language Teaching*, The University of Hong Kong, 1979, pp. 1–19.

Fung, Cheuk-yiu, "*Judicial Review from DSE Students Fails, Expectations of Thousands of Students become Empty*," July 3, 2020, in DSE 考生司法覆核敗訴 數以千計學生願望落空 -教育- 明周文化 (mpweekly.com), access date: July 24, 2021.

Fung, Dennis and Liang, Tim, "The Legitimacy of Curriculum Development in Post-Colonial Hong Kong: Insights from the Case of Liberal Studies," *Oxford Review of Education*, vol. 44, no. 2 (2018), pp. 171–189.

Fung, Dennis Chun-Lok and Lui, Wai-Mei, "Is Liberal Studies a Political Instrument in the Secondary School Curriculum? Lessons from the Umbrella Movement in Post-Colonial Hong Kong," *The Curriculum Journal*, vol. 28, no. 2 (2017), pp. 158–175.

Fung, Dennis Chun-Lok and Lui, Wai-mei, *Education Policy Analysis: Liberal Studies and National Education in Hong Kong* (Singapore: Springer, 2017).

Fung, Dennis, Lui, Wai-Mei, Liang, Tim, and Su, Angie, "The Way Forward for the Development of Liberal Studies: How Teachers Perceive Its Introduction and Implementation in Hong Kong Secondary Schools," *Asia Pacific Education Review*, vol. 18 (2017), pp. 123–134.

Fung, Yiu-cheuk, "From an examination paper to look at history subject: A chronology of the DSE history subject examination controversies," in www.mpweekly.com, June 30, 2020, access date: July 22, 2021.

Headline News (Hong Kong Chinese newspaper).

Hong Kong Commercial Daily (pro-Beijing Hong Kong newspaper).

Hong Kong Free Press (Hong Kong English website news).

Hong Kong Government, *Secondary Education in Hong Kong over the Next Decade* (Hong Kong: the Government Printer, 1974).

Hong Kong Government, "*Statement on Government's Policy on the Re-organization of the Structure of Primary and Secondary Education,*" tabled in Legislative Council on January 23, 1963 (Hong Kong: Government Printer, 1963).

Hong Kong Legislative Council, *Official Report Proceedings: Meeting of 20th May 1964*, in https://www.legco.gov.hk/1964/h640520.pdf, access date: August 1, 2021.

Huang, Zhongjing, Wang, Ting, and Li, Xiaojun, "The Political Dynamics of Educational Changes in China," *Policy Futures in Education*, vol. 14, no. 1 (2016), pp. 24–41.

Hung, Steven Chung-fun, "Financing Schooling Policy of the Hong Kong Government: A Historical Comparative Analysis with the Theories of the State," unpublished PhD thesis, Tarlac State University, 2012.

Hung, Steven Chung-fun, "Contextual Analysis of Hong Kong Education Policy in 20 Years: The Intention of Making Future Citizens in Political Conflicts," *Contemporary Chinese Political Economy and Strategic Relations: An International Journal*, vol. 3, no. 2 (July/August 2017), pp. 713–745.

Ip, Kin-yuen, "History Subject's Examination Controversy Showed White Terror in the Resignation of Two Officers," *Ming Pao*, August 5, 2021.

Johnson, Chalmers A., *Peasant Nationalism and Communist Power: The Emergence of Revolutionary China, 1937–1945* (Stanford: Stanford University Press, 1962).

Kam, Iris Chui-ping, "Personal Identity versus National Identity among Hong Kong Youths – Personal and Social Education Reform after Reunification," *Social Identities*, vol. 18, no. 6 (2012), pp. 649–661.

Kan, Vincent and Adamson, Bob, "Language Policies for Hong Kong Schools since 1997," *London Review of Education*, vol. 8. No. 2 (July 2010), pp. 167–176.

Lai, Manhong and Lo, Leslie N. K., "Struggling to Balance Various Stakeholders' Perceptions: The Work Life of Ideo-Political Education Teachers in China," *High Education*, vol. 62 (2011), pp. 333–349.

Lanford, Michael, "Perceptions of Higher Education Reform in Hong Kong: A Glocalization Perspective," *International Journal of Comparative Education and Development*, vol. 18, no. 3 (2016), pp. 184–204.

Lee, Min, "Hong Kong Catholic diocese fails in schools appeal," Associated Press, February 3, 2010, in *Hong Kong Catholic diocese fails in schools appeal* | Taiwan News | 2010-02-03 17:29:48, access date: August 29, 2021.

Li, Jun, "Fostering Citizenship in China's Move from Elite to Mass Higher Education: An Analysis of Students' Political Socialization and Civic Participation," *International Journal of Educational Development*, vol. 29 (2009), pp. 382–398.

Lo, Sonny Shiu-hing, *Hong Kong's Indigenous Democracy* (London: Palgrave, 2015).

Lo, Sonny Shiu-hing, *The Politics of Policing in Greater China* (London: Palgrave, 2016).

Lo, Sonny Shiu-hing, "Ideologies and Factionalism in Beijing-Hong Kong Relations," *Asian Survey*, vol. 58, no. 3 (June 2018), pp. 392–415.

Lo, Sonny Shiu-Hing, ed., *Interest Groups and the New Democracy Movement in Hong Kong* (London: Routledge, 2018).

Lo, Sonny Shiu-Hing, Hung, Steven Chung-fun, and Loo, Jeff Hai-chi, *The Dynamics of Peaceful and Violent Protests in Hong Kong: The Anti-Extradition Movement* (London: Palgrave, 2020).

Lu, Jie, "Ideological and Political Education in China's Higher Education," *East Asian Policy*, vol. 9 (2017), pp. 78–91.

Luk, Hung-kay, *A History of Education in Hong Kong: A Report Submitted to the Lord Wilson Heritage Fund* (York University, 2000), pp. 16–20.

Luk-Fong, Pattie Yuk Yee, and Brennan, Marie, "Teachers' Experience of Secondary Education Reform in Hong Kong," *International Journal of Educational Reform*, vol. 19, no. 2 (Spring 2010), pp. 128–153.

Ma, Eric, *"Top-down Patriotism and Bottom-up Nationalization in Hong Kong,"* the Chinese University of Hong Kong, 2003, in https://www.com.cuhk.edu.hk/project/ericsite/academic/top-down.pdf, access date: May 3, 2021.

Ma, Veronica Kit-ching, *"Implications of School Management Initiative: A Case Study of Teachers' Perspective,"* unpublished MEd thesis, University of Hong Kong, August 1993.

Marsh, R. M. and Sampson, J. R., *Report of the Education Commission* (Hong Kong: Hong Kong Government, 1963).

Meisner, Maurice, *Mao's China and After: A History of the People's Republic* (New York: The Free Press, 1999), pp. 312–351.

Ming Pao (Hong Kong Chinese newspaper).

Morris, Paul and Scott, Ian, "Education Reform and Policy Implementation in Hong Kong," in Ho, Lok Sang, Morris, Paul, and Chung Yue-ping, eds., *Education Reform and the Quest for Excellence: The Hong Kong Story* (Hong Kong: Hong Kong University Press, 2005), pp. 83–97.

New China News Agency, "Hong Kong Education needs to be rectified and cleared of its root, and it is necessary to dig out the 'poisonous fester' of the Professional Teachers Union," July 31, 2021, in 新华社：香港教育要正本清源必须铲除"教协"这颗毒瘤 (locpg.gov.cn), access date: August 1, 2021.

Oriental Daily (Hong Kong Chinese newspaper).

Po, Lanping, "*Hong Kong's Education System needs to be scratched in its bones and remedied for its poison,*" People's Daily, May 16, 2020, in 香港教育需要"刮骨疗毒" (peopleapp.com), access date: July 24, 2021.

Postiglione, Gerard A. and Lee, Wing-on, *Social Change and Educational Development: Mainland China, Taiwan and Hong Kong* (Hong Kong: Centre of Asian Studies, the University of Hong Kong, 1995).

Reed, Ray Garland, "Moral and Political Education in the People's Republic of China: Learning through Role Models," *Journal of Moral Education*, vol. 24, no. 2 (May 1995), pp. 99–112.

Sala, Ilaria Maria, "Hong Kong bookshops pull politically sensitive titles after publishers vanish," *The Guardian*, January 7, 2016, in *Hong Kong bookshops pull politically sensitive titles after publishers vanish* | Hong Kong | The Guardian, access date: August 22, 2021.

Sing Tao Daily (Hong Kong Chinese newspaper).

Spires, Robert, "Hong Kong's Postcolonial Education Reform Liberal Studies as a Lens," *International Journal of Educational Reform*, vol. 26, no. 2 (Spring 2017), pp. 154–172.

Sweating, Anthony E., "Hong Kong Education within Historical Process," in Postiglione, Gerard A., ed., *Education and Society in Hong Kong: Toward One Country and Two Systems* (Hong Kong: Hong Kong University Press, 1992), pp. 39–82.

Sweeting, Anthony, *Education in Hong Kong, 1941 to 2001: Visions and Revisions* (Hong Kong: Hong Kong University Press, 2004), pp. 377–378.

Ta Kung Pao (pro-Beijing Hong Kong Chinese newspaper).

Tang, Wing-lam, "DSE Controversy: Three Days before the resignation of two examination managers are making people shivering," HK01, May 16, 2020, in DSE 歷史科｜一文看清考評風波　兩經理辭職前三日間如何驚心動魄｜香港01｜社會新聞 (hk01.com), access date: July 24, 2021.

Tang, Wing-lam, "So Kwok-sang responds to non-renewal: Personal reasons without being pressured," HK01, September 1, 2020, in DSE 2021｜考評局秘書長蘇國生回應不續任：個人考慮、不涉施壓｜香港01｜社會新聞 (hk01.com), access date: July 25, 2021.

The Basic Law of the Hong Kong Special Administrative Region of the People's Republic of China, in Basic Law – Basic Law – Chapter VI (EN), in Basic Law - Basic Law (EN), access date: August 29, 2021.

The Committee on Education, "*Report of the Committee on Education,*" in The Hong Kong Government Gazette, April 11, 1902.

The Hong Kong Government, "*Education Ordinance 1913,*" in *The Hong Kong Government Gazette*, May 22, 1914.

"The Situation, Challenge and Prospect of implementation of National Education," in *Hong Kong: Report of Task Group on National Education of the Commission on Strategic Development* (Hong Kong: Task Group on National Education of the Commission on Strategic Development, April 2008).

The Sky Post (Hong Kong Chinese newspaper).

To, Hoi-ming, "Citizenship and Social Development studies was successfully opened, and this is a new turning point in education reform," Ta Kung Pao, September 3, 2021, p. A5.

Tse, Thomas Kwan-choi, "Remaking Chinese Identity: Hegemonic Struggles over National Education in Post-Colonial Hong Kong," *International Studies in Sociology of Education*, vol. 17, no.3 (September 2007), pp. 231–248.

Tung, Chee-hwa, *Chief Executive's Policy Address* (Hong Kong: the HKSAR Government, 1997), in https://www.policyaddress.gov.hk/pa97/english/paindex.htm, access date: August 1, 2021.

Wang, Qinghua, "Strengthening and Professionalizing Political Education in China's Higher Education," *Journal of Contemporary China*, vol. 22, no. 80 (2013), pp. 332–350.

Wen Wei Po (Hong Kong Chinese newspaper).

Wen Wei Po (pro-Beijing Hong Kong Chinese newspaper).

Westcott, Ben, "China's top political body met in secret and issued an ominous message to Hong Kong," CNN, November 1, 2019, in *China's top political body met in secret and issued an ominous message to Hong Kong – CNN*, access date: August 16, 2021.

Wong, Rachel, "'End of academic freedom': University of Hong Kong to fire pro-democracy activist and law professor Benny Tai," July 28, 2020, in *End of academic freedom': University of Hong Kong to fire pro-democracy activist and law prof.* Benny Tai – Hong Kong Free Press HKFP (hongkongfp.com), access date: September 12, 2021.

Wu, David Tai-wai, *"Investigating School-based Management in Hong Kong to Validate the Prerequisites for Successful Schools Using an Exploratory Sequential Design,"* unpublished PhD thesis, Hong Kong Institute of Education, October 2015.

Wu, Ka-yan, "Facebook saying Carrie Lam should go, two Examination Authority managers resign," HK01, May 16, 2020, in 【01獨家】FB發「林鄭滾蛋」 考評局評核發展部通識科兩經理辭職 | 香港 01 | 社會新聞 (hk01.com), access date: July 24, 2021.

Xie, Ailei; Postiglione, Gerard A., and Huang, Qian, "The Greater Bay Area Development Strategy and Its Relevance to Higher Education," *ECNU Review of Education*, vol. 4, no. 1 (2021), pp. 210–221.

Xu, Shuqin and Law, Wing-Wah, "School Leadership and Citizenship Education: The Experiences and Struggles of School Party Secretaries in China," *Education Research for Policy and Practice*, vol. 14, no. 1 (February 2015), pp. 33–51.

Yeung, Hans, "A Critique of the History Subject paper in 2021," May 8, 2021, in 眾新聞 - 盤點2021年歷史科試卷 (hkcnews.com), access date: August 6, 2021.

Yung, Andrew Man-sing, "The Policy of Direct Subsidy Scheme Schools in Hong Kong: Finance and Administration," *Hong Kong Teachers' Centre Journal*, vol. 5 (2006), pp. 94–111.

Zainab, Raza, "China's 'Political Re-Education' Camps of Xinjiang's Uyghur Muslims," *Asian Affairs*, vol. 50, no. 4 (2019), pp. 488–501.

Zenz, Adrian, "Thoroughly Reforming Them towards a Healthy Heart Attitude': *China's Political Re-Education Campaign in Xinjiang*," *Central Asian Survey*, vol. 38, no. 1 (2019), pp. 102–128.

Zhang, Guohua, Boyce, Gordon, and Ahmed, Kamran, "Institutional Changes in University Accounting Education in Post-Revolutionary China: From Political Orientation to Internationalization," *Critical Perspectives on Accounting*, vol. 25 (2014), pp. 819–843.

Zhu, Zhiyong and Deng, Meng, "Cultural or Political? Origin and Development of Educational Policy of the Tibetan Neidi Education in China," *Chinese Education & Society*, vol. 48, no. 5 (2015), pp. 332–340.

Index

A high degree of autonomy 71
Academic: debate 128; freedom 117, 130, 163–5, 186, 191
adaptation 3, 151, 173–7, 192
advertisements 177, 180–4
Alliance in Support of Patriotic Democratic Movements of China (ASPDMC) 116–18, 123
analytical framework 1, 3, 36
anti-China 20, 28, 116, 124–5, 132–3, 174
anti-governmental 30, 58, 116, 123
anti-national education campaign 1, 12, 20, 108, 118, 135
arrest 28, 35, 70–1, 73, 87, 90, 92, 114, 118, 105, 137, 157–63, 165, 177
Article 23 of the Basic Law 67, 103, 122, 197
assessment 15, 21, 25–7, 29, 31, 50–3, 56–7, 59, 63–4, 78, 82, 85, 87, 99, 105, 127, 129–30, 132, 141, 193–5, 198
Australia 92, 158, 163, 173, 186, 195
authoritarian 11, 136, 163, 188, 191
authority 12, 17, 27, 34, 51, 56, 64–5, 67–8, 82, 99, 108, 126–7, 129, 148, 154, 192, 194, 196–8, 202

Basic Law 1, 28, 37, 42, 50, 59, 61, 64, 66–7, 69, 71–2, 74–6, 84, 88, 102, 112, 122, 154, 191, 201
Beijing 35–7, 48–51, 55, 58, 60, 65–8, 70, 72–3, 77, 85–95, 97–8, 100, 102–3, 109–11, 114–20, 122–3, 125–9, 133–6, 147–9, 153, 156–7, 160, 164, 169, 174, 176–77, 184–5, 188–90, 199–202
Board of Directors 98, 100–2, 107, 111–2, 197

brainwashing 28, 34, 117
Britain 1, 43, 85, 112, 140
British National Overseas (BNO) 158, 185
bureaucratic politics i, 3

Canada 92, 158, 173
capitalism 17, 164; academic 164
Catholic Church 55, 64, 99, 126, 167, 200
censorship 93, 125, 142–3, 164–5, 191
centralization 21–4, 49
centralize 6, 23, 33, 37, 48, 189, 192
Chan, Johannes Man-mun 164, 186
Chan, Kin-man 35, 68, 133, 163
Cheng, Joseph Yu-shek 163–4
Chief Executive 13, 28, 32, 42, 51–2, 55, 60–2, 64, 67–8, 70–1, 91, 93, 100–1, 109–10, 122–4, 129–30, 132–3, 136, 154–7, 186, 189, 193, 202
Chinese Communist Party (CCP) 1, 68, 70, 103, 109–11, 116, 126, 128–9, 134, 136, 151–53, 157–8, 174, 185, 190, 194
Chinese history 2–3, 8, 10, 12–13, 19, 26–7, 30, 54, 59–62, 74, 76–7, 85–6, 100–1, 105, 113, 123–4, 128–9, 133, 135–6, 140, 142, 152, 155, 157, 176, 188, 191, 193
Chow, Agnes Ting 158–9
Chu, Yiu-ming 68
Chung, Tony Hon-lam 162
Citizenship and Social Development 2, 58, 64, 74, 78–86, 105–6, 121, 125–6, 140–2, 175–7, 188, 193, 199
Civil Human Rights Front (CHRF) 123, 125–6
civil servants 51, 73, 154, 174, 179
code of conduct 115

Index 205

colonial 12, 14, 24–5, 27, 31, 33–5, 37, 41–3, 45, 48, 50, 54, 62, 188–9, 191–2, 198
Communist Youth League (CYL) 15–16, 28
conflicts 40, 120
confrontation 17, 20, 42, 71, 120–1
constitution 10, 53, 61, 72, 75–6, 80, 88, 106, 153, 195
contract 111–13, 128, 144, 148, 163–4, 180, 186, 195–6
Court of Final Appeal 155
crime 76, 101, 118–19, 125, 147
criminal offence 73
crisis 33, 51, 53, 124, 139, 147, 196
Cultural Revolution 6–7, 20, 51, 108–11, 114, 120, 128, 134, 136, 138, 143–4, 189; Hong Kong-style 108, 114, 136, 143
curriculum reform 22–3, 25, 29, 33, 36, 40, 52, 54, 58, 62, 74, 76–8, 86, 151, 154, 184, 190–1, 199

decentralization 20–4, 49
decentralize 22, 24, 37, 48, 189, 192
decolonization 62, 151–7
democracy 11, 20–1, 28–9, 32, 41, 50, 57, 70, 73, 90–1, 93, 95, 98, 100, 104, 110, 114, 116–17, 121, 125–6, 141, 159–60, 162–4, 185–6, 189, 194, 200, 202
democrats 13, 35, 67–8, 73, 90, 121, 125, 149, 157, 160–1, 163, 165
Demosisto 129, 158–60
Deng, Xiaoping 7, 9–10, 14, 16, 49
depoliticization 10, 13, 191
Direct Subsidy Scheme (DSS) 49, 50, 63, 94, 100, 179, 181–2, 202
dismissal 113, 123, 163
dissolve 123–5
District Councils 60

Education: groups, 89, 94–102; national, 1–2, 6, 12–13, 20, 22, 25, 27–9, 32–5, 37, 41–2, 57–8, 60, 64, 66, 68, 75, 100, 103–4, 108–9, 117–18, 135, 154–60, 184, 188–9, 191, 195, 197–9, 202; patriotic, 9, 19, 65–7, 85, 103, 151, 153–7, 184, 189, 191, 197; political, 3, 6–16, 18–19, 24–5, 34, 38–9, 47, 199–202; policy, 13, 18, 25–8, 32–5, 37, 40–2, 45–7, 53, 60–1, 63–4, 109, 118, 120, 188–9, 191, 194, 199–201

Education Department Bureau (EDB) 11, 56, 59–61, 64, 72–3, 82, 84, 86–8, 105, 109–14, 117–19, 123–4, 126–7, 129, 131–4, 139–40, 142, 144–6, 155, 158, 166–7, 169, 173–6, 178, 184, 193–4, 196–8
Election Committee 98–100, 107, 189, 198
elections 28, 73, 159–60, 163
emigration 192; *see also* migration
ethics 54, 56, 66, 78, 110, 112, 114, 119, 145, 197
examination question 51, 108, 118, 126–36, 142–3, 148–9, 189, 193, 196
Executive Council 48, 120
executive-led 67, 154

fake news 162
Federation of Education Workers (FEW) 68, 72, 84, 94, 97, 100–2, 118, 125, 127, 129, 134, 138–9, 156, 161
flag-raising ceremony 142, 155, 174
France 92

German 50, 54
Governor 45
Greater Bay Area (GBA) 70, 85, 93, 121, 173, 176–7, 184, 187, 191
Guangdong 23, 61, 70, 92, 136, 187

hardline 1, 62, 67, 113, 123, 134, 186
History subject 74, 76, 126–8, 130–3, 135–6, 147–9, 155, 193, 199–200
Hong Kong and Macau Affairs Office (HKMAO) 35
Hong Kong Examination and Assessment Authority (HKEAA) 27, 51, 55, 108, 110, 118, 127, 136
Hong Kong Federation of Students (HKFS) 158, 160–1
Hong Kong Human Rights and Democracy Act 159, 162
Hu, Jintao 16
human rights 6, 20, 76, 84, 109, 116, 124, 154, 159–60, 162

identity 1–3, 12–14, 18–20, 24, 26–8, 31–4, 40–2, 50, 57–8, 60–2, 65, 70–2, 74–83, 85–6, 113, 129, 132, 134, 152, 154, 157, 162, 169, 174, 178, 188–92, 200, 202
ideological 15–16, 18–19, 21, 23, 35, 38, 55, 62, 109, 136, 151–2, 200

Index

imprison 35, 73, 157–65, 185
indoctrination 1, 7, 10, 13–14, 18, 24, 34, 46, 58, 151–2, 188, 191
integrity 17; academic 191; moral 114; territorial 69, 75
intellectuals 13, 28–9, 35, 41, 58, 134, 157, 188
interest groups 34–5, 41, 54–5, 65, 89, 97–8, 103, 129, 132, 157, 189
international schools 49, 138, 182
Internet 15, 29, 69, 78, 84, 87, 89–91, 110, 112, 162, 185, 190
Ip, Iam-chong 163

Japan 10, 14, 19, 45–6, 74, 76–7, 92, 126–8, 131–2, 134, 142, 153, 159, 165, 176
Japanese: 126; anti- 74, 76; army 77; invasion of China 45, 127–8, 153, 176; media 159; occupation of Hong Kong 46

kindergarten 47, 51, 53, 99, 102, 156–7, 165, 182–3, 188

Lam, Carrie 61–2, 70–1, 93, 122–4, 130, 132–3, 136, 148, 155–6, 202
Laswell, Harold xi, 192
Law, Nathan 158, 160–1
legalization 151, 157–64, 191
Legislative Council (LegCo) 68, 73–4, 78, 97–8, 100, 109, 118, 159–63, 186, 189, 194–5, 199
legitimacy 9, 12, 14, 19–20, 23–5, 33–4, 48, 58, 62, 65, 192, 199
Leung, C. Y. 28, 58, 62, 110, 120, 186
Liberal studies, 2, 8, 11, 23–4, 26, 28, 28–34, 41, 52, 56–9, 64–5, 74, 78–86, 105, 109–10, 117–19, 121, 125–6, 133, 140–4, 150, 188, 194–5, 198–9
Lo, Keith 128, 133–4
localism 1, 28, 37, 68, 70, 103, 122, 135, 162, 185, 196
localists 1–2, 20, 28, 42, 70, 93, 162, 189

mainlandization 1, 2, 6, 26, 34, 65–107, 135, 151, 169, 188, 190–91
Mao, Zedong 7, 16–17, 134, 153
Marxism 8, 10, 16, 152; Leninism, 16
media, 4, 58, 69, 84–5, 89–92
merit 164
middle class 18, 51, 109, 138, 140, 158
migration 151, 165–73, 177–84
military 5, 9, 14–17, 43, 46, 50, 65, 77, 92, 128, 185, 196

mini-constitution 1
Ministry of Education (MoE) 3–4, 7–9, 15, 23, 68, 88
Mongkok riot 1, 20, 28, 40, 57, 65, 135, 158, 188
music 13, 54, 111

Nanking 43, 76
national anthem 13, 61, 71–2, 74, 87, 104, 110, 154, 160, 185, 195
national emblem 74
National Security Commission: China 65; Hong Kong 164; Macau 67
national security concerns 68
national security education 3, 6, 8, 10–13, 19–20, 23, 26, 28, 30, 34–6, 42, 51, 58–9, 62, 65, 69–77, 87–9, 103–6, 113, 116, 119, 135, 142–3, 151–2, 155–7, 178, 184, 187, 189–91, 193, 195, 198
national security law 1, 3–6, 8, 10–11, 13–14, 19–20, 23, 23–6, 28, 30, 33–6, 42, 51, 58, 65, 67–73, 75, 84, 86–8, 90, 93–4, 103–6, 108–09, 112–16, 118, 122–3, 125–6, 134, 138, 140–3, 150–1, 154,57, 159–65, 169, 173, 175, 177–80, 184, 186, 188–92, 194–5
nationalism 14, 16–17, 19–20, 24–5, 27–8, 34–6, 48, 57–8, 62, 70, 74, 77, 93, 120, 146–7, 169, 188–90, 198, 200
Ng, Eddie Hak-kim 110

oath-taking 1, 28, 35, 57, 65–6, 154
Occupy Central 160–1, 163–4, 186, 188, 198
One-way permit holders 167–9

parents 3, 13, 171–8, 22, 24, 28–9, 34, 36, 43, 49, 51, 54–5, 58, 93, 112–13, 138–42, 151, 158, 165, 174, 184, 188, 190
patriotic 1, 5, 9, 16, 19–20, 27, 31, 34, 49, 58, 65–6, 73, 83, 85, 100, 103, 116, 124–5, 135, 143, 146, 151, 153–7, 175–6, 184, 189–91, 197
patriotism 3, 16–17, 19–20, 24–25, 27–29, 32, 34–6, 38, 48, 58, 62–3, 66, 70, 78, 84–5, 93, 155, 176, 188, 190, 199–200
pay scale 179–80
pedagogy 6, 9–18, 25, 58, 74, 78, 85, 111–13, 140–1, 154, 174
persecute 158

Index

police 5–6, 20, 28, 42, 45, 71, 87–8, 105, 109–11, 113–14, 117, 119, 122, 125–6, 132, 136–8, 142–5, 156, 159–62, 174, 185, 194, 197
political conflicts 40, 200
political control 45
political correctness 93, 113, 128
political culture 11, 15, 25, 30, 53, 108, 143, 157, 169, 191
political identification 157, 190
political neutrality 133, 163
political participation 82, 108, 118, 142, 157–61, 163–64
political reform 14, 25, 35, 122
political science 163–5, 191
political socialization 11, 14, 17, 19, 39, 188, 191
political struggle 108–9, 120, 135–6, 177
political system 2, 7, 11, 15–16, 32, 37, 53, 57, 61, 70, 98, 154, 189
politicization 2, 10, 13–14, 18, 29, 50, 57, 117, 128, 134, 191
politics of education reform 19, 20, 55, 133, 189, 192
populism: new right 50; radical 68, 103
power struggle 34–5, 55, 129, 180, 189
pro-Beijing 2, 29, 31, 36, 48–9, 55, 58, 65, 67–8, 72–3, 77, 85–6, 88–95, 97–8, 100, 102–3, 109–11, 115–16, 118–20, 122–3, 125–9, 133–6, 141, 149, 156–7, 160, 164, 169, 174, 176–7, 184–5, 189, 199
Professional Teachers' Union (PTU) 94–5, 108, 116–26, 146, 194, 201
professionalism 24, 36, 40, 123, 131, 174, 190, 198
protests 2, 26, 35, 37, 39, 65–6, 70. 106, 110–12, 116, 119, 121–2, 125–6, 143, 159, 175, 177, 186, 193, 200
public examination 13, 51, 108, 131–34, 142–3, 162, 189
public fear 13

radicals 28, 42, 67, 70
redness 68
regime 1, 8–11, 17, 25, 42, 73, 75–6, 190
retire 109, 139–40, 150, 164, 180, 194–6
ruling: authorities 148; elites 2, 17, 35, 48

Scholarism 20, 29, 32, 119, 132, 158–9
school management 22, 47, 50, 52, 55, 63, 72, 115, 137, 174, 200
school principals 30, 66, 95, 100–2, 139, 142, 155–6, 177

schoolchildren 153–5, 169
Second World War 10, 77, 153, 155, 176
secession 69, 76, 161–2
secondary schools, 95, 98–9, 101, 116, 119, 123, 138, 150, 156–7, 165, 167, 169, 178–9, 183, 188, 196
securitization 5–6
Shanghai 21, 45, 60, 101–2
socialism 7, 16–17, 66, 151–2
soft 123, 152: power 191
sovereignty 1, 12–13, 27, 34, 36, 40, 49, 62, 69, 74–6, 84–6, 94, 135, 152, 188, 198
Standing Committee of the National People's Congress (SCNPC) 19, 22, 28, 35, 42, 66, 73, 124
State Council 22, 35
student: enrolment 139, 165–7, 169–72, 178; population, 8, 25, 165, 169; union 88, 160
subversion 69, 73
subvert 35, 70, 76
suppress 14, 111, 125, 135, 174, 177, 189, 191

Tai, Benny 35, 68, 72–3, 104, 119, 163–4, 186, 193, 202
Taiwan 37, 62, 64, 70, 88, 90–2, 121, 151, 158, 160–3, 173, 185, 200–1
teaching vacancies 180–3
Tiananmen 5, 9, 50, 93, 135, 140, 153, 159–60, 164; tragedy 135, 190
Tibet 6, 18, 39, 121, 151, 165, 203
transmission belts 89
triads 111, 144, 174
Trojan Horse 70, 104
Trump, Donald 21
Tung, Chee-hwa 13, 51, 58, 60, 62, 64, 91, 202

underdevelopment 2
united front 6, 17, 65, 92, 184
United States 11, 19, 24, 70, 90, 92, 158, 162, 169, 173
universities 4, 7–11, 15, 18–19, 24, 48, 51, 57, 69–70, 87–8, 93, 97–100, 103, 106, 116, 123138, 143, 150, 157, 164–5, 169–174, 176–7, 184, 191, 194
unpatriotic 20, 34, 83, 125, 175

visual arts 54; teacher 114, 145, 194

Washington 169
White Paper 46, 48, 67–8
Wong, Benson 163
Wong, Joshua 20, 29, 32, 93, 119, 158–61

Xi, Jinping 1, 15–16, 65–7, 69, 70, 103–4, 151–2, 189, 197
Xinhua 67, 104, 116–21, 123–25, 127–8, 130–1, 133, 136, 146–7, 196–7
Xinjiang 4–6, 37, 121, 151, 165, 186, 202

yellow teacher 108–9, 113–14, 117, 121, 144, 174
Yeung, Hans 127–8, 131, 133, 136, 149, 193, 196
Yeung, Kevin 68, 72, 78, 83, 86–7, 113, 115, 124, 127, 131, 136, 144–5, 158, 178, 195–6
Yuan, Tiffany 158, 160

Zen, Joseph 55

Made in the USA
Middletown, DE
31 January 2024